Creating Effective Groups

Creating Effective Groups
The Art of Small Group Communication

THIRD EDITION

Randy Fujishin

ROWMAN & LITTLEFIELD PUBLISHERS, INC.
Lanham • Boulder • New York • Toronto • Plymouth, UK

Published by Rowman & Littlefield Publishers, Inc.
A wholly owned subsidiary of The Rowman & Littlefield Publishing Group, Inc.
4501 Forbes Boulevard, Suite 200, Lanham, Maryland 20706
www.rowman.com

10 Thornbury Road, Plymouth PL6 7PP, United Kingdom

British Library Cataloguing in Publication Information Available

Library of Congress Cataloging-in-Publication Data
Fujishin, Randy.
  Creating effective groups : the art of small group communication /
Randy Fujishin.—Third edition.
       pages cm
  Includes bibliographical references and index.
    ISBN 978-1-4422-2249-6 (cloth : alk. paper)—ISBN 978-1-4422-2250-2 (pbk. : alk.
paper)—ISBN 978-1-4422-2251-9 (electronic)
    1. Small groups. 2. Communication in small groups. 3. Group decision making.
  I. Title.
  HM736.F85 2013
  302.3'4—dc23 2013018304

Printed in the United States of America

For Vicky,
my gift for this lifetime.

Contents

Preface   xi

CHAPTER 1 **Working in a Group**   1

Working in Groups   2
Four Elements of a Problem-Solving Group   3
The Small Group as a System   4
The Power of One   6
Characteristics of Groups   7
The Power of Diversity   13
Individual and Group Exercises   16

CHAPTER 2 **Discovering Yourself**   19

Being Open to Self-Discovery   20
Spending Time by Yourself   21
Self-Discovery Inventories   23
Speaking Kindly to Yourself   27
Accepting Yourself   30
Accepting Others   30
Critically Thinking About Yourself as a Communicator   31
Individual and Group Exercises   33

CHAPTER 3 **Expressing Yourself Clearly**   35

Communication Is a Learned Behavior   36
Five Roles That Prevent Clear Expression   37
The Communication Process   38
I-Statements   42

Four Levels of Communication 43
Gender Differences in Conversational Strategies 45
Guidelines for Speaking Clearly 47
Reducing Anxiety When Speaking 49
Defensive vs. Supportive Group Climates 51
Individual and Group Exercises 55

CHAPTER 4 **Listening for Understanding** 57

The Importance of Listening 58
The Process of Listening 58
Poor Listening Styles 59
Barriers to Listening 60
Acceptance: A Requirement for Listening 61
Listening for Understanding: Active Listening 63
Advantages of Active Listening 68
Guidelines for Active Listening 69
Intercultural Awareness 70
S.O.A.R. Technique 73
Individual and Group Exercises 76

CHAPTER 5 **Problem Solving in Groups** 79

Myths of Small Group Problem Solving 80
Decision-Making Techniques 82
Discussion Questions 86
The Standard Problem-Solving Agenda 87
The Circular Nature of Problem Solving 91
Being More Creative 92
Individual and Group Exercises 95

CHAPTER 6 **Preparing for Discussion** 97

You Don't Know Everything 98
We Can Always Know More 99
Where to Research 99
What to Research 103
Constructing an Information Sheet 105
Using Visual Aids 105
Testing Evidence and Reasoning 107
Recognizing Logical Fallacies 111
Ethical Communication 113
Your Time Management 116
Individual and Group Exercises 119

CHAPTER 7 **Guiding Discussion**   121

Guiding Discussion to a Shared Path   122
Task-Guiding Behaviors   123
Social-Guiding Behaviors   126
Being an Effective Follower   128
Individual and Group Exercises   131

CHAPTER 8 **Leading a Group**   133

What Is Leadership?   134
Approaches to Leadership   134
The Attitude of the Servant Leader   138
Leading an Effective Meeting   140
Impromptu Speaking   144
Taking Care of Yourself as the Leader   148
Individual and Group Exercises   150

CHAPTER 9 **Building a Cohesive Group**   153

The Social Dimension   154
Feeling Successful   155
Feeling Connected   157
Feeling Valued   159
Feeling Supported   161
Trusting Others   162
Groupthink: When Groups Are Too Cohesive   164
Individual and Group Exercises   166

CHAPTER 10 **Managing Conflict**   167

A Different Approach to Conflict   168
Myths of Conflict   169
Advantages of Conflict   170
Three Types of Group Conflict   171
Dealing with Procedural Conflict   172
Dealing with Substantive Conflict   173
Dealing with Interpersonal Conflict   175
Specific Interventions for Dysfunctional Behavior   177
The Spirit of Collaboration   181
Forgiveness   185
Individual and Group Exercises   188

Afterword   191
Resources   193
Index   197
About the Author   201

Preface

WORKING in groups is a part of your life. Whether you're the CEO of a corporation, the chairperson of a committee, a volunteer in a fund-raising group, the manager of a work team, or the head of a family reunion planning committee, you will be working with others in groups to solve problems.

The degree of success or failure these groups experience is, to a large extent, up to you. Whether you realize it or not, your participation in a group influences the effectiveness and productivity of that group. Every word you utter and every gesture you make can have an effect upon the other group members. One harsh word or angry glance can send a group into confusion and conflict. One kind word or gesture of support can cultivate cohesion, encourage cooperation, and even bring healing to a group. One act can change the direction and destiny of any problem-solving group. You can help create an effective group no matter where you are.

Working with groups, however, is one of the most demanding activities we engage in during our life. Very few of us ever receive training in group problem solving and decision making. Additionally, most of us enter into a group problem-solving effort with little or no formal communication skills training. Finally, very few of us possess the enthusiasm and optimism necessary to guide, encourage, and even inspire a group to be successful.

The purpose of *Creating Effective Groups* is to provide you with the fundamental knowledge and skills to communicate more effectively and interact more productively in any small group problem-solving activity. This text was designed to give you a simple yet comprehensive introduction to the study of small group communication, group decision making, group dynamics, leadership, or team building for college and industry.

Several features of this book distinguish it from other small group communication texts. First, *Creating Effective Groups* focuses on fundamental concepts and practical skills, without getting bogged down in lengthy theoretical discussions. Second, it is based on the idea that every group member, not just the leader, contributes in significant ways in creating the task and social dimensions of any group. Third, the writing style is warm, friendly, and encouraging, which will keep you engaged and involved in the learning process. Fourth, utilizing the author's counseling as well as communication studies training, the psychological factors and variables of group interaction are discussed. Finally, each chapter begins with real-life stories that illustrate the need for the skills and concepts presented in the chapter.

Each chapter of *Creating Effective Groups* will provide you with the opportunity to practice, develop, and implement a variety of communication skills in the small group setting, so that your group will be effective and successful in solving problems.

You will also be given specific ways to increase your awareness, sensitivity, and supportiveness of the needs and feelings of others in your group. For what good is a group if it accomplishes its assigned tasks, but injures or diminishes the spirit of its people? To create a truly effective group, you must be attentive and responsive to the task and social dimension of the group. This book will enable you to accomplish both tasks, so you can create effective groups in your life.

I would like to thank Charles Harmon, executive editor at Rowman & Littlefield, for his guidance and assistance in the production of this third edition.

Steve Richmond has provided me with spiritual encouragement, good conversations on the road, and an introduction to the joys of riding a motorcycle to faraway places. Thank you, Steve.

And special thanks goes to Paul Sanders for being my good friend and brother for these past three decades.

Finally, I would like to express my deepest appreciation, gratitude, and love to my wife, Vicky, and our sons, Tyler and Jared. They have created the loving home that is the best place in the world for me.

CHAPTER 1

Working in a Group

The real voyage of discovery consists not in
seeking new landscapes, but in having new eyes.

—MARCEL PROUST

THE best journeys in life provide us with new ways of seeing the world. Whether it's a month-long expedition to the Himalayas or a thirty-minute visit with an old friend, we come away from these experiences with a greater understanding and appreciation of others and ourselves. We are changed. With new eyes, we see that we are capable of becoming more than we once believed—that we can be freer, happier, and stronger than we once thought.

The best journeys in life, we discover, bring us closer to our truer selves.

One such journey took place for me in a cramped, cheerless conference room in Santa Barbara many years ago. I was a part-time employee at a small electronics company during my sophomore year of college, and I was asked to participate in a problem-solving group that would recommend ways to boost employee morale.

My previous experience with problem-solving groups was limited to high school student government and two college group projects in psychology. All three experiences proved frustrating. The meetings were disorganized, adversarial, and long. Invariably one person would monopolize the discussion, while the rest of us would roll our eyes and watch the clock. We accomplished very little. At the end of these meetings, I often left the room feeling confused, frustrated, and angry.

So when I arrived at our first meeting in that small, cluttered conference room in Santa Barbara, I was not expecting to experience anything different. I was the youngest of the seven-member group. The other six were full-time employees in their 30s and 40s. I felt inadequate and unnecessary. Before we sat down, the team leader introduced himself to me and offered me a soft drink. Once the meeting began, I was surprised by the organized flow of the discussion. The leader skillfully kept us on track, occasionally summarized the ideas that were being considered, and often complimented us for contributing other ideas. He even asked me for my thoughts a number of times as I sat silently watching the dance of the discussion.

Before I knew it, the leader was highlighting the main proposals we had generated, previewing the next step in the process, and thanking us for our work. That first meeting ended in less than one hour!

There were five more meetings after this initial session, and each one ran as smoothly as the first. We had our moments of disagreement and conflict during the six hours, but our team leader was skillful in guiding the discussion and accepting of our differences, and insightful in focusing and synthesizing our ideas.

In the end, I no longer regarded working in groups as something to be avoided. Rather, working in groups was something that could be productive, exciting, and even fun. Because of that, I saw a different world and a different me.

This chapter will help you understand the basic nature and process of any problem-solving group you will participate in or lead. The most important concept you should keep in mind as you work with small groups is that you, one individual member of a group, can make a difference. Your individual contributions during the life of a group can help make or break a group, so strive to be positive, constructive, and encouraging in all that you do. Your efforts can contribute to creating effective groups.

Working in Groups

Since that journey into the conference room, I have worked with a variety of problem-solving groups, both as a leader and as a participant. As a college instructor, corporate consultant and trainer, and clinical therapist for over twenty-five years, I have worked with hundreds of groups. Of course, not every group runs as smoothly as the one I just described. In fact, I believe that problem solving in small groups can be one of the most challenging activities. But I am also convinced that you can learn skills and discover strengths within yourself to make this process more effective and rewarding.

Working in groups is a part of life. Whether you're the vice president of marketing, a member of a PTA group, or the head of the high school reunion planning committee, you will be working with others in small groups to solve problems.

At first glance, this activity may seem easy. All you do is sit around a table, talk, and accomplish things. What could be easier? But rather than experiencing unselfish cooperation, responsible preparation, and open communication in our problem-solving efforts, we are often shocked by the lack of cooperation, the inadequacy of preparation, and the poor communication skills of group members. If we are honest, we would also have to admit to our own inabilities and lack of understanding of this complicated process called group problem solving.

A life of frustration is inevitable for any coach whose main enjoyment is winning.

∞

CHUCK NOLL

The purpose of this book is to provide you with a basic understanding of solving problems in a small group and the skills necessary to participate in and lead effective group discussions.

Four Elements of a Problem-Solving Group

A problem-solving group is three or more people who share a common task, interact face-to-face, and influence one another. Let's consider each element.

Three or More People

The minimum number of individuals needed to constitute a small group is three people. Two people do not make a group because their interaction is that of a couple, or dyad. In a dyad, one person speaks, the other listens and responds, and then the original speaker considers what is being said. No third individual witnesses the event or influences the interaction. A dyad normally encourages more self-disclosure, simply because no audience or third party is present.

Most groups have little control over the number of participants. The size of the group might be determined by group policy, management, available people, or the size of the meeting room. Group membership can range from three to thirty people or more.

I believe the ideal number of members in a small group is five to seven. In a group this size, each member is encouraged to speak without the imposition of a large number of individuals serving as an audience. Also, a group of five to seven provides more input than smaller groups, while maintaining a comfortable level of intimacy that larger groups often lack. In this book, we'll examine and discuss groups of five to seven people.

Sharing a Common Task

The second essential element of a problem-solving group is that the group shares a problem it feels is worth solving. Whether it's brainstorming ways to generate money, selecting a candidate for a committee, or planning a coworker's retirement dinner, there is an identified task or goal the group must accomplish. That task is the primary purpose for the existence of the group.

Interacting Face-to-Face

The third element of a problem-solving group is that group members interact face-to-face. This means they will be able to see one another's faces. Usually, this meeting will occur in the same room with all members physically present.

But the advent of video technology, video teleconferencing, and the Internet permits the group members to see and hear one another without being physically present in the same room. Teleconferencing still satisfies our face-to-face criterion, although most of the nonverbal communication occurring in such interactions is lost. Nonverbal communication is all communication that is neither spoken nor written; it includes such variables as body movement, paralanguage (or the way we speak), clothing, punctuality, gestures, distancing or proxemics, facial expressions, use of time, and seating arrangements. Research has consistently reminded us that nonverbal communication has more impact on the receiver of a message than words themselves.

Ideally, the problem-solving group meets around a single table, thereby providing as much nonverbal information as possible. Being physically close to other human beings provides an immeasurable advantage as you interact and communicate. It's always better to be able to see the face and the body of the person you're interacting with, rather than hearing a tinny voice over a phone receiver, because without the nonverbal cues, much information about content and speaker can be lost.

Influencing One Another

This final element is fundamental to the definition of a problem-solving group. A group member does not exist and operate in a vacuum, isolated from the other members. Each member's statements and behavior affect every other group member in some way, be it small or great. A thoughtful compliment, a subtle criticism, a raised eyebrow, or a complaining moan can communicate a message of monumental proportions, and its effect can last a lifetime.

The reason people have gathered in groups to solve problems since the beginning of recorded history is that they benefit from the pooled skills, knowledge, resources, and experience provided by the group. The group, with its collective resources, usually stands a greater chance for survival and success.

An individual is also influenced and affected by the other group members. You can learn from their information and grow from their suggestions, be persuaded by their arguments and challenged by their proposals, be hurt by their remarks and healed by their praises. You can be deflated by others' bickering and inspired by their encouragement. Each member influences and is influenced by other group members, whether he or she acknowledges this fact or not.

> Example is not the main thing in influencing others. It is the only thing.
>
> ෴
>
> ALBERT SCHWEITZER

The Small Group as a System

A common illusion is to think we are separate from the other members of the group. We tend to see our individual needs, behaviors, responses, and communication as separate, unconnected to those of our group members. Most of our behavior and thinking are self-motivated, and we often lack awareness of the intricate and profound connections the group has established in its web of interactions.

There are two ways to look at group interactions. The first way sees each member as distinct and disconnected from any substantial and meaningful tie with the other people, like lone cowboys meeting on a hill to chat, then galloping off in different directions. In other words, I enter into the group being me, and I leave the group being me. Nothing has changed in me, except that I've spent some time with other people.

A second way of viewing group interaction is as if the group was a living organism. We are each a part of this living organism. You're the heart, I'm the lungs, and the other members serve their respective functions of the body. When something happens to one part, all the other parts feel the effects. This is the essence of the systems perspective of group interaction and is valuable in understanding and appreciating small group process.

A system is a collection of interdependent parts arrayed in such a way that a change in one of its components will effect changes in all the other components. The emphasis in a systems perspective is not on the individual members, but rather on the group as a whole. Any group of people working together to solve a problem meets this definition of a system. Now we'll consider four characteristics of a system: interdependence, mutual influence, adaptation, and equifinality.

> We are all connected to one another in ways both large and small. To deny this is to turn your back on one of life's greatest truths.
>
> ∽
>
> KARL MENNINGER

Interdependence

The first characteristic of a system is interdependence. Interdependence means that each group member depends on all the other members in one way or another. An obvious example is the absence of four of the five members at a meeting. Even though you are present, the absence of the other group members makes it impossible for you to participate in the meeting. Another example is a group member not researching or producing a critical piece of information the group needs in order to proceed. One member's behavior, or lack of behavior, prevents the entire group from progressing. In many ways, you are connected to and dependent upon the actions of the other group members.

Yet once the individual members form a working group, they acquire a collective life. The group can take on characteristics—productivity, creativity, and responsiveness—that may not be characteristic of any one individual member. The individuals can often become energized by the collective whole. They can achieve more productivity than any member could realize alone. This is often referred to as synergy—the group product is usually superior to the best individual product. In other words, two heads are better than one.

Mutual Influence

The second characteristic of a system is mutual influence. Mutual influence implies that cause and effect are interchangeable. Each action or behavior serves as a response to a previous behavior and a stimulus for a future action. This characteristic of systems theory makes any attempt to assign blame for any problematic behavior pointless, because that behavior was in response to a previous behavior. An example of this would be the "nag/withdraw" syndrome. A wife withdraws because her husband nags. But the husband insists he nags because she withdraws. Oftentimes, it is pointless to assign blame, to point the finger at who started this whole mess, because the behaviors are so intertwined. Rather than blame, the wife and the husband should explore ways to alter or modify the pattern of "nag/withdraw." The focus is on modifying behavior patterns instead of seeking to blame or punish.

Adaptation

Adaptation means that a system will seek to adapt to fit the demands of a changing environment. The group's flexibility to modify its procedures, rules, communication patterns, even its way of thinking and feeling, is indicative of its ability to survive and is required for its overall health. The problem-solving group must remain flexible and willing to change in order to cope with the changing environment (people, issues, and circumstances). Groups that are rigid, dogmatic, and unwilling to explore and discover new ways of operating are doomed to mediocrity and often failure. The flexible group is a healthy group.

Equifinality

Finally, the fourth characteristic of a system is equifinality. Equifinality is the ability of a group to accomplish a goal in many ways and from many starting points. The group must accept the fact that there are many ways to accomplish a goal or task, not just one right way. The concept of equifinality opens up the possibility and potential for creative approaches to solving problems, which includes seeing the "problem" from a variety of viewpoints. Many roads lead to the "good life." The secret is discovering the one that feels right to you.

The Power of One

Every behavior of each individual has its effect on the group—regardless of whether the behavior is negative and counterproductive, or positive and productive. In other words, your behavior, be it negative or positive, influences the group's interaction and final product. The beauty of a systems perspective on group process is that it serves as a reminder that you have the power to influence and determine the direction and outcome of the group.

Peter Senge supports this idea of the power of one in his book, *The Fifth Dimension: The Art and Practice of the Learning Organizations.* He believes that systems thinking is the key to understanding how groups and organizations work—the idea that all the parts of a group or organization are ultimately connected to one another and that "low leverage change can shift large structures within an organization." Senge encourages us to discover small ways to participate and contribute to actually affect and change large organizations and institutions. Your individual participation can play a very important role in creating an effective group.

> Whatever the ups and downs of detail within our limited existence, the larger whole of life is primarily beautiful.
>
> ∽
>
> GREGORY BATESON

Characteristics of Groups

To better understand how your individual participation influences the effectiveness of a group, you will need to become familiar with the basic characteristics of groups.

Group Formation

Whenever I see a group of businesspeople in a meeting, a cluster of Boy Scouts pitching tents at a campground, or a group of protesters picketing city hall, I am reminded why individuals join others to form groups—because each member receives something personally from his or her affiliation with the group. People join groups for a variety of reasons. William Schutz believes there are three basic needs that motivate individuals to become members of a group. He identifies these needs as inclusion, control, and affection.

Inclusion is the individual's need to feel wanted or to be a part of something bigger than himself. He wants to feel "in" and not "left out." The need for inclusion describes our desire to belong, to fit in, to be valued, and to be. We want to count, to matter. Inclusion in a group can often validate our worth in the world.

We want to be included in certain groups because we are attracted to the group's activities or even to the group members—not attraction in the sense of romance and love, but in terms of likeness and affinity. We join groups because of similarity in beliefs, ethnicity, economic status, or age. People join religious, social activist, or flying saucer clubs because of common beliefs. Others join groups such as the Japanese American Citizenship League, NAACP, and Mexican-American Youth Association for their ethnic similarities. Membership in a country club, the Millionaires Club, or a homeless shelter can be motivated by economic likeness. An individual might desire to join a group to participate in the activities. Groups such as a social-dancing club, a fraternity or sorority, a weight-lifting group, or a bird-watching club provide opportunities for people to gather with others and feel included.

Many people join groups to discover or strengthen their identity and purpose for living. We determine our self-identity to a great extent by the people with whom we associate. Birds of a feather flock together. Many of the groups identified above—churches, social organizations, businesses, and even the Hells Angels—can provide a person with a strong sense of identity and purpose.

Control provides the individual with the sense that she has some degree of personal influence and power over her environment and life—that what she says and does makes a difference, not only in the decisions and activities of the group, but also in other facets of life. To participate in a problem-solving group can provide an individual with opportunities to share opinions and feelings, to influence and persuade others, and to solve problems of significance.

Many people join groups so they can experience some degree of influence and contribution. The goal or objective the group seeks to achieve can provide this sense of influence and contribution. Groups such as a volunteer wilderness rescue team, a Little League fund-raising group, a corporate work team, or a politician's election campaign provide opportunities for individuals to help advance a cause or accomplish a goal. Once the goal is achieved, the group will often disband. But this isn't necessarily so. Examples of long-term groups are Mothers Against Drunk Driving, Alcoholics Anonymous, and Greenpeace, and these groups give individuals the sense that they can make a difference for a lifetime.

Affection is the need to be liked and to be able to initiate and maintain close relationships with others. This might be the most basic of Schutz's three interpersonal needs that motivate us to join groups. We have the need to form close friendships and ties with other human beings. Without these experiences of giving and receiving love and affection, our lives would be dull indeed. Oftentimes, our participation in groups can provide us with some level of affection. The interpersonal relationships that you experience during group work can be enjoyable, rewarding, and growing experiences in and of themselves. A friendship you make in a group might develop into a lifelong relationship. Who knows what can develop when you join a group.

As you consider these three basic needs for joining groups, you might have noticed some groups satisfy more than one purpose. For example, a religious organization can provide inclusion, control, and affection. This is true for the majority of groups people join; there is rarely only one reason for group affiliation.

Although many of the groups we have discussed are not necessarily problem-solving groups, they provide ample opportunities to make decisions and solve problems. Even a social-dancing club will occasionally need to plan a fund-raiser, arrange a dance with other clubs, or decide what to do with a member who makes others uncomfortable with overt flirting.

Task and Social Dimensions of Groups

Once membership in a problem-solving group is established, it is important to realize that interaction within the group occurs in two areas or dimensions, the task dimension and the social dimension. Each dimension covers a different aspect and purpose of the group's interactions.

The task dimension. Each problem-solving group must attempt to solve a problem. The task dimension is the work of the group. All efforts to this end are considered the task dimension of a problem-solving group. Researching the problem, analyzing the problem, brainstorming solutions, discussing the strengths and weaknesses of the solutions, reaching consensus on the best solution, and implementing the solution are all elements of the group's task dimension.

The social dimension. While the group is busy doing its work in the task dimension, the social dimension is occurring simultaneously. The social dimension is the interpersonal relationships of the group members. It consists of the feelings and interactions of the group members. The social dimension is not separate from the task dimension, but rather is intertwined with the task dimension. A change in one produces a change in the other. We don't really understand all the subtle relationships between the task and social dimensions, but we can be certain they do influence each other.

Norms and Conformity

In every problem-solving group, the behavior of all group members is determined and regulated to a great extent by the norms operating at the explicit and implicit levels. Conformity or adherence to these norms provides many benefits to the group. Challenging group norms can be an important task of the effective group member.

Norms. Norms are the rules that regulate the behavior of group members. They hold the group together, making smooth, predictable interaction possible. Norms provide the basic building blocks of group interaction. Without norms of behavior, the group could easily be thrust into confusion, alienation, and even hostility. We need to understand two types of norms in problem-solving groups.

The first type is implicit norms, which are norms not announced verbally or in writing by the group. They are understood by group members, either consciously or unconsciously, but are not orally stated. Norms such as keeping quiet when others are speaking, being polite, sitting face-to-face with other members, and avoiding obscenities are examples of implicit rules or norms.

The second type is explicit norms, which are orally stated or written down as a code of conduct or expected group behavior. Many groups will establish formal rules of behavior that members are expected to follow. For example, military organizations, weight reduction groups, and religious sects might provide new group members with a list of expected behaviors, either verbally or in writing.

Conformity to norms. Conformity is the adherence to group norms. Why do group members obey or adhere to the norms of the group? There are many reasons for this. First, conformity to norms makes our lives easier. Rather than always having to consider and decide from circumstance to circumstance when to talk, whom to face, and which hand to shake, norms prescribe these behaviors. Conformity to norms makes life orderly, predictable, and organized. Second, adherence to norms makes the interactions within the group more productive. Rather than spending time debating which behaviors are acceptable and which are unacceptable, the efforts of the group can be directed to the task dimension. Third, conformity to norms provides each member with a sense of belonging and acceptance. Whether it's a secret group handshake, a Moose Lodge hat, or a certain style of dress, norms of behavior can make us feel like one of the group.

Clarifying a norm. When in doubt about an ambiguous or confusing group norm, a simple technique for clarifying an implicit norm is to simply raise the question to the group. For instance, let's assume that for the past three meetings, most group members, including the leader, arrived ten to fifteen minutes later than the agreed-upon meeting time, but you have been punctual to every meeting. You could bring the implicit norm (arriving late to meetings is acceptable) to the group for discussion. You might say, "I've noticed many group members arrive ten to fifteen minutes after our agreed-upon meeting time. Is this the accepted norm of the group? I need to have clarification on this, because if it is the accepted norm, I too will arrive late."

Most group members are not used to having implicit norms brought to the explicit level of oral discussion. Many issues of substantive and interpersonal conflict can be resolved during the early stages of group development if the group puts the issue on the table for all to see and discuss. Don't be afraid to make the invisible visible.

> It is by risking that
> we live at all.
>
> ∽
>
> WILLIAM JAMES

Challenging a norm. It's also important for you and the group to challenge any explicit norm you feel is illegal, unethical, or harmful to group members or others. History is filled with examples of men and women who without question or challenge followed the rules or norms of a group that brought pain and suffering to others. Just as you can challenge an implicit norm, you can challenge an explicit norm before the group. This requires some courage, because you might be challenging the leadership and power structure of the group. But if you feel deep in your heart that a particular norm is harming others, you owe it to yourself and others to speak.

Four Phases of Group Development: Perspective 1

Every problem-solving group changes during the course of its existence. It has a life all its own. No two groups are exactly the same. However, Aubrey Fisher identified a four-phase sequence of group development. This four-phase model consists of periods of orientation, conflict, emergence, and reinforcement.

1. **Orientation**. Most members of new groups spend their first meeting or two getting to know one another. Group members often feel a high level of anxiety and uncertainty because they have little or no previous history with one another. The orientation phase is devoted to letting the group members "break the ice" and get acquainted. Humorous remarks, polite behavior, social chitchat, and conflict

avoidance are characteristic of this group development phase. This phase is often referred to as primary tension—the uneasiness group members feel because they are unfamiliar with one another.

The social dimension of the group is overemphasized during this time because the establishment of a warm, supportive, and trusting environment is crucial to the group's task dimension in later phases of its development.

It is also during the orientation phase that members begin to initiate discussion about the task before them. Discussion about the nature and scope of the problem or task begins. Group members will often state their opinions and feelings in tentative, vague language, because they might not yet be comfortable fully disclosing their positions on issues.

The group is not just "spinning its wheels" or wasting time during the orientation phase. It is actually establishing a foundation of group member knowledge and interaction that will make it perform more effectively in the later phases.

2. **Conflict**. After group members are comfortable enough to share their opinions and feelings at a deeper level, they can begin the second phase of group process, the conflict phase. Conflict is a natural and expected part of group process, since it is during this phase the group members begin to express their individual opinions and feelings. During this phase, group members discuss the nature and background of the problem, propose solutions, debate the relative merits of the solutions, and select the best solution or solutions. During the conflict phase, group members begin to clarify their opinions and feelings about the issues. More energy is devoted to sharing differences of opinion, arguing positions, and debating the issues. It is also during this phase that members critically evaluate evidence presented and the reasoning for the solutions proposed. Uneasiness experienced here is called secondary tension—the tension caused by disagreement or criticism over one's ideas, evidence, or proposed solutions.

Groups that develop a safe, supportive social dimension during the orientation phase are more likely to successfully weather the secondary tension experienced during the conflict phase. Groups that have not devoted sufficient time to the orientation phase can buckle under the pressures of conflict. Also, groups that have developed an overly cohesive social dimension might see conflict as a threat to their tight-knit, happy family and will avoid the conflict that is necessary to be effective in the task dimension. This concept of groupthink will be discussed in greater detail in Chapter 9.

3. **Emergence**. During the third phase, group members move from debate and conflict to a possible solution that is acceptable to all members. It's a time when the group negotiates, compromises, and begins to discover common ground. Whereas the conflict phase emphasizes differences of opinion, the emergence phase focuses on similarities. During this phase, decisions emerge. Members increasingly make statements of agreement, acceptance, and approval, and then decide on or adopt a solution.

4. **Reinforcement**. The final phase occurs when group members congratulate themselves on a job well done. During this time, the group also constructs an

implementation plan and timetable for the agreed-upon solution. The social dimension is reinforced in this phase with the expression of positive feelings about the group and its accomplishments. Members often feel a strong sense of group identity and belonging. Disagreement, conflicts, and arguments were successfully negotiated and the group
is stronger, more effective because of it.

If you've ever worked in small groups, however, you know that they rarely follow the exact steps Fisher identified. A group may go through these phases for each issue it addresses. One group might devote the majority of its time to orientation and socializing, whereas another group will bypass orientation altogether and focus solely on

> If we really understand the
> problem, the solution will come
> out of it, because the answer is
> not separate from the problem.
>
> ∾
>
> KRISHNAMURTI

the task at hand. Groups can get sidetracked, abandon their discussion, or disband as a group altogether. In real life, the journey a problem-solving group takes is much more complex and the stages it experiences are not as clear-cut as one might hope.

Multiple Sequence Model of Group Development: Perspective 2

To take this complexity into account more accurately, Marshall Poole described group development differently. Rather than a linear model, he proposed a multiple sequence model of decision emergence. This model of group process envisions a group moving along three activity tracks: task, relational, and topic. The task track is the structure or the phase of the discussion, the relational track is the social dimension of the group, and the topic track is the specific issue content of the discussion at that moment. A group on the task track might decide to return to the analysis of the problem, take a vote on an issue, or postpone discussion of an item. A group involved on the relational track is devoting its focus and interaction on the social dimension of the group, such as sharing personal information, taking a break, or joking with one another. Finally, the topic track is the actual discussion of the task issue the group is attempting to solve, such as sharing information and evidence, questioning, negotiating, and reaching consensus.

In this model, groups do not necessarily move along these three tracks at the same rate or in the same way. Some groups invest a great amount of time on the relational track before moving to the task track, while other groups may focus primarily on the task track and devote minimal time to the relational track. Breakpoints are the transitions when groups switch activity tracks.

Fisher's Four Phase Group Development perspective and Poole's Multiple Sequence Model perspective each provide helpful insights into the life and activity of problem-solving groups. Fisher gives us four phases of group development that help us understand and establish goals for group work, and Poole reminds us that we don't always proceed along a single, predictable path, but rather shift the focus of group activity depending upon the needs of the group. Specific goals of group development and flexibility in the attainment of those goals are important points to remember as you problem solve with others.

The Power of Diversity

As our society becomes more diverse, the membership of our groups will also reflect this diversity. In the coming decades Non-Whites—Hispanics, African Americans, and Asians will constitute the majority of the U.S. population and White Americans will be in the minority. This shift will also be reflected in the memberships of every group you will be involved with at school, at work, and in your neighborhood. This is a fact of life. Groups will continue to become more diverse.

Ethnicity will not be the only difference we will experience, as differences in culture, gender, age, socioeconomic status, education, knowledge, and experience will also add to the diversity of all groups you will participate in. And the richness and depth of these differences will provide every group with advantages that far outweigh their disadvantages.

The primary advantage of diversity is in group decision-making, problem-solving, and productivity. Heterogeneous groups provide far greater perspectives, experiences, information, and skills than homogeneous groups. To be able to draw upon the different ideas, backgrounds, and ways of doing things increases the probability of making better decisions, solving problems, and being more productive in the long run.

A second advantage is that a more diverse group can serve to counter-balance possible bias and prejudice that is more prevalent in groups that are homogeneous. For instance, in a group of seven females and one male, the lone male could experience greater bias and exclusions by the female group members than if there were three males and four female members. I once served on a college committee as the only male with seven female colleagues and I experienced bias expressed in a few of their responses to my contributions such as, "Well that's because you're a man" and "You men always want to jump in and solve the problem." Even though we all smiled at those light-hearted remarks, perhaps I would have responded differently if there had been one or two other men present. Diversity in group membership can reduce the expression and display of bias and prejudice in group interactions.

A third and very significant advantage that diversity can bring to a group is an enhanced view of the world. Working with people who are different from yourself, whether that difference is gender, age, culture, or ethnicity, can actually serve to increase your awareness, appreciation, and maybe even your affection for those whom you once might have perceived as being very remote and distant from your mind and heart.

In my life, I've discovered that my experience working in very diverse groups has broadened my knowledge of others, increased my appreciation for different cultural practices, and most importantly, opened my heart to welcome and cherish those I once regarded as distant and even suspect. This is the greatest lesson diversity has taught me and I'm a better person for it.

There are, however, some disadvantages that diversity can present. One disadvantage expresses itself in communication behavior. Different cultures have very different ways of communicating in the small group setting. For instance, in Asian cultures, communication tends to be more indirect and less confrontational when compared to American culture. Asians are less assertive, more compliant, and less expressive in their nonverbal communication behavior than Americans. These differences could increase the potential for misunderstanding and conflict. We will be examining these cultural differences in a later chapter.

Gender differences can also increase communication difficulties in groups when men demonstrate a tendency to make more declarative statements and ask less questions than women do. And I might add, most men do in fact focus their initial attention to solving a problem rather than researching and analyzing a problem before setting out to solve that same problem. Maybe my female colleagues were right.

Age is another diversity challenge that can present challenges in a group. An older group member might value authority, rules, punctuality, and conservative attire, whereas a teenage member of that same group might question or challenge authority, think outside the box, disregard punctuality, and wear whatever fits his mood. You can see where these different values attributed to age could be fertile ground for misunderstanding and conflict as these two individuals attempt to communicate and work together.

These are just a few of the ways diversity can present challenges to any group. Here are five things you can do to maximize the advantages and minimize the disadvantages that diversity can have on the members of a group.

First, prepare mentally for participation in a diverse group, regardless of the kinds of diversity present. Adopt the mental frame of reference that diverse groups can provide a much richer opportunity for more effective decision-making, problem-solving, and social interaction than more homogeneous groups confronting the same tasks and challenges. Remind yourself that you are only one of billions of people inhabiting this earth and this new group will give you the opportunity to meet new people, learn new things, and discover new experiences. It all begins with a thought—that diversity gives you the opportunity to grow.

Second, show warmth and friendliness during the initial phases of your group's process. Greet the other members of your group with a smile, a handshake, and a warm hello when you first meet. Don't wait for the other person to make the initial move. Take that first step towards friendship. People make strong and lasting judgments of you when you first meet, so make a positive, friendly impression. Put out the welcome mat and greet them warmly.

Third, put others first. This begins by asking questions of the other group members, regardless of how different they might be from you. Take a genuine interest in others. Put others first and yourself second. Listen to what they have to say, even though their beliefs, values, thoughts, and feelings may seem vastly different from yours. Ask yourself the question, "What can I learn from them?" rather than "What can I teach them?" See the difference? That little difference in putting others first can be the first step in growing and maybe even making a new friend.

Fourth, establish common ground whenever you can. By common ground I mean those experiences, beliefs, and feelings you both share. Although your age, gender, culture, or ethnicity may be different, there are many things you both have in common that can serve to build a bridge that you can both stand upon. Maybe you both like video games, root for the same athletic team, enjoy similar food, love to go to movies, were both middle children, or desire to pursue similar professions in the future. Whatever you have in common, discover and acknowledge those commonalities. The common ground you establish can serve as a bridge for understanding and appreciation, reducing psychological and emotional distance.

The fifth and final thing you can do is to serve others, no matter how different they may be from you. Find ways you can be of support and encouragement to them. This final suggestion goes beyond merely acknowledging and appreciating those things you both have in common. Serving others is a willingness to do something to make someone else's life better. To sacrifice so that someone else might benefit. There's an old saying that, "To have a friend you have to be a friend." And there's no better way to be a friend than to be of service to another human being.

So, whatever you might do to support or encourage another person in your group, no matter how different he or she might be, take that opportunity to be a blessing. Whether it's providing them with some encouraging words, helping them with a group task, giving them a ride home from a meeting, or treating them to a cup of coffee, your support will not only be appreciated, but it can open the door to an entirely different kind of relationship between the two of you.

The power of diversity in groups cannot be overemphasized. Diversity can be viewed as a reason for mistrust and conflict or it can be seen as an invitation for productivity, growth, and even friendship. It all depends upon your point of view. See the power of diversity when you work with others in groups.

The purpose of this first chapter is to provide you with a basic understanding of small group process and, more important, to explain how groups operate systemically. When you find yourself participating in any problem-solving group, you can keep in mind the reasons why people join groups, the dimensions of group interaction, and the stages of group development. Working in a group is no easy matter, so hopefully these basic concepts will enable you to participate in constructive, positive, and caring ways so you can help create a more effective group.

◇ Individual and Group Exercises ◇

Family of Origin Rules: Your Original Group

EXERCISE
1.1

Consider what your life was like growing up in your family of origin. Did your parents plaster rules to the refrigerator and the bathroom mirrors? Did you receive long lectures about what to do and what not to do? Or did your parents even talk to you? Make a list of five spoken (explicit) or unspoken (implicit) rules or norms of behavior you remember from your family of origin. Be as specific as possible.

Could you list five rules from your family of origin? What do you think of them? What did you think of them when you were a kid? Do you still operate under these communication rules as an adult? As you examine the rules you listed, do you see any that might interfere with how you communicate today?

Group Problem-Solving Permission List

EXERCISE
1.2

Read each of the following statements pertaining to some aspect of communication or interaction in small group problem solving. Then indicate whether you agree or disagree with the statement using the ratings below. Respond to each statement based on what you think about your communication behavior, not on what others have said.

(1 = strongly disagree, 2 = disagree, 3 = unsure, 4 = agree, 5 = strongly agree)
I give myself permission to . . .

1. participate in a small problem-solving group.	1	2	3	4	5
2. share my thoughts and ideas with the group.	1	2	3	4	5
3. share my feelings with the group.	1	2	3	4	5
4. disagree with other group members.	1	2	3	4	5
5. listen to the opposing ideas of other members.	1	2	3	4	5
6. listen to criticism from other members.	1	2	3	4	5
7. respond to criticism from other members.	1	2	3	4	5
8. consider points of view different from my own.	1	2	3	4	5
9. compromise when it will benefit the group.	1	2	3	4	5
10. facilitate negotiation within the group.	1	2	3	4	5

How did you rate yourself on these 10 statements? You need to discover how you feel about each behavior if you work in a problem-solving group for any length of time. Think about each item before you enter into any group process.

Sharing in Your Group

EXERCISE 1.3   In your small group, share your findings to Exercise 1.2. Prepare a one- or two-minute statement summarizing your response to this exercise; highlight three strengths and three weaknesses you see in yourself. When others share their responses and lists, refrain from judging or evaluating them. Simply listen and learn.

Research Another Culture Online

EXERCISE 1.4   Go online and type in the name of a country or culture that is different from your own. Select a website that gives background information on that country or culture's communication behavior or customs. Spend a few minutes reading about how their communication behavior is different from your own. After reading about that country or culture, spend a few moments reflecting on how you might identify, appreciate, and acknowledge those communication behaviors in future small group work. You might even think of ways to welcome and make that individual feel appreciated and valued.

Discovering Yourself

Knowing the self is enlightenment.

—LAO TSU

THE morning sun feels warm on my face. There is no sound, no movement, only this gravel road stretching in a straight line for twenty miles in either direction, like a gray ribbon disappearing into the distance. I'm sitting on the tailgate of my pickup, listening to the silence of the desert, somewhere between Tonopah, Nevada, and the Utah border.

This is my second day in the desert. Last night I camped about three miles from here, on a smooth ridge overlooking this valley. Most of the evening I sat in my beach chair and gazed at the stars overhead. I made no fire, played no music. I simply sat and watched the stars, as the gentle breeze came up from the southwest. I listened to the silence all around.

I find the desert silence beautiful. Like a celestial choir from a distant galaxy, its anthem speaks to my heart, calms my body, and once again I hear my own breathing deep and true. I soon discover my thinking ceases and my heart expands to greet the silent stars above.

The solitude of the desert puts me in touch with myself. Far from the responsibilities of family and friends, work and community, I can sit and breathe. And do nothing for a period of time.

Once or twice a year, I venture into the desert alone for two or three nights. Leaving the comfort of my wife and children and all that is familiar, I withdraw from my regular life. The experience replenishes my spirit. It makes me feel whole, alive, and connected to those things that give my life meaning upon my return.

The desert experience also enables me to detach a little more from my usual tendency to want to control others—especially the students I teach in group work, the families I work with in counseling, and the trainees at seminars I conduct in industry. I've discovered that I return from the desert with a stronger desire to watch the process of the group unfold, rather than force my own agenda. I am more willing to listen to the opinions and feelings of others, rather than advocate or advance my own position, because I have gotten in touch with a quieter, deeper part of who I am, the part of me that isn't rattled or shaken by debate, disagreement, criticism, or conflict. This enhances my ability to face the rigors and requirements of small group problem solving.

Working with others in a small group can be one of the most demanding, challenging, and frustrating tasks we can perform. The close proximity, the different personalities, the heated discussions, the misunderstandings, both large and small, can and do provide the ingredients for all kinds of conflict within any group. If you do not possess some degree of perspective, self-awareness, and calm, the rigors of working with others can quickly get the best of you. Successful group participation not only demands a basic understanding of group process, it also requires a level of self-knowledge. This chapter will provide you with the opportunity to know yourself a little better.

Being Open to Self-Discovery

Before you can really be open to the ideas, opinions, and feelings of the others, you must first be open to your own ideas, opinions, and feelings. This might seem obvious at first glance. Of course you're open to your own thoughts and feelings. Who knows me better than me? But do you really?

It's been my experience while training, leading, and working with groups that most people go into a problem-solving group with a limited level of self-awareness and self-knowledge. During the course of group work, little things irritate them without their realizing that they do the same things. They are upset by the different opinions of others. They are hurt when someone criticizes them. They are frustrated when someone interrupts them in mid-sentence. And they get angry when the group doesn't decide in their favor. Sound familiar? It's as if the entire world has to agree with us for us to be happy. If not, we're upset. You'll soon discover that very rarely will the other members of your group see the world the way you do. In fact, the more you listen to the ideas and opinions of others, the more you'll realize just how different we all are.

So are you destined to be frustrated, angry, and hopeless while you work with others in groups? Not at all. But it requires that you open yourself to a little self-discovery before you enter into the wild world of working with other human beings. To know yourself—your strengths as well as your weaknesses, your beauty as well as your ugliness—is helpful in getting to know others. To be open to yourself is the first step in being open to others. So let's learn something new about you.

When was the last time you discovered something new about yourself? Maybe you recently broke off a friendship because you realized you didn't want to invest the energy the relationship required. Perhaps you enrolled in an art class and discovered you really enjoy painting with watercolors. Or maybe you watched a documentary on television and found yourself for the first time in your life thoroughly engrossed in the history of the Japanese samurai warriors.

Every day you have countless opportunities to discover fascinating, beautiful, and even surprising things about yourself. Whether it's the gradual unfolding of a new love or a new appreciation for classical music, you are discovering things about yourself from moment to moment—if you are open.

> All of the troubles of life come upon us because we refuse to sit quietly for a while each day in our rooms.
>
> ∽
>
> BLAISE PASCAL

However, many people are closed to new discoveries about themselves and the world around them. There's an old story about a college professor of religion who visited a Zen priest. The old priest invited the young professor to sit down in his simple yet tasteful room. The professor immediately began talking about Zen. He talked and talked. The old priest began to pour tea into the professor's cup as the young man droned on. Even after the cup was full, the old man continued to pour the tea. The cup overflowed and the tea eventually spilled on the young man's lap.

The professor shouted, "Master, why are you still pouring the tea? Can't you see the cup is already full?"

"You are very observant," replied the priest. "The same is true for you. If you are to receive any of my teachings, you must first empty the cup of your mind, for it is already full of your old learnings."

Like the professor, we too are not always open to self-discovery, or any kind of discovery for that matter, because we are full of old learnings. Old learning can be any idea we have about ourselves and who we think we are. The majority of these ideas came from others—parents, teachers, coaches, friends, and acquaintances. They came from movies, television, radio, magazines, and books, telling us who we should be and what we should want.

Very little of our learning comes from deep within ourselves, because we spend very little of our waking moments completely alone with our thoughts and feelings. We are constantly listening to the television or music. We would prefer the company of just about anyone rather than spend an evening by ourselves. But we can benefit from a fundamental knowledge of who we are, rather than who everyone else says we are. Without this knowledge, our interactions with others will lack connection, depth, and maturity. We need to take time to rediscover who we are. Spending time by ourselves is the most powerful way to accomplish this goal.

Spending Time by Yourself

Not everyone has the desire or the time to go off to the desert for a couple of days of solitude. But I believe there are countless other ways we can experience periods of solitude in our daily lives. Spending time by yourself doesn't necessarily require a solo trip to the Himalayas or joining a Benedictine monastery. Solitude can be discovered right where you are, if you are open to it. Here are some suggestions of simple ways you can experience solitude. Don't feel that you have to try them. But if you'd like to get a feel for who you are without the interruption of others, you might want to try one or two of these activities. I think you'll enjoy them.

Waking Up Earlier

No matter how busy or cramped your life is, you can give yourself the gift of ten minutes of solitude by waking up earlier in the morning. Experiment with your morning ritual by setting the alarm ten minutes earlier for one week. Instead of waking up at 6:30, try 6:20. That might not sound too appealing, but you'll discover you're much more

> The worst loneliness is not to be comfortable with yourself.
>
> ∞
>
> MARK TWAIN

flexible than you thought. You can use those extra ten minutes to sit in the kitchen or living room and watch the sunrise, listen to the birds sing, or hum a song of your own, while the rest of the world sleeps.

Going to Bed Later

Try going to bed ten minutes later in the evening, especially if you're a night owl. So, instead of going to bed at 11:00, you hit the sack at 11:10. During those extra ten minutes, you are to do nothing. Bundle up in a big coat, sit in the backyard or on the roof, and look at the stars overhead. Don't do anything. Just sit. This is your gift to yourself.

Taking Time Out

During the course of your day, give yourself a ten-minute mini-vacation by taking time out to stroll around outside of the office or on campus, instead of visiting with your colleagues at the water cooler or the snack shop. This ritual can become the most peaceful and restful ten minutes of your workday.

Turning Off the Radio

Another way you can be alone is to turn off the radio or stereo (and the cellular phone) when driving to and from work. It's amazing how different your driving experience can be without the constant intrusion of other people's voices and music. In the silence you will hear other things. I think you'll be surprised by the experience.

Stopping for Decompression Time

Returning home from a day at work or school also provides an opportunity to give yourself the gift of solitude. I call it decompression time. Usually, we rush out of work or school, fight the traffic for thirty to sixty minutes, skid into our driveway, and rush into the house, only to be met by family or roommates. We do all this without a quiet transition or decompression time.

    Try doing it differently for a while. Before pulling up to your driveway after a day at work or school, you can stop at a nearby park, elementary school, or quiet spot in the neighborhood for ten minutes to catch your breath, collect yourself, and decompress before entering into the next phase of your daily life. This can transform you back into a pleasant, even charming individual whose arrival at the end of the day will be anticipated with joy!

These are just five simple things you can do to give yourself the gift of solitude. You can probably brainstorm a number of other ways to get some time alone. Don't forget the traditional ways of experiencing solitude, like a solo afternoon trip to the lake, an overnight safari, meditation, prayer, or a stroll through the neighborhood after dinner. There are many ways to incorporate a little alone time. No matter what form of solitude you select, the important point is to get away from the hustle and bustle of life and open yourself to your own music.

I've discovered in my work with problem-solving groups that individuals who experience the greatest amount of disagreement, conflict, and hostility with others are often those people who are in conflict with themselves. Their relationships with others tell me a great deal about their relationship with themselves.

We need to be at peace with ourselves before we can be at peace with others. One of the best ways to begin this journey is to spend time alone, before entering any group process. Once you've experienced solitude, you can begin to discover some things about yourself.

Self-Discovery Inventories

There are countless ways to discover things about yourself. Personality tests, IQ scores, feedback from family and friends, report cards, job reviews, handwriting analysis, and career placement tests are but a few of the hundreds of methods people use to provide you with information about who they think you are. Advertisements in magazines, billboards, television, and radio, as well as the heroes and heroines in the evening news, movies, and paperbacks, also provide a steady diet of images of whom we should strive to emulate if we are to be worthwhile, desirable, and loved. The information from "out there" telling us who we are and who we should be is never-ending.

I want to leave these sources of information that claim to know who you are and who you should be for a moment and have you look to yourself for the same information. You will not know all there is to know about yourself after completing these exercises, but you will become more familiar with yourself.

> The unexamined life
> is not worth living.
>
> ⁂
>
> SOCRATES

Inventory 1: Who Are You?

Complete the following statements with the first idea, noun, adjective, verb, and so on that come to mind. Don't think about your response; just jot it down. Give yourself only sixty seconds.

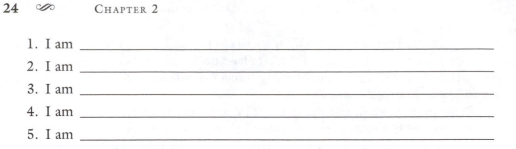

1. I am _____
2. I am _____
3. I am _____
4. I am _____
5. I am _____

Were you able to write down five responses about who you are? Do you notice any patterns in your responses? For instance, are most of your responses nouns (roles) such as student, wife, Buddhist, engineer, secretary, cowboy, or brain surgeon? Or are most of your responses descriptions such as caring, loving, resentful, lonely, twenty-seven years old, redheaded, or inquisitive? Are there any characteristics or roles you listed that are essential to who you are? Are there any you would like to change or modify? How do you see your responses affecting your interaction with other individuals and groups?

Inventory 2: What Do You Believe?

Complete the following statements with a belief you hold. Take a bit more time to consider each response than you did in Inventory 1. Give yourself five minutes.

1. I believe _____
2. I believe _____
3. I believe _____
4. I believe _____
5. I believe _____

Were you able to write down five beliefs? If not, what does this mean to you? Do you notice any patterns in your responses? Do your beliefs concern yourself, other people, ideas, or things? Are your beliefs stated positively or negatively? If someone held the opposite opinion or belief, how would you feel about the person? If someone held the same opinion or belief, how would you feel about the person? How do you see your beliefs affecting your interaction with other individuals and groups?

Inventory 3: Six Months to Live

Write down five things you would like to do if you discovered you had only six months to live. Assume you will experience no physical pain until the final week of life.

1. _____
2. _____

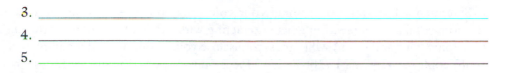

3. _____

4. _____

5. _____

Do any of your responses surprise you? How do you feel about your responses? Do your responses involve people, places, or things? Which item would you most want to accomplish before dying? If you were going to die in six months, how would that affect your communication with others? How would it affect your attitude toward working with a problem-solving group?

Inventory 4: Your Communication Behaviors

Read the following statements carefully; then circle the number that most accurately describes your response to the statement. Base your response on what you think, not on what others have said about your communication behavior.

(1 = strongly disagree, 2 = disagree, 3 = unsure, 4 = agree, 5 = strongly agree)

1. I speak in a pleasant tone of voice. 1 2 3 4 5
2. I speak at an adequate rate (speed) of speech. 1 2 3 4 5
3. I speak without verbal fillers ("um," "like," etc.). 1 2 3 4 5
4. I have a relaxed posture when speaking. 1 2 3 4 5
5. I use expressive gestures when speaking. 1 2 3 4 5
6. I smile when I speak with others. 1 2 3 4 5
7. I make eye contact when speaking with others. 1 2 3 4 5
8. I nod my head in agreement when listening. 1 2 3 4 5
9. I share my opinions with close friends. 1 2 3 4 5
10. I share my opinions with acquaintances/associates. 1 2 3 4 5
11. I share my feelings with close friends. 1 2 3 4 5
12. I share my feelings with acquaintances/associates. 1 2 3 4 5
13. I share my needs with close friends. 1 2 3 4 5
14. I share my needs with acquaintances/associates. 1 2 3 4 5
15. I am comfortable when I disagree with others. 1 2 3 4 5
16. I can disagree without disliking others. 1 2 3 4 5
17. I can verbally admit I'm wrong. 1 2 3 4 5
18. I can ask for forgiveness when I have hurt others. 1 2 3 4 5
19. I make others feel good about themselves. 1 2 3 4 5
20. I am optimistic and positive in my interactions. 1 2 3 4 5

    Statements 1 through 3 examine your voice. Statements 4 through 8 look at your nonverbal communication when interacting with others. Statements 9 through 14 examine your ability and willingness to disclose your thoughts and feelings to different people. Statements 15 through 18 focus on your behavior and attitudes when you are in disagreement or conflict with others. They also examine your ability to admit mistakes. Statements 19 and 20 look at your overall attitude and effect on others. Do you see any categories of communication behavior where you are especially strong? Are there any categories where you are weak or could use improvement? How would your weaknesses affect communication with others in a group work? How do you feel about your overall communication skill level?

Inventory 5: You're Not Perfect

List five communication behaviors, personal habits, personality characteristics, relationships, and anything else you can think of that you feel needs improvement. Solicit input from family and friends, coworkers and neighbors. Just the mere fact you would ask others for feedback will change your relationship with them.

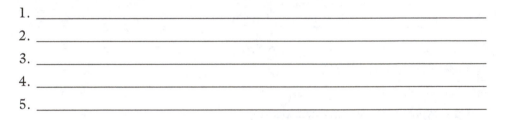

1. _____
2. _____
3. _____
4. _____
5. _____

    Well, how did you do on this exercise? I hope that you were able to identify five specific weaknesses or shortcomings. Once you can admit you're not perfect and there are things you need to improve, the criticism or threat of criticism from others will have less effect on you. Once you can freely admit to one weakness (or all five!), and not invest great amounts of energy and time defending or denying your weakness, you may experience a new freedom that allows you to be more open to the communication and feedback of others.

Inventory 6: Your Thanksgiving List

List two things you are thankful for about your physical self, two things you are thankful for about your psychological self, and two things you are thankful for about your spiritual self. Choose conditions or attributes you already possess, not those you are striving or hoping to achieve.

1. I'm thankful for my (physical) _____
2. I'm thankful for my (physical) _____
3. I'm thankful for my (psychological) _____

4. I'm thankful for my (psychological) _____

5. I'm thankful for my (spiritual) _____

6. I'm thankful for my (spiritual) _____

Was it easy or difficult to think of six things to be thankful for? If you found it difficult, you may not have taken enough time to be aware of and appreciate all the things that are working in your life. There are countless things about our bodies, minds, and hearts worth appreciating and being thankful for, but we are usually too busy to take time out to marvel at all the wonderful gifts we already possess.

Speaking Kindly to Yourself

In your journey to increased self-awareness, you always run the risk of discovering thoughts, ideas, and feelings that are not always positive, enlarging, or encouraging. These negative thoughts can bring us down, interfere with our communication with others, and in general, make our lives miserable. These negative thoughts can not only disrupt our participation and effectiveness in group work, but also hinder our level of self-acceptance and personal growth.

In his book *A Guide to Rational Living*, psychologist Albert Ellis outlines the ten most troubling thoughts Americans have that make their lives unsatisfactory, frustrating, and depressing. He calls them our ten irrational beliefs, and I believe that many of these commonly held ideas prevent us from communicating and interacting in effective and healthy ways with others in our group work. See if you hold any of these beliefs:

1. You should be liked/loved by everyone.
2. You should be competent, adequate, and achieving in all possible respects if you are to consider yourself worthwhile.
3. Happiness is externally caused, and people have little or no ability to control their sorrows and disturbances.
4. Your past history is an important determinant to your present behavior and that because something once strongly affected your life, it should indefinitely have a similar effect.
5. There is only one right solution to a problem, and it is catastrophic if this perfect solution is not found.
6. If something is or may be dangerous or fearsome, you should be terribly concerned about it and should keep dwelling on the possibility of it occurring.
7. Certain people are wicked and they should always be severely blamed and punished for their villainy.
8. It is awful and catastrophic when things are not the way you would like them to be.
9. It is easier to avoid than to face certain life difficulties and self-responsibilities.
10. One should become quite upset over other people's problems and disturbances.

Ellis discovered that almost all of the psychological and emotional distress his clients were experiencing was based upon one or more of these ten irrational beliefs. In fact, beliefs 1 and 2 accounted for almost seventy percent of his clients' presenting problems in therapy—the idea that one should be liked by everyone and the idea that one should be competent in all possible respects.

> We must always change, renew, and rejuvenate ourselves, otherwise we harden.
>
> ⸏
>
> GOETHE

Ellis instructs us to identify any irrational belief we might hold, challenge that belief with its opposite idea, and ultimately replace the old belief with a healthier belief. Maybe you've told yourself one or two of the ten statements listed above. Or maybe you believe one of these ten ideas to be true for you. Well, if you do, you might want to challenge that particular belief and substitute a different, more rational belief for the irrational one you might be holding.

Here are the ten statements presented in their opposite form. Read over the list and see if any of the ideas are helpful in creating a new way of talking kindly to yourself and, hopefully, increase your level of acceptance, understanding, and effectiveness when communicating with others in your group work.

1. *You don't have to be approved of by everyone.* Not everyone has to like or love you. It is irrational to strive for universal approval or affection. No one is liked, loved, or approved of by everyone. To strive to be approved of by everyone in your work group is not always a desirable goal. People who try to win the approval of everyone will sacrifice their own principles, values, and happiness to placate or satisfy others.

2. *You do not have to be perfect or competent in everything you do.* No human being is perfect. There will be some activities in which you will achieve competency, even mastery, but no human being is competent in everything. In fact, experiencing failure can be one of the best teachers you will ever have as you work with others in small groups.

3. *Your happiness comes from within you, and you can change your feelings by changing your thinking.* Your feelings are determined by your thinking, not by external events. You can change your feelings by changing your thinking. In fact, almost all the negative feelings you will experience can be modified or eliminated by seeing the truth of these ten beliefs.

4. *Your current behavior is not determined by the past.* Human beings can unlearn old behaviors and replace them with new behaviors. Although many habitual ways of behaving and thinking can be deeply rooted and difficult to change, they can be changed with focused thinking and concentrated effort. So, if your past small group work experiences have been frustrating or unsuccessful, you can open to the fact that your future group experiences can be very successful and rewarding. The past is the past. You create the present and the future!

5. *There can be many solutions to any given problem.* It's irrational to think there is only one solution to any problem. Most likely, there are a variety of ways to solve any problem. Remember the notion of equifinality from Chapter 1? Many ways exist to solve any problem. This is one belief that requires your creativity when solving problems in your group.

6. *Don't worry.* It's irrational to worry and be overly concerned about every little thing that can go wrong in your life. The vast majority of the things you will worry about during your lifetime will never come to pass. Much of your worry is born from fatigue and loneliness. Get enough sleep, rest, and relaxation. Participate positively and optimistically when you interact with others.

7. *Most people are good at heart.* The first response when things go wrong in groups is to look for someone to blame and punish. We desire to vilify and demonize those we hold responsible for our problems. But very few people are totally hateful, mean, or evil. The vast majority of people are basically good, hardworking, honest folks.

8. *Its okay if you don't get your way.* We don't always get our way. Can you imagine if you got everything you ever wished for? You'd be a gluttonous, wealthy, overindulged mess! We need to get beyond ourselves and begin to be aware of and responsive to the needs of those around us. In this life, we need to move from self to others. Don't get too hung up on what you want or what you desire. Learn to think of others too.

9. *It's better to face your problems and responsibilities than avoid them.* It's irrational to avoid or deny actual problems or responsibilities facing you. Physical illness, relationship conflicts, and emotional distress need to be acknowledged and addressed. The same holds true for your responsibilities. You need to keep your promises, meet your legal obligations, and carry out your duties. This is especially true when you work with others in groups, because the success of the group depends upon each member taking responsibility to do his or her part.

10. *Let others be responsible for themselves.* It is irrational to be overly concerned about the lives of other people. Human beings need to take responsibility for their own lives. We can be responsive to others, but not responsible for them. Each person needs to live his or her own life. There's an old saying, "Every time you help someone, you make them a little weaker, a little more dependent upon you." Let others be responsible for themselves.

These ten beliefs constitute a much more positive and healthy way of viewing yourself and others. You might find many of these beliefs helpful in talking to yourself in a more positive way. If you discover that an irrational belief is running through your mind and causing you some distress or pain, try to consciously hold the opposite belief in your mind and heart for an equal amount of time. Remember, your words create what you become, so learn to speak more positively and kindly to yourself.

Accepting Yourself

Even though we can invest a great deal of effort into increasing our self-awareness and speaking more kindly and positively to ourselves, we will never come to a complete understanding of ourselves. It's not possible in this lifetime, and I think a little mystery is good. What's important is that you take the time to ask yourself some important questions about your life every once in a while. Who are you? What do you believe? What are your priorities? How do you communicate to others? What do you want to improve? And for what are you thankful? The six inventories you just completed earlier in this chapter are invitations for self-discovery—not for you to consider just once, but rather as a way to stay in touch with yourself in the years to come.

Knowing yourself—having a sense of who and what you are—is important in your interactions with others in your small group problem-solving activities. It is important for you to have a familiarity with yourself before you enter into group work. You are less apt to look to other group members for approval, for you have already taken the time to examine and accept your strengths as well as your weaknesses. You will be more familiar with your skills, behavior, personality, and maybe even your soul. You will have attempted to accept the good with the bad. That's who you are, and no one's perfect.

> We cannot change anything unless we accept it. Condemnation does not liberate, it oppresses.
>
> ∽
>
> CARL JUNG

I'm not suggesting we neglect or turn a blind eye to those areas we can improve or correct; just the opposite. I'm suggesting we acknowledge and accept those things we can improve rather than deny or defend their existence. The first step in changing something is to accept its existence.

It's okay to have weaknesses—areas we want or need to improve. When we can acknowledge this in ourselves, we are more likely to accept imperfection in others as well. And accepting others is the first step in working with others. Self-acceptance means we don't have to be perfect.

Accepting Others

We need to accept those whose manners irritate us, whose ideas annoy us, and whose goals disturb us. Usually, we try to distance ourselves from such individuals. We build walls or fences to keep them out, but in the end we cage ourselves in. More and more, we become prisoners of our own limited and ethnocentric view of the world, when in reality there are countless ways of seeing and experiencing life—ours being just one of the multitude.

The acceptance of others requires us to suspend judgment for a while. This doesn't mean we never evaluate, criticize, or blame. It means we silence our judging, condemning mind for a while and listen to others, even if their ideas are diametrically opposed to ours. It means we become more open to others—to broaden our definitions of what is acceptable, eligible, and tolerable. It means we overlook differences and seek similarities. It means we lighten up and open up to others.

Without this acceptance of others, our interactions in groups can be rigid, intolerant, and blaming. Our relationships with others can be marked by detachment, apathy, and even suspicion, except with those individuals who share our beliefs and goals. Without the acceptance of others, our commitment to the group and our participation in negotiation and compromise will be feeble and insecure. The acceptance of others is crucial to successful group work.

Critically Thinking about Yourself as a Communicator

In this chapter you've examined what your perceptions are regarding your beliefs, values, likes and dislikes, achievements, roles, talents, and goals. That's helpful in developing an awareness of self that can increase your communication effectiveness in group process, especially when your opinions, beliefs, or behaviors are being questioned or challenged by other group members.

Yet, it is equally important for you to be willing to stand back and re-examine those same perceptions you hold about yourself, especially those perceptions regarding your communication abilities. It's good every once in a while to have a reality check of sorts. This is a process we often overlook or are reluctant to engage in—to critically think about our self-concept. And this is a process we will conclude this chapter on—critically thinking about yourself as a small group communicator.

Here is a three-step process that can help you more honestly and critically think about your self-concept as a communicator within a small group.

Step 1: Awareness.

The first step in critically thinking about your self-concept as a group communicator is the awareness that it is important to engage in this process. It is not uncommon for human beings to go through their entire lives without serious reflection or systematic examination of who they are. They simply wander through life with some vague, unconscious notion that they're okay, not okay, or something in between. But that's not going to be you.

Be courageous and realize that it's important for you and for those with whom you interact, to occasionally pause from the hustle and bustle of your busy life and take an honest look at yourself. This awareness of your need for an occasional re-examination of who you are as a small group communicator is the first step.

Step 2: Reflection.

The second step is to honestly rate and reflect upon your small group communication attitude and behaviors. Just the mere fact that you are willing to rate yourself and reflect upon these items accurately and honestly is more than most people are willing to do. Good for you!

Here are seven items that you can reflect upon. I'm sure you can think of more behaviors, but I believe that these seven are essential to your effectiveness in small group communication. Read each statement and rate yourself honestly in terms of your self-perceived behavior in the group. *Circle* the number that represents your response.

1. I am <u>NONVERBALLY RECEPTIVE AND WARM</u> to others.

   Never 1   2   3   4   5   6   7   8   9   10   Always

2. I <u>demonstrate a POSITIVE ATTITUDE</u> toward others.

   Never 1   2   3   4   5   6   7   8   9   10   Always

3. I <u>ENCOURAGE OTHERS to express</u> their ideas and feelings.

   Never 1   2   3   4   5   6   7   8   9   10   Always

4. I <u>LISTEN to the ideas/opinions</u> of others with an open mind.

   Never 1   2   3   4   5   6   7   8   9   10   Always

5. I <u>SPEAK in a respectful, informed, and succinct manner</u>.

   Never 1   2   3   4   5   6   7   8   9   10   Always

6. I <u>fulfill my RESPONSIBILITIES</u> and duties to the group.

   Never 1   2   3   4   5   6   7   8   9   10   Always

7. I <u>demonstrate LEADERSHIP in helping the group</u> reach its goals.

   Never 1   2   3   4   5   6   7   8   9   10   Always

Your honest reflection and rating of these seven behaviors will provide you with a more accurate and structured shaping of a small group communicator self-concept than simply saying to yourself that, "I did a good job," "I did okay," or "I was horrible at today's meeting." The benefit to responding to these seven small group communication behaviors is that it not only focuses your attention to how you did in past meetings, it will focus your attention and efforts in future group interactions. Awareness and reflection are foundational to positive growth.

Step 3: Feedback.

This third step requires some courage and a few bucks to treat someone to coffee. It's one thing for you to rate yourself as a group communicator, but it's another thing to solicit the perceptions of someone else from your group to also rate you.

The perceptions of another person regarding your communication behavior can be extremely informative and maybe even a little surprising as you listen to their feedback. And remember, their perceptions are simply that—their perceptions. Receive their responses gratefully and graciously as additional input for you to consider as you evaluate and reflect upon your communication behavior. Treat your evaluator to coffee and make the time together a positive, fun event.

Have your fellow group member rate you on the same seven items on page 32 to provide specific feedback on your small group communication behavior. And remember not to defend, debate, or dispute as you receive their ratings. Most of their feedback will be positive I'm sure, and if they rate you low on one or two items, ask for specific reasons for their ranking and listen without defending yourself. Remember, the purpose is to receive feedback and learn how others see you. Your self-concept can be modified with the help of others. Be open to those opportunities. And don't forget to pay for their coffee.

Your willingness to occasionally reflect upon your small group communication behavior and attitude is a healthy perspective and can provide the opportunities for significant growth and improvement in your communication life. Be gentle on yourself as you critically think about your communication behaviors and attitudes.

In this chapter we examine the idea of being open to solitude and self-discovery. We look at ways you can spend time by yourself and discuss the importance of accepting yourself and others in group communication. Now that you've had an opportunity to discover yourself a little more, you can create a more accepting, understanding, and compassionate atmosphere in your group work.

∞ Individual and Group Exercises ∞

How Others See Your Communication Behavior

EXERCISE 2.1

Have someone who knows you well, such as a family member, coworker, or friend, review your responses to Inventory 4 in this chapter. Briefly explain the inventory. Then have this person comment on your responses to each statement. Withhold judgment as you listen. Let the person talk about how he or she sees you and your communication behavior. Ask for suggestions on how to improve communication. Thank the person for sharing.

Communication Behaviors for You to Improve

EXERCISE 2.2

Based on the responses you received in Exercise 2.1 and your own thoughtful consideration of your responses to Inventory 4, list three specific behaviors you would like to improve.

1. _____

2. _____

3. _____

Before participating in any future group work or interpersonal interactions, remind yourself about these three behaviors. Make a conscious effort to improve them.

Group Sharing of Individual Communication Behaviors

EXERCISE 2.3 Make copies of Inventory 4 for members of a group you are working with. Ask group members to complete the inventory. When they have finished, make copies of each inventory and distribute them to group members. Distribute your inventory as well. One by one, have group members provide feedback to each member's inventory. This activity can prove very insightful in helping the group communicate more effectively.

Reviewing Communication Feedback Online

EXERCISE 2.4 Go online and post an invitation on your Facebook page to solicit communication feedback from friends. This invitation takes courage, but the feedback can be very enlightening. You might use the seven items provided in the small group communication behavior list from this chapter or make up your own list of communication behaviors. Don't go overboard. Five to seven behaviors are enough to provide you with some valuable information on how others see your communication behavior. And remember to be open to their perceptions. You don't have to disagree, defend, or debate. Just receive the feedback with an open mind. You might just learn something new and helpful.

CHAPTER 3

Expressing Yourself Clearly

Speak your truth clearly and kindly.

—Thomas Merton

Every time she entered the conference room, the rest of us in the group would cringe, for we knew we'd be in for a long evening.

Janet was one of nine members of an advisory board for a new teacher credential program at a local university. I also sat on the board, which met once a month to oversee the program.

Although the other members and I observed the usual norms of communication, Janet seemed to delight in breaking many of the rules. She would interrupt speakers in mid-sentence, criticize anyone who questioned an idea she had advanced, and scowl when others objected indirectly to her behavior.

What disturbed me most was Janet's controlling behavior. She would attempt to dominate the discussion with monologues supporting her position, misinterpret the remarks of others to fit her design, and challenge the chairperson with regularity. In short, Janet was a problem-solving group's nightmare.

She attended those meetings for six months. During the sixth meeting, Janet conducted herself in her usual domineering manner and many of us offered subtle, and not so subtle, objections to her behavior. I felt sorry for her. Yet I realized her conduct was detrimental to the task and social dimensions of the group.

During our break, I took a walk out to the parking lot to stretch my legs and saw Janet, in tears, hurrying to her car. I could hear her crying as she unlocked her car, not far from where I stood in the shadows of a building. Within a moment or so, I heard her engine roar as she sped out of the parking lot.

Apparently, during the break, she and the chairperson had argued about her behavior, and Janet had resigned from the board right then and there. I was told

Janet calmly strolled out of the room, without uttering a word to any of the others in the group. That was the last they saw of her.

But I had seen Janet cry.

In this chapter we will explore the importance of communicating your thoughts and feelings effectively to others when you work in groups. Many people think that effective communication requires only that we tell others what's on our minds and our messages will be received accurately. But this is not always the case, especially during heated group discussions in problem-solving groups. Special attention needs to be paid to avoiding dysfunctional ways of communicating, owning your messages, understanding gender differences in conversation strategies, and giving feedback to others. By learning to send clear and effective messages, you can create more effective group interaction.

Communication Is a Learned Behavior

I've often thought about Janet's tears in the parking lot that Tuesday night so many years ago. Her confident exterior, I thought, hid a troubled, perhaps lonely interior. Over the years, I've been haunted by the image of her crying in her car. Did she treat her loved ones in the same controlling way? Were there any loved ones in her life? Had she always been this way? Where did she learn to be so pushy?

Janet, like you and me, learned most of her communication behavior in her family of origin. By the age of five, the fundamental structure of our personality has been established. Also by the age of five, the majority of our daily adult language has been learned and our basic communication patterns have been firmly established.

Can our communication patterns be changed? Yes, I believe they can, and people can learn new ways of speaking, listening, and interacting with others. I've spent twenty-five years teaching communication courses and have witnessed thousands of students improve the way they speak and listen. I have also been a marriage and family counselor since 1986 and have seen how individuals and families can correct dysfunctional patterns of interaction and replace them with more effective methods of communication. But change is not easy.

> When old patterns are broken, new worlds emerge.
>
> ∽
>
> TULI KUPFERBERG

Most people are unaware of their own communication patterns and behavior. They often assume that communication skills are something they're born with—like breathing and walking. They believe they're talking when their mouths are moving and they're listening when their mouths are shut. What could be simpler than that? However, you'll see that the communication process is actually more complex than you might first think.

Before we explore the process of communication and look at specific ways you can express yourself more clearly, it will be helpful to review five communication roles that prevent you from expressing yourself clearly.

Five Roles That Prevent Clear Expression

Family therapist Virginia Satir has suggested four dysfunctional communication roles family members can adopt in their interactions with one another. She refers to these four roles as the computer, blamer, placater, and distractor. The computer is the cool, collected, intellectual family member who uses logic and reasoning as the primary method of communicating. The blamer is the family member who finds fault and casts blame on others. The placater is the peacemaker who tries to avoid or diffuse conflict at all costs by complying with the wishes of others. And the distractor is the one who attempts to get the focus off the conflict issue, using humor or irrelevant communication to accomplish the task. This is a simplified explanation of Satir's communication roles, but it presents a valuable means for examining communication patterns.

I've constructed a modified version of Satir's model for groups: the controller, blamer, pleaser, distractor, and ghost. Upon examining these five roles and their characteristic patterns of behavior, you might recognize some aspects of yourself.

Controller

The controller tries to dominate, regulate, and manipulate the interaction of the group. The controller's verbal communication patterns are usually issuing orders and directives. She tends to give directions and explain the superiority of her ideas and solutions over all others presented. The controller often uses logical appeals and intricate reasoning to get her way. She can be a master of words and persuasion. No matter what methodology she uses, her ultimate goal is to control the group and achieve her objectives.

Blamer

The blamer usually finds fault with others and their ideas and suggestions, although he tends not to offer suggestions of his own. He generally blames others for the group's shortcomings and failures. The blamer casts a shadow of doubt and gloom on solutions the group proposes and is the first to say "I told you so" when a solution fails.

Pleaser

In my model, the pleaser is similar to Satir's placater. The pleaser attempts to avoid all conflict by giving in to the wishes of the others. The pleaser agrees to just about anything the others ask or require. When a conflict begins to arise, he does whatever it takes to dissolve or neutralize the disagreement. He is generally uncomfortable asserting opinions, defending positions, and sharing feelings. The pleaser backs down rather than fights.

Distractor

The distractor doesn't give in, blame, or control. The distractor's role is to draw or deflect attention away from the issue at hand. When the group experiences stress or conflict, she usually jokes about the situation or redirects the discussion to an unrelated

> When you blame others, you give up your power to change.
>
> ∽
>
> ELEANOR ROOSEVELT

issue or topic. The distractor is just as uncomfortable with conflict as the pleaser, but her method for handling discomfort is different. Whereas the pleaser placates or gives in, the distractor utilizes some avoidance technique to change the subject.

Ghost

The ghost is an individual who neither shows up to meetings nor participates when he does attend. Just as the word suggests, this group member's participation is nonexistent. He is often labeled the nonperformer, the low-verbal, and the passive-aggressive personality. I simply refer to this person as the ghost, because he is not really there to contribute to the group's efforts.

Do any of these role descriptions sound or feel familiar to you? Do they remind you of someone from your family of origin? A friend or coworker? More important, do you see yourself described in any of these five dysfunctional communication roles? If so, you may want to explore your reasons for these behaviors and consider modifying or eliminating them if they no longer serve a purpose in your life.

These five basic dysfunctional roles will appear from time to time during your work with others in groups. Your awareness and ability to recognize these roles will greatly enhance your understanding and effectiveness in your small group work.

The Communication Process

Very few people would welcome the thought of living the rest of their lives in complete isolation from other human beings. The prospect of spending life alone on a desert island or facing the horrors of solitary confinement would be intolerable for many of us. The purpose of life is found in our relationships with others during this lifetime. The primary way we initiate, develop, and maintain these relationships is through the communication process. Communication is a transactional process in which communicators attempt to influence and are influenced by others. It's the give and take of life. This process takes two forms—verbal and nonverbal communication. We will explore both, as well as examine the communication process within which they operate.

Verbal Communication

The first form of communication is verbal communication. Verbal communication is all spoken and written communication. These are the words of communication, whether they are being boisterously delivered in a speech or silently read in a book. From the moment you vocalize your first word as a toddler to the last words you utter on your deathbed, your verbal communication is essential in your efforts to live your life.

When you work in groups, keep these four principles of verbal communication in mind: it's symbolic, it's rule governed, it defines and limits, and it lets us create. Verbal communication is symbolic, in that words stand for or symbolize things in the real world. They are not the actual things they represent. Verbal communication is rule governed. There are syntactic rules that govern the order of words in a sentence. For instance, "I am turning off the computer" is syntactically correct, whereas "Off the am I turning computer" doesn't make much sense.

Verbal communication defines and limits. Language is used to define things, which also limits the thing being defined. For instance, if I said that Lisa is an ineffective manager, I have defined her as a manager and limited her to the status of ineffective as opposed to outstanding, effective, or satisfactory. Finally, verbal communication lets us create. We can arrange the thousands upon thousands of words contained in the English language in an endless variety of combinations and structures to communicate our thoughts and feelings. Different combinations of words enable you to express a message in a way that reflects your attitude, mood, and personality. This is one of the joys of life—to create messages that are uniquely yours.

Nonverbal Communication

The second form of communication is nonverbal. Nonverbal communication is all communication that is not spoken or written. Although we spend a great deal of our formal education learning to communicate verbally with others through reading, writing, and sometimes even speaking, we rarely receive any specific coaching or training in nonverbal communication. The entire universe of nonverbal messages above, below, around, and through the verbal messages is usually neglected in our formal education, and yet researchers have been telling us for years that nonverbal communication can have more impact on us than verbal messages in many situations.

Nonverbal communication comes in myriad forms and is delivered in immeasurable ways. It's embedded in the clothes you wear, the tone of voice, the posture you present, the gestures you use, the facial expressions you flash, or the car you drive. It's your silence, your gentle touch, your downcast eyes, or your deep, relaxed breathing. It's all these things and a thousand others that constitute nonverbal communication behavior.

When you work in groups, keep in mind the following principles of nonverbal communication: it is continuous, it conveys emotions, it is more universal than verbal communication, it is multichanneled, and it is ambiguous. Nonverbal communication is continuous; it is always present. Whereas a sentence ends and talking stops, your body posture, your facial expressions, and your clothing can communicate messages long after you've stopped speaking. Nonverbal communication conveys emotions much more effectively and quickly than verbal communication. Your facial expressions, tone of voice, and posture can communicate your feelings of tenderness, anger, frustration, or joy much more quickly and profoundly than words could ever accomplish.

Nonverbal communication is also more universal than verbal language. Emotions such as anger, sadness, joy, surprise, and boredom can be communicated to others by one's facial expressions and body language, regardless of language barriers or cultural differences. Nonverbal communication is also multichanneled in that messages can be sent in all five sensory channels, whereas most verbal communication must flow through auditory and visual channels. Finally, nonverbal communication is ambiguous. By that I mean that it really is impossible to "read someone like a book." Nonverbal communication is far too complex and difficult to interpret to convey any one specific message or meaning to a given behavior or act. Someone's folded arms during a business meeting can be interpreted in a variety of ways. It can mean the person is cold, bored, comfortable, defensive, or angry. It can even mean that he's hiding a food stain from lunch. One thing you can do when nonverbal communication is ambiguous is to ask questions. Rather than guess at the meaning of a particular behavior or act, you can always choose to ask the other person and open up the lines of communication.

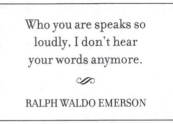

Who you are speaks so loudly, I don't hear your words anymore.

∞

RALPH WALDO EMERSON

The Transactional Nature of Communication

By using the verbal and nonverbal forms of expression, we participate in the most important activity there is: communication. Communication is transactional; that is, each person communicating is sender and receiver simultaneously, not just sender or receiver. As communicators, each person communicating has an effect on the other. In addition to this mutual impact of the communicators, the context of the communication setting or environment has an influence upon the communication act also.

In communication, you are attempting to influence the other communicator in some way. Maybe not as obvious, but equally important, is that by interacting with another human being, you are also opening yourself up to the influence of others. In this sense, communication is a transactional process—there is a constant give and take, an interdependent influence upon both communicators by one another during the process of communication. This is the transactional model of communication—the dance of life.

The Components of Communication

To understand more specifically how the transactional communication process works, let's examine the components of communication. The communicators are the individuals who are sending and receiving messages simultaneously from one another during the communication event. The message is the thought or feeling a communicator wants to convey. This message can be an idea, thought, or feeling. The communicator must encode or convert this thought or feeling into verbal and nonverbal symbols that others will understand. This encoding process is highly complex. The words selected, rate of speech, tone of voice, facial expressions, and body language are determined by the source's relationship with the receiver, purpose, speaking situation, and countless other variables. The decoding process involves making sense out of messages. The receiving communicator must decipher the words and the nonverbal cues sent by the other person so they have meaning for him. After decoding the message, the communicator encodes a return message and sends it on its way. Noise is any physical or psychological interference that reduces the accurate decoding of a message, such as the sound of ambient talking, a jackhammer nearby, or multiple meanings for a given work.

The most important aspect to remember about this encoding/decoding process is that it occurs simultaneously within each communicator. As one individual is formulating a sentence to express his thought or feeling (encoding), he is simultaneously observing and trying to make sense (decoding) of the nonverbal behaviors or feedback from the other communicator. The effective communicator will read the feedback accurately and adjust his or her messages appropriately. In this sense, the process of communication is transactional, in that each communicator influences and is influenced by the other communicator.

A channel is the medium by which the message is communicated. A communicator can use the channels of sound, sight, smell, touch, and taste to send a message. For instance, if you want to communicate affection to another person, you can use a variety of channels or combinations of channels. You can say, "I like you" (sound). You can wink your eye (sight). You might hug the individual (touch). You could send some cookies you baked to the person (taste). Or you could send a bottle of perfume (smell). Usually, the more channels you use, the more effect your message will have on the receiver.

The encoding and decoding processes of both communicators are influenced by their individual backgrounds. The personal history of the communicator, personality, gender, race, age, knowledge, experiences, attitudes, beliefs, and emotions influences his or her communication experience. It determines to a great extent how he or she will encode and decode messages during the communication process. In addition to the personal background of the communicators, the physical environment of the communication setting affects and influences the communicators and how they will process the communication interaction. The physical surroundings, the specific occasion in which the communication occurs, the noise level, the temperature, and the interruptions from machines and people all contribute to having an influence on the communication process.

The most important thing to keep in mind as you communicate with others in your groups is that what you choose to say and how you choose to behave will have an effect on the other group members—not only as they modify and readjust their messages to you, but also their behaviors. In the transactional model of communication, your words and behaviors can influence others and you can indeed create more effective groups.

I-Statements

To ensure a message is encoded accurately, communicators must be sure to encode clear messages. I-statements are the first step in communicating clear messages. With I-statement language you personally take ownership of your thoughts and feelings. Here are some examples of simple I-statements:

> I believe trucks are the most useful vehicles.
> I think education is important to personal growth.
> I feel upset by what I heard at this morning's meeting.
> It's my opinion that you're correct.

Do you notice how the speaker takes ownership of the opinion or feeling expressed? Do you also notice an I-statement doesn't necessarily have to contain the word I to qualify as an I-statement? For example, "It's my opinion that you're correct" shows ownership even though it doesn't contain the word I.

I-statements provide several advantages. First, when a speaker uses I-statements, the listener of the message knows who the originator or owner of the statement is. If I-statements are not used, the ownership of the message is often uncertain or overstated.

A second advantage to I-statements is they provide a target for the listener of the message to respond. If a speaker says, "Everyone thinks the Forty-Niners are the best team," the listener might be less likely to disagree, because the speaker uses the word everyone as the source of the message. At a subconscious level, it might be difficult to confront or argue with "everyone" rather than with an individual.

A third advantage to I-statements is that they let you know when people are speaking for others. For instance, the statement "My wife likes to go camping" shows the husband is speaking for the wife.

A fourth advantage to I-statements is that they are more thoughtful statements. Because they show ownership, I-statements force the speaker to weigh his remarks more cautiously. I think (I-statement) it's easier to flippantly say, "Everyone really likes you," rather than owning the statement and saying, "I like you."

> To know oneself, one must assert oneself.
>
> ∞
>
> ALBERT CAMUS

Another advantage to I-statements is that they help prevent blaming others. Many times a speaker uses what is called "you-language" instead of I-statements. The speaker sends "you" messages such as "You make me mad" and "You're a grouch," directing blame to the listener of the message. If the speaker were to use I-statements, such as "I get mad when you call me chubby" or "I notice you're not smiling," the tone of the statement is much different. There is less of a blaming and faultfinding tone to these statements. Ownership of thoughts and feelings is the purpose of I-statements.

Four Levels of Communication

Now that we know how to construct an I-statement, the next step in learning how to speak clearly is to examine the four levels of communication, which are surface talk, reporting facts, giving opinions, and sharing feelings.

Each level of communication contains different levels of information. The surface talk level merely acknowledges others without really sharing. The reporting fact level shares information we know can be verified or proven. The giving opinion level deals with our opinions and beliefs. The sharing feelings level involves our most intimate information—our feelings and emotions.

We are not restricted to communicating at just one level. We can communicate from all four levels of disclosure during the course of one conversation. Let's examine the four levels of communication.

Level 1: Surface Talk

In this first level of sharing, we keep our conversations to a minimal level of disclosure. The surface talk level of sharing includes greetings, casual acknowledgment of strangers and acquaintances, chitchat with a coworker, and so on. The primary goal is to acknowledge another human being without having to provide any personal information about ourselves. Listen to the following surface-level remarks:

> How's it going? / Fine. / How about you? / Fine. /
> Looks like rain, huh? / Maybe. /
> Have a good day. / You, too. / Thanks.

As you can see, there isn't any real disclosure going on in these statements. That's not bad. Their purpose wasn't to conduct some deep, involved conversation. Both parties were merely acknowledging one another in a socially acceptable fashion.

Surface talk is just another way of saying, "I see you and I want to acknowledge you," and usually nothing more. It's a way of being polite to people we come in contact with. It would be humanly impossible to conduct in-depth discussions with everyone we saw in a given day. We probably wouldn't want to, anyway.

Level 2: Reporting Facts

The second level of communicating involves the reporting of facts. Reporting the outside temperature, giving directions to a stranger, demonstrating how to tune a carburetor, giving a lecture on the mating habits of moths, providing information about a car you're selling through the papers, and answering questions during an interview are examples of reporting factual information.

Facts are different from opinions in that they can be verified. A thermometer can verify the temperature. A map can verify the directions you're giving. A car manual can verify your directions on tuning a carburetor. Scientific research can verify the information in your lecture. Your tune-up receipts can verify your statements about the car's maintenance history. Your previous employers can verify your information regarding past employment performance. The key to identifying communication at this level is that the content of the messages can be verified or proven. The following statements are reporting facts.

> I weigh 162 pounds.
> I was employed by Apple Computer from 1998 to 2000.
> It rained two inches in San Francisco during December.

At the reporting fact level, there isn't usually a great deal of personal information being shared. Sure, there could be exceptions, such as, "I've been in a mental hospital for twenty years," but the majority of factual information reveals little concerning your personal opinions or feelings.

Level 3: Giving Opinions

Giving opinions is a little more risky than surface talk or reporting facts. By giving your opinions about topics, people, or events, you are exposing more of who you are. You are allowing others to see more of you by sharing your opinions, attitudes, and beliefs with them. This level is much more threatening to you, because there is a greater chance of disagreement, disapproval, and conflict brought about by opinion differences with others.

> More words count less.
>
> ∾
>
> LAO TSU

But disagreement is natural. We couldn't possibly agree on every topic we discuss with others. And once again, we wouldn't want to. That's the beauty of life. It's often our differences that make people interesting to us. They complement our weaknesses and show us new ways of seeing, thinking, and feeling. The following statements are giving opinions:

> It's my opinion gun control would not lower violent crime.
> I know this plan will work.
> I believe if we go to counseling, we'll continue our relationship.

Level 4: Sharing Feelings

The deepest level of communication is the sharing of feelings. It's at this level that two people really communicate for connection—the feeling level. Sharing feelings can be extremely beneficial in your communication with a problem-solving group, because it directly invites discussion about the social dimension of the group. Many difficulties experienced in the social dimension of the group could be avoided if individuals would be more willing to share their feelings before anger, resentment, or hurt got in the way of effective communication.

Here's a list of feeling words to get you in the mood. This feeling list can provide you with a richer look at the emotional world in which you live. Have fun!

accepted	ecstatic	intense	restless
afraid	edgy	intimidated	sad
annoyed	elated	irritable	sensual
anxious	embarrassed	jazzed	sentimental
ashamed	enthusiastic	joyful	shaky
bashful	excited	lonely	shy
bewildered	fearful	mean	silly
bitter	foolish	miserable	strong
bored	free	moving	subdued
brave	frustrated	needed	tender
calm	furious	neglected	tense
confident	glum	nervous	terrified

Sharing feelings is the most intimate way we can verbally connect with others. It provides others with information about our hearts—our joy, our fear, our anger, and our love. Without this information, we are merely two-dimensional stick figures who never reveal the deeper dimensions of who we are.

Gender Differences in Conversational Strategies

During your life, you have no doubt observed differences in the conversational strategies of men and women. The findings of numerous communication researchers have discovered that there are differences in the conversational strategies used by men and women. Linguistics professor Deborah Tannen in her book, *You Just Don't Understand*, believes that "the communication between men and women can be like cross-cultural communication, falling prey to a clash of conversational strategies." It's not so much that men and women desire to be in conflict with one another; it's just that their conversational strategies are so different. Tannen adds that "women speak and hear a language of connection and intimacy, while men speak and hear a language of status and independence." These are of course generalizations, and we should keep in mind that there are many exceptions to the rules. We must also remember that there are additional differences attributed to age, culture, economic background, education level, etc., that influence our choice of communication strategies, but for our purposes here, we will be focusing our attention on the gender differences between the communication strategies used by men and women.

Men seem to use more competitive strategies, whereas women use more cooperative strategies, and this can be the source of misunderstanding and conflict. Tannen further clarifies these conversational style differences by making the distinction between symmetrical and asymmetrical relationships.

A symmetrical relationship is one that is characterized by cooperation, equality, rapport building, acceptance, listening, questioning, empathy, exploring problems, encouragement, mutual understanding, complimenting, and negotiating. Tannen's research indicates that women most often demonstrate these behaviors in their conversational strategies, which encourages and maintains connection and a sense of community. Women tend to invest effort in establishing rapport, asking questions, listening without interrupting, being supportive, agreeing, complimenting, and sharing feelings. Their focus is more on the quality of relationship, rather than problem solving or competing with others. The symmetrical relationship is one of equality, connection, and cooperation.

The asymmetrical relationship is characterized by lecturing, giving advice, directing, commanding, evaluating, problem-solving, challenging, and competing. Tannen believes that men most typify these communication behaviors in their conversational style. Men tend to report facts and information, lecture, use more commanding language, ask fewer questions, interrupt, give advice, evaluate, challenge, and problem solve. The focus is more on reporting, lecturing, fixing, and competing.

> To become fully human,
> we must learn to develop the
> other parts of ourselves.
>
> ✑
>
> CARL JUNG

The relationship between the speakers in an asymmetrical conversation is secondary to the task at hand or the subject being discussed. In fact, competition characterizes much of the male conversational style, where the desire to know, to be right, and to win is foremost in their minds. The asymmetrical relationship is brought about by the competitive nature of the male conversational style because there is often a constant jockeying for the top position, the endless struggle to win in this competitive activity of talking.

How can all this information help you in your small group work? Plenty! You can become aware of and appreciate the differences in conversational strategies between men and women. Rather than blame, punish, or withdraw from a disagreement or argument brought about by differences in conversational strategies, you might be able to establish new lines of communication. Here are some suggestions you might consider as you attempt to create new ways of talking and listening:

Men:
Put the newspaper down when someone is talking.
Listen without interrupting, judging, or fixing.
Ask open-ended questions (How? Why? What?).
Paraphrase to prove understanding (Are you saying . . . ?).
Communicate agreement (I agree . . . , I see your point . . . , You've got a valid
    point . . .).

Communicate empathy (That must have felt . . . , I know how you feel . . .).
Encourage exploration (What else . . . ? How else . . . ? How did that feel?).
Compliment (I appreciate your . . . , I like your . . . , I admire the way you . . .).
Negotiate (How can we . . . ? What other solutions . . . ? Can we live with . . . ?).
Share your perceptions (especially strengths) about your relationships.
Share your feelings.
Listen again, without interrupting, judging, or fixing.

Women:
State your opinions more often (I think . . . , I believe . . . , It's my opinion that . . .).
Label a transaction when interrupted (May I speak? You're interrupting me.).
Label a transaction when being lectured (I believe you're lecturing me.).
Invite your own participation (Would you like to hear my opinion/feeling? I want to share my opinion/feeling.).
Disagree (I'm not convinced . . . , I have a different opinion . . . , I see it differently . . . , This is what I think . . .).
State a need (May I state a need? I need . . .).
State a boundary (No, that's not okay with me. This is unacceptable . . .).
State a boundary with a consequence (If you continue to . . . then I'm prepared to . . .).
Give advice (I think you should . . . , You might consider . . . , What if you . . .).
Give a command (I want you to . . . , Please get me . . . , Don't say . . . , Don't do . . .).

These suggested communication behaviors can be used to provide you with different conversational strategies than you might be accustomed to using in your group work. The goal is to expand the use of all the communication options available, so you can exercise more creativity as you interact with others.

Guidelines for Speaking Clearly

When you are communicating with others, you will find these guidelines helpful for expressing yourself clearly:

Be Specific

When speaking, try to use specific language. A common mistake is to assume the listener will visualize the same picture that you have when you say a word.

When I say, "I see a dog," you hear my sentence and decode the meaning of my words. The word dog is a relatively abstract, vague term. The dog you "see" in your head could be big, small, shaggy, or short-haired. You could "see" a bulldog, a collie, or a mutt. What I saw in my mind, and intended to communicate, was a German shepherd. Notice the difference between your picture and mine?

Use specific language to communicate what you think and feel to others. It will prevent a great deal of misunderstanding in your interactions with others.

Communicate Observations, Not Inferences

Observations refer to what your five senses have gathered: what you have seen, heard, smelled, felt, and tasted. Inferences, on the other hand, go beyond what you have observed and make assumptions about what you think and feel. Notice the difference between the following observation and inference statements:

> That couple is in love. (inference)
> The two people are walking arm in arm. (observation)

Communicate about a Behavior, Not the Person

It's important to communicate about a person's behavior, rather than comment on what you imagine he is or what he is like. Use adverbs (relating to actions) to describe people rather than adjectives (relating to qualities). Communicating in this way is more specific by reporting behaviors rather than attempting to label the person. Notice the difference in the following statements:

> Harvey is a loudmouth. (describes the person)
> Harvey has been talking for ten minutes. (describes the behavior)

Communicate in Terms of "More or Less," Not "Either-Or"

We tend to use polar terms when communicating with others. It was either the most wonderful event or the worst event. Either she was smart or she was stupid. Our laziness often displays itself in our communication. Rather than force descriptions of people, places, and things into extreme terminology with "either-or" language, try to communicate in terms of degree ("more or less" language). For example, rather than saying, "Terry is the loudest person on earth" (either loudest or softest), you could restate your opinion: "Terry speaks louder than Kevin" (matter of degree).

Share Ideas, Don't Give Advice

Avoid the tendency to evaluate and give advice to others. Rather, communicate the sharing of ideas and alternatives instead of giving advice and solutions. For example, instead of saying, "You should get a divorce" (advice), you could suggest, "There are a number of things you can do to improve your marriage, such as take a vacation, enroll in a communication class, or enter into therapy" (suggesting options). This approach lets the other person consider and decide for himself. It also allows the person to save face rather than be proven wrong and be instructed by you.

Communicate What Was Said, Not Why It Was Said

Try not to assess motive or reasoning behind what another person says. Once again, this gets us into the area of inference and assumption. Instead, focus your communication on observable information introduced by such language as "what, how, when, and where." This will keep the discussion on a level that is more effectively communicated and debated, rather than entering into the domain of motive and assumptions.

Match Nonverbal and Verbal Communication

When speaking, try to match your voice, body, and gestures with the content of your verbal message. Mixed messages—inconsistent nonverbal and verbal messages—confuse the listener and threaten clear communication. When you say, "I enjoy spending time with you," your face, voice, and body should also communicate the same message with a smile, cheerful voice, and relaxed and open body posture.

Keep these seven suggestions for clear communication in mind when you work in your problem-solving groups. You will discover that your communication, as well as your thinking, will be more specific, congruent, and nonthreatening.

Reducing Anxiety When Speaking

Even though you have kept these seven suggestions in mind, you might find yourself in this situation. You have researched your topic thoroughly, prepared ahead of time, and arrived to the meeting early, and are prepared to contribute to the group's discussion, but when the time arrives, you begin to perspire, your mouth gets dry, and you feel dizzy, while everyone else appears to be speaking so effortlessly. And you feel frozen. You want to say something, you want to contribute to the discussion, but the words just don't come. So you sit silently listening to everyone else in the group speak, because you're feeling anxious, apprehensive, or frightened. What can you do in this situation? Well, here are a few things you might consider the next time you discover yourself in this situation.

It's Natural to Be Anxious

The human body reacts to any new experience or perceived threat with certain physical, psychological, and emotional responses. If your body didn't, that would be cause for serious concern. It's natural to feel some anxiety and fear when you talk in a group. So just accept the fact that some level of anxiety, apprehension, or fear is natural. Welcome to the club.

You Appear Much More Relaxed Than You Feel

When people view a video playback of their group discussion, they are all, with very few exceptions, surprised at how relaxed they appeared on the monitor. Feedback from other group members immediately after a discussion or work session confirms this interesting phenomenon. Each speaker experiences a great deal more internal anxiety than he or she exhibits externally. You may feel really nervous on the inside, but chances are you don't appear nervous to the other members of the group.

Have Something Important to Say

If you feel strongly about what you are going to share with the group, you are less likely to be fearful of them. People often feel anxious or nervous because they feel that their comments don't warrant serious consideration. And they're often right. So speak only when you have something important to say. That's an essential rule of thumb for group discussion, as well as in your daily life.

Practice What You're Going to Say

Here's an idea. Practice what you're going to say during the discussion. Now I realize that a discussion isn't scripted like a conversation in a play or movie. A discussion is more spontaneous, more impromptu in nature. But you could practice saying just one idea or one piece of information or evidence you would like to share during the discussion. It could be as simple as "I'd like to share that the Centers for Disease Control just last spring discovered that cell phone use severely compromises driver attention." Practice saying it two or three times. Experiment with different volume, pitch, rate, and inflection. Notice what it feels like to say those words. Hear the words from your own mouth. Get a handle on that one statement you'd like to share with your group. Practice can be one of the most important factors in overcoming stage fright during discussions. There is no substitute for practice. Remember, speaking is a physical skill, as well as an intellectual or psychological skill.

Release Your Tension Before You Speak

Some people might jog, walk, or simply stretch the morning of an important discussion or meeting. I know of one college administrator who goes for a brisk walk around campus before she attends a particularly stressful or demanding meeting. This helps her loosen up and, as she says, "get a more positive frame of reference than a stuffy conference room can create." One effective relaxation exercise you can try is to simply breathe deeply from your stomach. Keep your eyes open, but don't fix your gaze at any one thing. Just breathe deeply, evenly. You'll discover that all your bodily rhythms will become more calm and centered. Experiment and discover what works best for you.

Experience Reduces Anxiety

The more experience you have speaking during a discussion, the less likely you are to be frightened during your next group meeting. It's like that with most things. The more you do it, the less frightening it is. I remember when I first started chairing department meetings at the college years ago. I was really anxious and intimidated by the more experienced educators in those meetings, but as I got more meetings under my belt, those experiences made me less anxious. In fact, the more I participated, the less anxious and more confident I became. Experience reduces anxiety.

The Group Is on Your Side

Think of your own reactions when you've participated in a group. Did you want the other group members to fail? To look like fools? Most likely not. The vast majority of us want the best for others. We want others to succeed. Group members really are supportive and encouraging if given half a chance. One of the most uplifting thoughts you can have as you share your ideas with your group is the belief that they wish you well and they want you to succeed. They really are on your side.

Defensive vs. Supportive Group Climates

Have you ever attended a business meeting, a problem-solving session, or study group where the atmosphere felt cold, unfriendly, or even hostile? The interactions were focused on debate, evaluation, and control, and your emotional response was to feel defensive or guarded.

Then there are other business meetings, problem-solving sessions, or study groups that feel just the opposite. They generate an atmosphere of warmth, friendliness, and even caring. The interactions of the group focused on open communication, with an emphasis on exploring ideas and alternatives, sincere listening without judgment, and a sense that people understood and respected you, even if their ideas differed. Your emotional response to this more supportive climate was to feel safe, open, and willing to participate enthusiastically.

Every work group creates a kind of atmosphere or emotional tone that permeates the interactions and dealings of its group members. Like the first example, some groups create an atmosphere of defensiveness, mistrust, and evaluation, whereas other groups create an atmosphere of supportiveness, openness, and trust. This group atmosphere doesn't just mysteriously appear out of nothing. It is created by the communication behaviors of the individual group members themselves.

Jack Gibb studied small group interactions and discovered that every group creates an atmosphere that can be rated on a continuum between a high level of defensiveness and a low level of defensiveness. Gibbs found that some groups were more positive in their member interactions with "face saving" types of communication behaviors, whereas other groups were more negative in their member interactions with "face threatening" types of communication. The important finding was that there were specific communication behaviors that created a defensive group climate and another set of communication behaviors that fostered a supportive group climate. Here is a summary of these defensives and supportive behaviors:

Defensive Climate:
1. Evaluation
2. Control
3. Strategy
4. Neutrality
5. Superiority
6. Certainty

Supportive Climate:
1. Description
2. Problem Orientation
3. Spontaneity
4. Empathy
5. Equality
6. Provisionalism

Let's take a brief look at each of these six categories of communication behaviors so we will have a better understanding of specific behaviors we can use and others we can avoid in our efforts to create a healthy and productive group climate.

1. Evaluation vs. Description

Evaluation arouses feelings of defensiveness within group members. Such statements as "You're always late," "You don't ever have any helpful ideas," and "How can you be so irresponsible?" are evaluative statements that immediately arouse feeling of defensiveness to say the least. More than likely, the recipient of those kinds of statements might also want to retaliate, attack, or even leave the group. No one likes to be put down or criticized, especially in the presence of others. Many of these evaluative statements begin with the word, "You," followed by the judgment or criticism. Be careful when you use "You-language" that your statements don't focus on the negative.

Description is the opposite of evaluation in that the focus is not directed at the other person, as in "You-language." Rather, you keep the focus on yourself, the speaker. In this approach, try using your "I-statements" and describe your own perceptions, opinions, and feelings instead of labeling. Describe your experience rather than judge or evaluate the other person.

These following statements focus on description rather than evaluation: "I get frustrated when you arrive fifteen minutes late," "I feel disappointed when you offer the same solutions time and time again," and "I'd appreciate it if you would contact one of us if you can't locate the equipment yourself." Notice how these descriptive statements focused on the speaker's feelings and thoughts, without blaming or name calling?

2. Control vs. Problem Orientation

Group members will often try to impose or force their solution to a problem. This behavior of insisting or controlling can make the recipient of the message feel like a child being scolded by a parent. An example of a controlling statement would be, "I don't want to hear another word from you for the rest of the meeting!" Controlling statements communicates the message that, "What I want is all that's important" and everyone else in the group is secondary.

Problem-Orientation takes a different attitudinal approach that says, "We're all in this together." It doesn't insist on getting its own way or controlling the behavior of others. Instead, it attempts to discover solutions that meet the needs of everyone in the group. More of a Win-Win approach rather than a Win-Lose approach. A problem-orientation statement would sound like this, "Ted, could we hear some other opinions, so we can get a more comprehensive view of the options available to us?"

3. Strategy vs. Spontaneity

Sometimes people can be manipulative or dishonest in their communication with the other group members. It's almost as if the individual is trying to bend the truth or the rules to achieve his or her goal or purpose. Perceived manipulation or dishonesty in communication can cause defensiveness within a group. Listen to this manipulative statement: "Well, the men in the other groups treat their female group members to coffee after their meetings." The men in the group could feel somewhat manipulated by that woman's comment and could feel more defensive as a result.

The opposite strategy would be spontaneity, which simply put is, "Say what you mean." Rather than trying to package your message strategically or manipulate a desired response, spontaneity is more open with its statement or request. The more spontaneous statement would sound like this, "Hey, how about you guys treating us to coffee?" Spontaneity in communication can add to the supportiveness in a group and maybe bring more fun and life to its members.

4. Neutrality vs. Empathy

Indifference to the thoughts, feelings, and actions of others is one of the most discouraging and demeaning ways you can respond to other group members. Neutrality communicates that the other person "doesn't matter." He or she doesn't care what the other person thinks, feels, or experiences. Responses such as, "So what?" "Do you think I care?" and "Oh well, bad things will happen to you" are examples of neutrality.

Empathy, on the other hand, communicates a willingness and ability to put yourself in another person's situation. You attempt to feel what they feel and experience what they experience. Unlike an indifferent response, with empathy you communicate caring. Listen to these empathetic responses: "I'm so sorry for you. That must have hurt your feelings," "I do care what happens to you very much" and "Of course that was disappointing to you. Let me treat you to coffee so you can talk about it."

5. Superiority vs. Equality

One of the quickest ways to make other group members feel defensive is to act superior to them. Superiority communicates the message that "I'm better than you." Whether it's in your words or behavior, the message that you're superior to everyone else is not only a recipe for defensiveness, but a barrier for the group. Here are some samples of superior statements: "That's not the way I told you to do it," "Must I do everything around here?" and "You people couldn't survive without me."

The opposite of superiority is equality. You can still be better at something or know more than someone else in your group, but communicate in a way that emphasizes equality. This lets the other person save face and feel equal to you, even if they lack the knowledge or skills that you possess. Here are some examples of statements of equality: "If you'd like, I can show you a solution that worked for me," "This would be difficult for anyone to do, but can I share an approach that helped me," and "I'm glad I can finally assist you with something. Here's what I'd do in this situation."

6. Certainty vs. Provisionalism

Certainty or dogmatism is the mental attitude that "I know it all." "I know all the answers and I'm right. And you're wrong." That last sentence is the one that really creates a defensive atmosphere within any group—that everyone else is wrong. These know-it-all people have difficulty interacting with anyone. Here are examples of statements of certainty: "You're wrong," "That will never work," and "Just ask me because I will have the answer." Wouldn't you love to work with someone like that?

Provisionalism means temporary or interim. Unlike the group member who is certain that he or she is always right, a group member who operates under the attitude of provisionalism, communicates by qualifying statements and avoiding absolutes. Words such as possibly, maybe, occasionally, perhaps, and sometimes are the language of a person who operates under provisionalism. Here are some examples of provisionalism: "Maybe I'm wrong," "Perhaps that will work, if we test it a few more times," and "We could ask the other group members for their input before we make a decision."

Your ability and willingness to send clear messages when you interact with others is essential to making groups work effectively. To own your statements and share information, opinions, and feelings in specific, nonthreatening ways will enable you to communicate clearly and invite others to share more openly with you also. Use these skills to create effective group interaction.

❧ Individual and Group Exercises ❧

Family of Origin Communication Roles

EXERCISE 3.1 Think back to your family of origin and see if you can identify who may have played the roles of controller, blamer, pleaser, distractor, or ghost during times of stress or crisis. Identifying family members and their roles is not meant to blame them, but to discover patterns of behavior—theirs and yours. Write their name(s) beside the dysfunctional communication role.

Controller: _____

Blamer: _____

Pleaser: _____

Distractor: _____

Ghost: _____

Did your family members fit any of the dysfunctional communication roles? Did some play more than one role? What, if any, role(s) did you play within the family? Do family members still play these roles?

One important discovery you can make is the role you played (or still play) in your family of origin. Because if you did, there's a good chance you play a similar role when working in groups. A controller in the family will often try to control others in groups. Likewise, a pleaser in the family will often try to please others outside the family. Be aware of the roles you play when you communicate with others.

Making I-Statements to Two People

EXERCISE 3.2 This chapter discussed I-statements and levels of communication. The assumption is that disclosure of your thoughts and feelings is important for others in their attempts to work with and understand you. It's even more important for you to get a sense of who you are. You achieve this sense of self-intimacy, paradoxically, by sharing your thoughts and feelings with others, not by holding them in or hiding them from the listening ear of others.

List two individuals from your personal or professional life you'd like to communicate a thought or feeling to, but haven't had the courage or the opportunity to do so yet. These can be positive or negative thoughts or feelings. Write the name of the person and then briefly note what you would share with them (one sentence only).

Name: _____

Message: _____

Name: _____

Message: _____

How did you feel writing these thoughts or feelings down? What do you think or feel as you see these messages on the page before you? Would you ever consider sharing these messages with the people you listed? If yes, when will you share with them?

Reducing Speaker Anxiety

| EXERCISE |
| 3.3 |

Have your group members take 20–30 minutes to discuss their perceptions and feelings about speaking in a group. What uncertainties, anxieties, and fears do they have? Are there similarities in your perceptions and feelings? Have the members of the group share any previous speaking experience they have had in public speaking or group discussion. What have they learned about reducing their speaking anxiety in those settings? Discuss the suggestions for reducing speaking anxiety presented in this chapter. How might your group members support and encourage one another during an actual discussion?

CHAPTER 4

Listening for Understanding

No one can develop fully without feeling
understood by at least one person.

—PAUL TOURNIER

THE oak log crackles and snaps in the fireplace as the orange flames dance softly above the wood. I stare into the fire, feeling its heat on my face and hands. We both sit silently in overstuffed chairs, while an occasional red ember shoots out from the fire and bounces onto the stone floor in front of us.

Being here in this small, rustic cottage feels good to me. The warm, golden glow from two kerosene lanterns and the sound of the crackling fire soothe me, as a light winter rain falls outside. But what feels best is the way Winston listens to me.

Winston has been my friend and mentor now for twenty years. I trust his counsel. I appreciate his friendship. But most of all, I like being heard by him—to be understood at the deepest level.

I've come to this cottage to talk to Winston. Or rather, to be heard by him. You see, Winston has that rare ability to listen for understanding—to listen without interruption, evaluation, or advice. When Winston senses I need to be heard, he listens with an acceptance of who I am, not what he wants me to be.

When he listens to understand, I can hear myself think. He doesn't interrupt my story with his story. He doesn't pass judgment, offer criticism, or give advice. He won't even try to rescue, teach, or assist. Winston simply sits and listens in silence. And when he does speak, he'll ask a question. His questions invite me to explore and discover, not defend, justify, or even explain. Like a mirror, he lets me see myself, and I am better because of it. I'm a better husband, father, teacher, and therapist because he has listened for understanding.

In this chapter we'll explore the skill of listening for understanding. Your ability to listen and understand what other people in your group are saying will directly determine the success of your interactions with them. Without your ability and willingness to suspend judgment long enough to really hear what others are attempting to communicate, you will forever be destined to hear only the echoes of your own thinking and evaluation. The ability to listen for understanding lets you create the basis for an effective group.

The Importance of Listening

An old saying observes that "we were given two ears and only one mouth, so that we might hear more than we speak." Can you imagine having it the other way around? Attempting to communicate with only one ear and two mouths? The possibilities are humorous, and even a little frightening. Yet the attitude and behavior we carry into our discussions in group work is exactly that, trying to talk more and listen less. In our culture, talking is valued much more than listening. The individual who is articulate, persuasive, and even inspirational while addressing the group is regarded as wielding influence and power.

That makes sense, you might be saying to yourself. Speaking is important. We can't be successful without developing this skill. But listening is just as important. In fact, it might be more important than speaking in terms of the amount of time we spend in this activity. Studies show that we spend forty-five percent of our communication time in daily life listening, and only thirty percent speaking, sixteen percent reading, and nine percent writing. To make matters worse, studies also suggest that we remember only twenty-five percent of what we hear after two days. Listening is important and we don't do it very well.

During our communication in group work, we probably don't even realize that our listening isn't very effective. We don't listen to others in ways that encourage them to disclose more deeply. Instead we get in their way, we switch the discussion to our point of view, and the opportunity for them to speak is lost. How can we improve our listening?

The Process of Listening

Many of us think that listening comes as naturally as breathing, but it requires much more attention and skill than just keeping quiet while someone else speaks. Listening is the process of receiving, attending, understanding, responding, and remembering. The first step in the listening process is that of receiving or hearing sounds from your environment. Hearing is limited to the physiological process of receiving and processing the sounds. The second step is attending, which is the process of paying attention to some of the sounds you receive and disregarding or filtering out the others. For instance, you might hear a number of individuals talking at the same time during a discussion, but you attend or single out one particular person.

Understanding is the third step, and it involves comprehending the message. The fourth step is responding, and that includes asking questions or giving feedback to the speaker. And the final step in the listening process is remembering what was said. Listening is a process that requires your active participation.

Take a tip from nature, your ears aren't made to shut, but your mouth is.

✑

MALCOLM FORBES

Although there are many ways you can listen to another person, there is no one style of listening that ensures effective communication in every circumstance. However, there are four poor listening styles you should avoid.

Poor Listening Styles

Poor listening habits may prevent others from opening up to us. We might give the impression we are listening, when in fact, we are daydreaming, arranging our rebuttals, or changing the subject to accommodate our interests. Four styles of listening you must avoid when you are trying to be receptive to another person are refusing to listen, pseudolistening, listening selectively, and listening to evaluate.

Refusing to Listen

The most obvious behavior that prevents effective listening is to refuse to listen to the other person. Here are some examples of refusing to listen.

> Simply walking away when someone begins speaking.
> "I've had enough. I don't want to talk about this anymore."
> "I don't want to hear what you have to say."

Pseudolistening

Pretending to listen, or pseudolistening, is the second style of poor listening to avoid. In this style, the listener might demonstrate many of the nonverbal behaviors of true listening—an open posture, eye contact, nodding, and appropriate facial expressions—but make no attempt to receive, attend, or understand the content of what the speaker is saying. Here are some comments suggesting this style of listening.

> "You bet, I got the message."
> "Okay, dear."
> "Whatever."
> "Ah hum . . ."

Listening Selectively

The listener only attends and responds to those subjects he or she is interested in and skips the rest. We've all endured the individual who listens to us just long enough to bring up a topic he's interested in and then continues to dominate the conversation. Here are some examples of statements suggesting this style of listening.

"That reminds me of a time when I . . ."
"Now you're talking about something I'm interested in."
"I'm glad you finally brought that up because I had that happen to me . . ."

Listening to Evaluate

Rather than hear and try to understand the speaker's opinions, feelings, and frame of reference, a listener can be primarily focused on judging the message from his or her own point of view. Listening to evaluate focuses on judging the correctness, rightness, or worth of the speaker's statements. It doesn't matter whether the listener's evaluation is negative or positive; the goal is to judge what the speaker is saying. Whether the listener's response is "That's a wonderful point!" or "That's the most ridiculous opinion I've ever heard!" the deeper message is "I am the judge of your comments."

> If you judge people, you have no time to love them.
>
> ⌀
>
> MOTHER TERESA

Listening for the purposes of judging does not encourage or provide a basis of understanding. Here are some common responses that suggest listening for judgment.

"That's a good point. I agree."
"No one should say that."
"You're wrong. How can you say that?"

There might be occasions when using one of these four styles of listening might be appropriate. But when your primary purpose for listening is to create an open atmosphere in your group discussions, then avoid these four styles.

Barriers to Listening

In addition to avoiding poor listening styles, there are specific barriers to listening you should be aware of if you are to be an effective listener. The first barrier is the abundance of messages that bombard us every day. Messages crying out to be heard, to be listened to: the sounds of the radio, television, endless conversations, business meetings, phone messages, phone conversations, and the list goes on and on. There are just too many things to listen to in our lives.

External noise or interference from outside sources is the second barrier to listening. Some examples of external noise are traffic, barking dogs, machinery, and the music from our neighbor's stereo. These external noises make listening difficult.

Our rapid thought is the third barrier we experience. We can understand a person's speech up to 500 words a minute, while the average person speaks about 125 words per minute. With all this spare time on our hands, our thoughts can drift: we can think about our response to what is being said or just daydream about food. Our rapid thought can be a barrier to listening.

> Man's inability to communicate is a result of his failure to listen effectively, skillfully, and with understanding to another human being.
>
> ∽
>
> CARL ROGERS

The fourth barrier to listening is our preoccupation with self. We think in terms of how communication affects us, what it means to us, whether it agrees or disagrees with what we think, feel, and believe. The focus of our attention is on what we think, feel, and believe, and it is through this filter that we listen to what others say. The final barrier to effective listening is that listening requires effort. Effective listening demands that we pay attention, process what is being said, and interact appropriately.

Listening for understanding ultimately requires that we put aside our ego, pay attention to what is being shared, ask questions to clarify the messages, and respond in ways that demonstrate understanding. More than anything else, listening requires our acceptance of others.

Acceptance: A Requirement for Listening

The basis of all listening is acceptance, to be open to receive whatever it is that the speaker is sharing with us. Let's define acceptance as "receiving what is." No effective listening can occur without being open to the other person.

When it comes to listening to others, we often feel the urge to judge, fix, blame, control, help, criticize, or rescue them, rather than accept what they have to share. These urges surface most noticeably in our listening habits. Instead of listening in silence, with an open mind, ready to receive "what is," we judge, blame, criticize, tell our story, or give advice. We are rarely open and receptive to what the speaker wants to share.

We must be willing to listen to the different ideas, thoughts, and feelings when we listen to others, or forever be at odds with them, ourselves, and the world. By your being more open minded and receptive to what others in your group have to say, you will be creating an atmosphere in which more effective communication is encouraged. Here are two ways you can communicate acceptance.

Nonverbal Signs of Acceptance

Would it be easy for you to hold a conversation with an individual when all he did was frown and look away every time you tried to speak? Can you imagine what it would be like to talk and have him respond with labored sighs of disgust and disapproval? Not a pretty sight.

Your nonverbal behavior sets the tone of acceptance or rejection long before you speak. The manner in which you make yourself available to another person by your non-interference, posture and gestures, eye contact, facial expressions, nodding, and tone of voice demonstrates your acceptance of them.

Posture and gestures. How you stand or sit can communicate acceptance or rejection. By facing away from or speaking over your shoulder can communicate rejection, whereas facing the person directly can communicate more acceptance. When seated, a slouched, withdrawn posture can communicate negative messages, whereas an erect posture or one in which you lean in the direction of the person can communicate more positive messages. Your arms and hands can also be a source of acceptance by being open, rather than crossed over your chest or placed over your ears.

> With an open mind, you will be open-hearted; being open-hearted, you will know the divine.
>
> ✐
>
> LAO TSU

Eye contact. Eye contact can communicate acceptance in this culture. It can be a sign of acknowledgment, approval, and agreement, especially when accompanied with a smile. To refuse to look at someone can be interpreted as a sign of rejection. When you are listening, your eye contact should be direct. As someone speaks to you, maintain eye contact to demonstrate your interest and involvement. Don't look away or close your eyes and fall sleep. Look at the speaker for three or four seconds at a time. Don't stare for long periods of time, however. Staring can make others feel uncomfortable, so maintain direct eye contact for short periods of time. When interacting with individuals from other cultures, be as sensitive to the norms and expectations as possible, for direct eye contact can be regarded as impolite or rude in many Asian cultures.

Facial expressions. Your face can communicate a great deal about how you're feeling and what you're thinking. A frown, raised eyebrows, and rolling eyes are just a few of the ways your facial expressions can convey your thoughts and feelings. So, if you are trying to communicate acceptance, remember to reflect the appropriate facial expressions as someone else speaks. Supportive facial expressions are another way to create a sense of acceptance when listening to others.

Nodding. You can communicate acknowledgment by nodding. Your occasional nod is an encouraging nonverbal message that says you are paying attention and acknowledging the words of the speaker. Don't overdo this behavior, but use this form of nonverbal communication as a way of saying, "I hear you" and "What you're saying is important."

Your posture, eyes, and face are some of the most important tools you possess that will enable you to demonstrate and create an attitude of acceptance when someone speaks.

Verbal Signs of Acceptance

There are a number of verbal ways to communicate your acceptance while listening. These verbal signs of acceptance are no interrupting, non-evaluative listening, words of acceptance, phrases of acceptance, and invitations to share.

No interrupting. Two people cannot speak at the same time and expect communication to occur. Whenever someone speaks, someone needs to listen for communication to occur. So your willingness to listen is a very important message. Don't interrupt the speaker as he or she talks. Instead of interrupting or adding your own comments every twelve to fifteen seconds, let the speaker talk for thirty to sixty seconds without interrupting. In some instances, it might be beneficial and helpful for you to remain silent for a minute or two without interrupting.

Non-evaluative listening. By withholding your evaluation or judgment as the speaker talks, you are listening non-evaluatively. Many people are inclined to evaluate everything that is being shared. Like a judge, they listen with gavel in hand, ready to pronounce judgment even before the speaker has finished her sentence. Don't interrupt, give your opinion, or offer your advice. Just keep silent and listen.

Verbal responses of acceptance. There are verbal responses of acceptance. Words or phrases like "Oh," "Um," "Really?" "Okay," "I see," "Is that so?" "That's interesting," and "Say more" are some verbal responses of acceptance. They are not evaluations of right or wrong, good or bad, or agreement or disagreement. They are intended to communicate your attentiveness and your acceptance of what is being shared. It is your way to cheer the speaker on and say, "Keep going; you're doing a great job sharing!"

Invitations to share. You can invite others to share by issuing invitations such as "How's it going?" This invitation is relatively neutral and gives the person the choice to disclose and talk or to decline. Either way he responds to your invitation, honor his decision. If he decides to talk, listen non-evaluatively. If he declines, accept that also. What's important is that you are inviting him to share. You are creating the opportunity for him to talk. Other invitations to share are:

"Share your thoughts with me."
"Tell me about it."
"I'm interested in your point of view."

These are just a few ways you can encourage someone to open up. Your invitations to share can create a group atmosphere of openness.

Listening for Understanding: Active Listening

Once you have communicated nonverbal and verbal signs of acceptance and have encouraged the other person to talk, you can begin to listen for understanding. The primary goal of listening for understanding is to discover how the speaker thinks and feels. What does she experience, desire, need, and want? How does the world look from her singular perspective? What does it mean to be her, in her world?

This kind of listening, listening for understanding, is how therapists, psychologists, and psychiatrists are trained to listen to their clients. That's the way group members need to be heard by you at times. They need to be listened to for understanding.

The secret to listening for understanding is to test the accuracy of your message reception. The meaning of messages is not in the words of the message, but rather in the person sending the message and in the person receiving the message. In other words, meaning is in people, not in words. For example, the word ball can mean a football to me, a fun time to you, and a formal dance to someone else. The symbol or word ball was the same for all three of us, but the meanings we individually assigned to that word were very different. Meaning is not in words, but in people.

> The most basic of all
> human needs is the need
> to be understood.
>
> ✑
>
> KARL MENNINGER

Active listening is the process in which you restate in your own words what the speaker has said to clarify or confirm the accuracy of the message. Active listening involves the skill of paraphrasing, which is simply a restatement in your own words of the speaker's message.

Listening can mistakenly be viewed as a passive activity; the speaker talks and the listener listens. The speaker is active and verbal and the listener is passive and silent. When the speaker finishes talking, the assumption is that the message has been accurately received by the listener, with no observable effort or participation on the listener's part. What could be simpler? The speaker talks and the listener listens. But it's not so simple.

To ensure that the listener has accurately understood what the speaker has said, the process of active listening can be used. Active listening is the process in which the listener is an equal participant in the communication process. True communication requires the active participation of the listener as well as the speaker. There are two types of active listening: active listening for content (accuracy) and active listening for feelings (empathy). The four basic steps to the active-listening process are the same for either content or feelings. If you follow these four simple steps in your communication with others, you will have mastered one of the fundamental skills in creating receptive communication as a listener.

The Four Steps of Active Listening

Step 1. Speaker makes a statement.

Step 2. Listener paraphrases speaker's statement ("Are you saying . . . ?")

Step 3. Speaker accepts paraphrase ("Yes, that's what I meant.") or rejects paraphrase ("No, that's not what I meant.")

Step 4. If rejected, the speaker clarifies the original statement (the process repeats). If accepted, the listener is free to express her thought/feeling.

When you use active listening, don't overdo it. You don't want to sound like a parrot, repeating every sentence the speaker says. This can be irritating to the speaker and discourage communication as much as interrupting or judging. Use active listening like you would spices in cooking. Don't overdo it. Just use it enough to clarify those statements you're unsure of.

Active Listening for Content

The first type of active listening is listening for content or the accuracy of what is being shared. Here are some examples of active listening for content:

TIM: The solutions we've proposed to the problem don't make it in my opinion.
SARAH: Are you saying the solutions are not feasible?
TIM: That's exactly what I mean!
THUY: I'm out of here if you guys don't include everyone in the discussion.
CHIP: You mean you're going to quit the group if everyone isn't consulted?
THUY: Yes. I feel very strongly about this.

Did you notice how, in both examples, the listener actively reflected what he thought he heard by asking "Are you saying . . . ?" and "You mean . . . ?" Remember not to parrot word for word what the speaker has said. Just try to restate, in your own words, what the speaker has said.

The next dialogue provides you with an example where the first paraphrase is incorrect and the listener and speaker negotiate for shared meaning by using Steps 3 and 4 of the active listening process.

TAMMY: I think you should include Mark more in our group discussions.
HASSAN: Are you saying that I don't let Mark talk?
TAMMY: No. You let him talk. But I'd like you to acknowledge some of his comments.
HASSAN: You mean acknowledge or compliment some of his proposals?
TAMMY: I'd love that! It'd make him feel more valued.
HASSAN: I guess I don't acknowledge others enough. Sure, I'll try it.

Did you see how the listener and speaker had to repeat the process to get the message accurately communicated? This simple technique of actively reflecting the content of the message back to the speaker is effective in assuring the accurate reception of the thought or idea sent by the speaker.

There are three variations of the active-listening technique for testing the accuracy of the content sent by the speaker: the you technique, active-listening questions, and active-listening statements.

The "you" technique. The most basic form of active listening is mirroring to the speaker the content of the message with a question beginning with the word You. Here is an example of an active-listening question:

JARED: I think I need to step back from my involvement in our group.
TYLER: You think you need to take a break from chairing our group?
JARED: That's right. I'm getting a little burnt out.

Active-listening questions. The second type of active listening involves asking the speaker if what you heard is correct by beginning your interpretation with statements such as "Do you mean . . . ?" "Are you saying . . . ?" "Do I understand you to say . . . ?" "Are you feeling . . . ?" Here is an example of an active-listening question:

LEN: Researching this problem is a blast.
SUE: Are you saying you're having fun interviewing the experts?
LEN: Yeah, I'm actually enjoying talking to the engineers.

Active-listening statements. You can also reflect the content of the speaker's message by using statements that introduce your interpretation. Here are some examples of phrases you can use: "I hear you saying . . . ," "What you're saying . . . ," "What you're feeling is . . . ," "I understand you to mean . . . ," "It sounds like you . . . ," "I'm feeling that you . . ." Here are a few examples of active-listening statements.

"I hear you saying that you want a break from working Saturdays."
"It sounds like you wish you were in charge of the group."
"What you're saying is that you'd like to increase their stock options."

All three of these active-listening techniques for content will help you more clearly understand the thoughts and ideas presented by others. They will enable you to make certain that the pictures you construct in your mind's eye are the same as the ones they are attempting to communicate from their point of view. This same technique of active listening can also reflect our understanding of another person's feelings.

Active Listening for Feelings

Communicating in groups can involve sharing feelings and discussing emotions. This is especially true if you're trying to help someone through a problem or difficulty. Rather than clarify and validate the content accuracy of the speaker's message, the communication shifts levels to the speaker's feelings. To go beyond the content of what someone is saying and be sensitive to the feelings he or she might also be attempting to communicate is a powerful way to encourage deeper connection and relationships.

Three ways you can listen for feelings in your communication with others are by observing the speaker's nonverbal communication, reflecting the speaker's nonverbal behavior, and responding to the speaker's verbal communication.

Observing the speaker's nonverbal communication. The first way you can listen to the feelings is not with your ears, but with your eyes. An individual's posture, physical position relative to you, facial expressions, eye contact, gestures, tone of voice, rate of speech, breathing pattern, and touching behavior are just a few of the numerous nonverbal cues that communicate messages to you.

> It is with the heart that one sees rightly, what is essential is invisible to the eye.
>
> ✍
>
> ANTOINE DE SAINT-EXUPÉRY

Feelings and emotions are communicated primarily at the nonverbal level, so during your next conversation, pay attention to their facial expressions, posture, gestures, tone of voice, breathing, eye contact, and anything else you might observe. Be creative and listen for feelings, with your ears and eyes!

Reflecting the speaker's nonverbal behavior. An individual is often unaware of a downcast eye, raised voice, increased breathing rate, or reddening of the face. Many times these nonverbal behaviors go unnoticed by speaker and listener. If, however, you are observing any significant nonverbal behavior in the other person, you might want to share it. Share your perception without attaching any value judgment with it. Rather than say, "It looks like you're getting scared and frightened," you might say, "I notice that you keep looking out the window and your breathing is getting faster." This statement could invite the individual to talk about his or her feelings. Here are some phrases you might want to use when listening to feelings:

"I notice that you're arriving later and later to our meetings."
"I see that you're looking at the clock."

"I hear you sigh when I . . ."
"I notice that you're smiling when I talk about . . ."

Responding to the speaker's verbal communication. There are two instances when the speaker will verbally invite you to communicate at the feeling level of communication: first, when the speaker shares a feeling statement with you, and secondly, when the speaker asks you how you're feeling. In the first instance, the speaker will share a feeling statement with you, such as "I'm feeling happy," "I'm feeling upset," or "This situation makes me feel discouraged." Be sensitive to such feeling statements and respond to them by reflecting the speaker's feeling statement with a paraphrase to encourage him or her to explore or comment further. Here are some examples.

"I'm feeling a little tense."
"So you're feeling uptight?"

"This situation encourages me."
"Sounds like you're feeling optimistic?"

The purpose of paraphrasing or reflecting a speaker's feeling statement is to prove that you have received the message and to encourage the speaker to remain at the feeling level by having him or her explore or expand upon the statement.

The second way you can listen for feelings is to respond to specific invitations to communicate at the feeling level. When the speaker asks you how you're feeling about a particular issue, person, or situation, you will hopefully respond with an appropriate feeling response, instead of remaining at the content level. Here are some examples.

"Are you happy with the group's decision?"
"Yes, I'm pleased we decided to donate the money."

"Am I making you feel comfortable?"
"Yes, I'm not feeling nervous or frightened."

In addition to these two ways to respond to the speaker's invitation to talk about feelings, you can also issue an invitation yourself. You can follow up a speaker's content statement with a feeling-level question. This is one of the basic tools of therapists and counselors, especially when the client is unaware or unwilling to explore his or her feelings. Here are some examples of feeling-level questions:

"I might be promoted to manager." (content level)
"How are you feeling about that?" (feeling-level invitation)

"I'm discovering that the job is requiring more time than I thought." (content level)
"Are you feeling overburdened?" (feeling-level invitation)

By responding to the speaker's content statement with a feeling-level question, you can encourage the speaker to share at a deeper level. There are times during group discussion when the sharing of feelings is beneficial, especially when emotions are running high during disagreement or conflict. By inviting the speaker to share his or her feelings, you might be inviting a deeper level of sharing and understanding.

Advantages of Active Listening

Active listening has a number of advantages. First, and most obvious, it proves understanding. It assures speaker and listener the message sent was indeed the message received. That is what is meant by listening for understanding.

Second, active listening involves the listener. No longer does the listener passively sit and assume he has received the message accurately. He must participate in the process of communication and become involved in the message negotiation.

Third, active listening relieves the listener from having to act as judge, teacher, or rescuer. The listener simply reflects the message back to the speaker, but doesn't problem solve, judge, give advice, or perform a hundred other activities listeners are inclined to do.

Fourth, the speaker has a safe place to disclose thoughts and feelings without being threatened, criticized, or punished. The speaker can share, explore, and consider her thoughts and feelings without fear of evaluation.

> The first duty of love
> is to listen.
>
> ∽
>
> ERICH FROMM

Fifth, active listening develops trust between the speaker and the listener. It isn't very often individuals are given the opportunity to share what's really on their mind or deep in their heart without being attacked, rejected, or rescued. This is the most important reward of listening for understanding. The speaker trusts you.

Guidelines for Active Listening

Your skill in reflecting the content and feelings of other group members will greatly enhance the accuracy of the group's communication and will serve to create a more open and productive group atmosphere. As you use your active-listening skills, keep these guidelines in mind.

Avoid Parroting

A common mistake the beginning active listener makes is to paraphrase, word for word, the speaker's statement. Just like a parrot, the listener will reflect verbatim the words of the speaker. Here are a couple of examples of parroting:

HECTOR: I feel happy.
SAM: You feel happy?

SALLY: I'm having second thoughts about leaving.
TIM: You're having second thoughts about leaving?

The main disadvantage to parroting is that the listener doesn't prove true understanding of the speaker's statement. He merely repeats the exact wording of the statement and does not process the statement into his own words. A second disadvantage of parroting is the "echo" effect, which quickly becomes tiring to hear. Be creative! Put the speaker's statement into your own words.

Avoid Overuse of Active Listening

Nothing is more irritating than having someone use active listening to mirror every statement you make during a conversation. This can drive people crazy. You should reserve active listening for those occasions when you need to clarify the speaker's message, the speaker needs to feel understood by you, the speaker needs to vent or process feelings, or you and the speaker are in conflict.

If you use active listening about once every five statements you make during a conversation, you will not only improve the quality of the communication; you will also dramatically improve the quality of your relationships in your small groups.

Avoid Inappropriate Active Listening

Sometimes active listening is inappropriate. Although there are no fast and easy rules on when it is inappropriate to use active listening, you'll soon get a gut feeling after you've practiced it for a while. Here are some obvious examples of when it would be inappropriate to use the understanding response:

ANN: What time is it, Omar?
OMAR: Are you asking what time is it?

NANCY: The house is burning!
TED: You're saying the house is burning?

In each example, the listener inappropriately used active listening. The speaker was making a request or statement that did not require clarification from the listener. If these were real conversations, very few people would blame the speaker if she kicked the listener in the shin!

Intercultural Awareness

In addition to your listening skills, there is one important area of group communication that would be beneficial to examine in order for you to be genuinely receptive to all the possible members of your group, and that is intercultural awareness.

Every member of a group is different. We differ by gender, age, education, income, beliefs, attitudes, and experiences. But there is one difference that is playing an increasingly significant role in group interaction in the United States, the role of culture.

Recently, I was observing a group of students in one of my group discussion courses during the first week's activities, and I was once again reminded of the important role culture plays even in the most basic communication interactions. The six-person teams were assigned a twenty-minute in-class task of planning a hypothetical group vacation and reaching agreement on where to go, when to go, how much to spend, and what activities to include.

The group I was observing consisted of five white students—three women and two men—and one woman from Taiwan. All six students were in their late teens or early twenties. As I watched the first five or six minutes of their discussion, all five white students expressed their opinions while the Asian woman remained silent. The five students continued their lively discussion, while completely ignoring Rose, the young Asian woman. It was as if she wasn't even present.

Now I don't believe the five talkative students were being purposefully rude or mean. I think each of them was simply trying to get his or her point across and was oblivious to the fact that Rose hadn't said a word.

After a few moments, I interrupted the group and asked if all the members had been given the opportunity to voice an opinion. Immediately one of the women asked Rose what she thought. Rose took a deep breath, said a couple of words, then smiled awkwardly, and returned to her silence. The other group members smiled back, then concluded their discussion without soliciting Rose's opinion again, nor did Rose volunteer to speak. A difference in cultures could explain this often-repeated group discussion experience.

Intercultural communication is communication that involves different cultures within a country. In the case of the United States, a Judeo-Christian European heritage serves as the foundational cultural basis, with English as the primary language. But the United States is rapidly being modified and transformed with the swelling immigration by people from many countries and cultural backgrounds. To increase our awareness and to more effectively interact with those of different cultures, three important dimensions of culture should be examined. Those three dimensions are individual vs. collective, low context vs. high context, and competitive vs. cooperative.

Individual vs. Collective Dimension

Perhaps the most significant and deep-seated value that separates one culture from another is the individual vs. collective dimension—the degree to which the individual or the group is perceived and regarded as being most important. In an individualistic culture, the individual is regarded as being of paramount value. Being number one! Being all that you can be! Standing head and shoulders above the rest! Climbing the ladder to success! Looking out for number one! These are the slogans of an individualistic culture. The expression of the thoughts and feelings of the individual is highly valued. Self-actualization is the life goal. Self-promotion is expected. And the striving and sacrifice to achieve one's highest potential is encouraged and admired. Sound familiar? It should. The American culture is the most individualistic culture in the world, followed by other Western countries such as England, Australia, Canada, the Netherlands, and New Zealand.

On the other hand, a collectivist culture views commitment to the group as the paramount value. In a collectivist culture, the theme is "we," not "me." The emphasis is placed on the group, whether it's the family, the community, or the nation, never on the individual. In fact, the individual is expected and encouraged to use his or her talents for the good of the group and not for the good of the self. Self-expression, self-promotion, and self-actualization are perceived as selfish and even disloyal to the group. Such individualistic behavior brings shame to the individual, as well as to his or her family and community. In a collectivist culture, individualistic behavior is even punished. The Japanese have a saying, "The nail that sticks up is pounded down." Perhaps as much as seventy percent of the world's population lives in collectivist cultures, such as China, India, Japan, Latin America, Africa, Indonesia, and Taiwan.

Low-Context vs. High-Context Dimension

Cultures can also differ in their communication styles. Individualistic cultures, such as the United States and England, use what is called a low-context communication style. A low-context communication style is message content oriented, in which the listener is assumed to know very little and it is the speaker's responsibility to tell the listener everything. Words are very important. In a low-context style, verbal communication is very direct, precise, explicit, and literal. The nonverbal aspects of the context or setting of the communication act is not regarded as important, whereas the words are viewed as supremely important.

A will or living trust is an example of low-context communication. The words are important and the setting in which you read the will or living trust is almost irrelevant. In a low-context culture, public speaking would be a course that is highly valued, teaching and providing experience for the student in the art of saying anything to anybody.

A high-context communication style has a message context orientation. That is, the cultural context or setting of the communication act is important. Verbal communication is indirect, subtle, implicit, and figurative. Silence can be perceived as the preferred behavior or response, rather than talking on and on. In a high-context communication style, you are expected to understand the implicit rules and the unspoken rituals of the culture. You are expected to "read between the lines" and understand what the speaker is intending to communicate without being told or instructed in explicit detail.

In Japan, it is understood that if a person does not wish to do business with you he will simply say, "You have a very good product," or, "Let me think about your offer," rather than saying no directly or explaining in depth why your product or offer is not acceptable. To the Japanese businessman, it is important for you to "save face" and not be embarrassed by a direct rejection. This is understood in the context of Japanese business practice. In a high-context culture, it would be considered rude or offensive to be too direct, explicit, inquisitive, or verbally persistent. Consider the warning of Lao Tsu, "The more you say the less you say. And the less you say the more you say." "Silence is golden" might be even more instructive.

Competition vs. Cooperation Dimension

The third dimension of culture we will examine is that of competition vs. cooperation. In an individualistic culture like the United States, winning is prized above all else. We are taught that winning is good and losing is bad. Those individuals who have made it to the top of their fields are constantly being paraded before our eyes in the magazines, on television, in advertisements, and in movies. If we don't finish at the top, there's something wrong with us. But not all cultures are as competitive as America's.

Collectivist cultures are far more cooperative than individualistic cultures. In Asian, Latin American, and Native American cultures, cooperation among individuals is expected and encouraged. The individual cooperates with others to help the group realize its goals. Children help the family, relatives support one another, workers pitch in to assist coworkers, and even strangers are more inclined to lend a helping hand to those in need. Studies have shown that in collectivist cultures, the family is more highly valued than any individual within the family and this value permeates all social interaction within that culture.

In contrast to the cooperative culture, the members of a competitive culture are much more inclined to want to win at any cost, even if that cost involves loved ones and even ourselves. We, in America, sacrifice our families for our own careers and material accumulation. We drop off our babies at day-care centers for eight to twelve hours five and six times every week so we can work, not to earn the basics of life, but to get ahead, to acquire a bigger home, to purchase bigger cars, or to obtain more toys. We compete in our daily conversations to express our views and opinions. We want things done our way. We want to be the boss.

This cultural desire to win, to come out on top, to be the boss can express itself in and influence our communication within a group. This cultural desire to compete can affect the way we speak, interrupt, and listen to one another. It can encourage and reward high verbal behavior while devaluing or even punishing those who do not speak up, interrupt, or assert themselves. We need to be aware of these possible cultural differences when we work with others in groups.

S.O.A.R. Technique

To raise our awareness of group members from other cultures, I have designed the S.O.A.R. Technique, which includes four steps:

Seek
Observe
Ask
Relate

By using these steps, you can transcend the usual ways we ignore, judge, and even punish those from different cultures. We can soar above our usual way of marginalizing those who might want to contribute to the group task at hand, but possess a different way of seeing the world and communicating within it. Let's look at these four steps.

Seek

The first step to increase our awareness of those from other cultures is to actively seek them out rather than ignore or avoid them. If a person from another culture is in our group, we ignore them because they might dress differently, exhibit low-verbal behavior, or act with deference to our more outgoing speaking style. Sometimes we even consciously avoid interacting with them because that might require venturing out of our comfort zone, going into unfamiliar territory, and even questioning our own thinking, behavior, or culture. Rather than ignore or avoid, you might want to seek those of a different culture.

First, be consciously on the lookout for individuals of another culture. You can tell by skin color, dress, accent, or behavior. Don't be so self-centered that all you see during the group discussion is yet another opportunity for you to express yourself, for you to control the meeting, and for you to get your way. Instead, seek out others, especially those who might not feel as included or welcomed.

Seek out those from other cultures. Invite them to sit next to you as they enter the room. Sit next to them if there's an empty seat or if they're seated by themselves. Smile. That's a universal welcoming behavior that can transcend culture, invite inter-action, and build a bridge to another human being. Your first step is not to ignore or avoid, but to seek.

Observe

The second step is to observe rather than control. As Americans, we have a tendency to want to get our way, to express our desires and wishes, to influence interaction, and even to control others. This is deeply ingrained into our individualistic, low-context, and competitive culture. Too often, this tendency to control rather than observe can intimidate, threaten, and frighten those from less competitive and indi-vidualistic cultures.

Instead, you might try unplugging, even for a few minutes, from your desire to control communication, events, and others and simply observe the behavior and communication of those from other cultures. Keep your mouth shut and observe.

A great deal can be learned just by observation. You might notice that those from other cultures are listening attentively, approving or disapproving subtlety, or simply smiling to show their involvement in the process of the group. In your attempts to increase your intercultural awareness, try becoming more aware by observation. Slow down, keep silent for a while, and simply observe.

Ask

After seeking and observing, the third step to increase your awareness of those from other cultures is to ask questions rather than give answers. As Americans, we have a tendency to impatiently finish the sentences of others, to speak for others, and to tell others what they should think or do. And this is especially true in small group discussion in which we feel the need to tell more than ask, especially when controversial or divisive issues are being discussed.

In an effort to become more aware of and sensitive to those of other cultures in our group work, we can use questions as tools to make them feel welcomed, to encourage their participation, and to learn more about them. You can make them feel welcome by asking them how they're doing, what's happened to them since you last met, and whether there's anything you can help them with before the meeting begins. You can encourage their participation by asking the entire group if everyone has voiced his or her opinion. If they don't respond to that general invitation to speak, you might directly ask them if they had anything to share or contribute. When they speak, ask appropriate probing questions that encourage their participation. When someone from another culture contributes to the discussion, find specific things to compliment or praise. You can ask that person to share or explain his cultural perspective on the issues being discussed, on his observations of the communication process of the group, or about facts about him personally, if the situation allows for some more personal or intimate sharing. Use questions to get to know others.

One really wonderful question you might consider asking is, "Could I treat you to coffee (or tea, soda, or even lunch) and learn more about your culture?" An invitation to coffee can offer much more than an opportunity for you to learn about another culture. It can be the first step to a lifelong friendship.

Relate

The fourth step in this process is to relate to the individual from another culture in ways that establish common ground. By relate, I mean establish a connection with the other person by discovering things you have in common. This can be one of the quickest and most powerful methods to establish a connection with someone from another culture.

Even though you differ culturally in many ways, there are many things you have in common. You both had parents, were most likely raised in families with siblings, attended school, played sports, had friends, went on vacations, participated in religious activities, had extended family gatherings, celebrated birthdays, enjoyed foods, were involved in hobbies, overcame difficulties, realized goals, experienced life turning points, had mentors or heroes, hold similar fears and apprehensions, and cherish deeply held aspirations.

By asking questions and sharing, you both can discover that you have much more in common than you once thought. In this life, you generally find what you're looking for, and if you're setting out to relate to another person with the goal of finding common ground, that's what you'll discover. And perhaps you'll realize one of life's great truths: It's easier to like someone who is like you.

Choose to S.O.A.R. above our usual way of overlooking, disregarding, or ignoring those from other cultures. Instead, choose to seek, observe, ask, and relate to those who have a different cultural background so that you might understand and interact with them in more sensitive, inviting, and encouraging ways.

In this chapter we examine the skill of active listening—a method of listening for understanding—so you can make others feel understood when they speak to you. Your ability to listen for understanding in your group work will not only ensure that you have understood what others are saying; you also demonstrate an openness and desire to encourage others to express themselves, regardless of their ideas, beliefs, and cultural backgrounds, without judgment or evaluation. This might be one of the most important ingredients in creating effective groups.

❧ Individual and Group Exercises ❧

Listening the Wrong Way

EXERCISE 4.1 The next time you're talking with a friend, try listening the wrong way—a non-understanding listening style. Don't tell your friend what you are doing. Listen for your ego. Judge everything your friend says in terms of whether you agree with her or not. Try not to be too obvious or obnoxious. But in a gentle way, verbally judge the content of what she says during the conversation. See if you can listen the "wrong way" for a minute or two.

Did your friend notice your listening response style? What did she say or do to indicate she noticed your change in listening? (At least I hope this isn't your normal style of listening.) How did listening the wrong way affect or modify the content of the discussion? How did listening the wrong way affect or modify the way your friend communicated? How did it feel to you? Did it feel familiar? Did it feel strange? Who listens to you in this style? How does it feel to you to be judged when you share with another? Did the two of you discuss this experiment after you shared its intent? What did you discover about yourself?

Listening for Understanding

EXERCISE 4.2 With a different friend, try listening for understanding (active listening) during a conversation for four or five minutes. Don't tell your friend about your experiment. Simply slip into an active-listening style of communicating without verbally noting the change. Carry on your part of the conversation. If he asks you a question, reply. But the primary purpose of the experiment is for you to listen in a way that provides you with a greater understanding of what your friend thinks and feels. Use questions or statements that begin with "You're saying . . . ," "You're feeling . . . ," "What I hear you saying is . . . ," "You feel that . . . ?" "Sounds like you . . . ," and so on. Use some variety in your listening for understanding. And don't reflect every statement your friend makes.

Try active listening once or twice every minute—that's enough. The rest of the time, carry your end of the conversation. See if you can listen for understanding for four or five minutes without letting on that you're experimenting. After the conversation is over, feel free to share with your friend that you were experimenting with a new way of listening, a method that would improve your understanding.

Did your friend notice your listening response style? What did he say or do that indicated he noticed your change in listening? How did listening for understanding affect or modify the content of the discussion? How did listening for understanding affect or modify the way your friend communicated with you? How did it feel to you? What did you discover about yourself as you attempted to listen for understanding?

Making a New Friend from a Different Culture

EXERCISE
4.3
In the next week, invite a fellow student, coworker, or neighbor from another culture out to coffee or lunch (your treat). Take the twenty to thirty minutes to ask questions about that person's culture and perceptions and feelings about American culture. Remember to be warm, friendly, and nonjudgmental as your guest shares with you. What did you learn from your time together? What specific perceptions, attitudes, beliefs, or values did you notice were different from your own? What specific perceptions, attitudes, beliefs, or values were similar? What was the most important lesson you learned about yourself during your time with this individual?

CHAPTER 5

Problem Solving in Groups

> Every problem provides an opportunity
> for you to do your best.
>
> —Duke Ellington

IT was two hours into a meeting that seemed to drag on forever. I sat in one corner of the room observing seven men and women, all assembly line production team managers at a local computer company, discussing the problem of employee language barriers. Some managers had to cope with six different languages in their production crews of thirty individuals. I was one of a three-member communication consulting team hired to observe three two-hour meetings and then suggest specific ways this group could improve its communication behavior.

After three meetings, the managers had yet to agree on a solution to the problem. Our observation team met later to compare notes and view segments of the videotaped discussions. We made five interesting observations about the group's problem-solving behavior.

First, the group spent only twenty minutes of the six-hour discussion time analyzing the scope and nature of the problem. The members took two and a half hours to explain, clarify, and defend their individual proposals. The group generated only five solutions during the three meetings. More than eighty minutes of the discussion time were spent sharing tangential complaints, company gossip, and other topics not directly related to the topic. The group made only six attempts to provide any structure to the discussion in the form of summaries or reviews.

The production managers were surprised by our observations and most astonished by the self-centered nature of each individual's behavior and the group's inability to keep the discussion focused.

In the workshops we presented, our team trained the managers in problem analysis, active listening, brainstorming techniques, and discussion-guiding behaviors. The problem-solving sessions after the training were much more focused, creative, and productive. The eventual solutions to the language barrier problems were far different from and more effective than the ones originally proposed. And what was most heartening to us were their increased skills and confidence in working as a team.

This chapter will provide you with a systematic approach to solving problems in a small group. Like life, however, there are many roads that lead to a satisfying and worthwhile experience. The problem-solving agenda we will explore is one of many approaches, but it is the one most universally used in our culture to find workable solutions to problems challenging small groups. As you work in problem-solving groups, it is my hope that you will remain as open, flexible, and creative as you can while addressing the problems you will have to solve.

Myths of Small Group Problem Solving

The assumptions we bring into the small group problem-solving process directly and powerfully influence the manner in which we participate and how we feel about working with others in groups. The following are some myths or false assumptions about small group process.

Myth 1: There Is Only One Solution to a Problem

When a group gets together to solve a problem, there is a tendency for the group to think there can only be one right answer to the problem. Maybe this is a carryover from our school days, when each question on a quiz or examination had only one correct answer. When working in a problem-solving group, don't limit yourself by looking for only one solution to a problem; look for as many as you can. Challenge all group members who feel they have discovered the "right" answer. Always work to broaden and increase the possibilities and solutions. Think big! Think of the many!

Myth 2: Our Solution Is the Best Solution

Once the group has weathered the storms of the problem-solving process, there is often a feeling or attitude of invincibility or infallibility. Taken to an extreme, this phenomenon is known as groupthink—the group attitude that it can do no wrong—examined in Chapter 9. Be aware that the assumption that the group's decision or solution is the best, simply because the group invested effort in its creation, can be false.

The group needs to challenge the myth of "our solution is the best." It would be of greater value for group members to adopt a more tentative attitude or approach to their solution by saying, "This is the best solution we can come up with at the moment. But we are staying open to the possibility of discovering other solutions, maybe even

> Nothing is more dangerous than an idea, when it's the only one you have.
>
> ∽
>
> EMILE CHARTIER

better solutions, in the days to come." This attitude of openness and discovery, rather than arrogance and closed-mindedness, will keep the group healthy, wealthy (in the spiritual sense), and wise.

Myth 3: Two Heads Are Always Better Than One

Getting together with other people to solve problems is based on the notion that two heads are better than one, and that a group of people can provide more information, experience, and creativity than a single person. But for this to occur, the members must possess some level of mutual respect, cooperation, and skill. There must exist a minimal level of willingness to come together and join forces so their pool of information, experiences, and resources can be shared, built upon, and expanded in a spirit of cooperation.

If this minimal level of willingness, mutual respect, cooperation, and goodwill is not achieved, then the consequences can be harmful, counterproductive, and even disastrous. Working in groups is no picnic, as you are well aware. It exacts a price from each of its members in time and effort. But the benefits can outweigh the costs.

Myth 4: No Conflict Will Arise

Another assumption many people bring to group work is that there should be no conflict during the process of problem solving. Aren't we grown, mature adults? Aren't we rational, logical people? Well, we are, and we aren't. I am beginning to think I'm not as rational, logical, and mature as I once thought when I was younger—especially when I'm working under pressure or during times of extreme stress. The more honest I am with myself in matters like this, the more willing I am to admit to my occasional self-centeredness, my unwillingness to listen, and my reluctance to compromise.

Groups can experience greater conflict after members feel a certain level of security and trust within the group. This is natural. Whenever people share ideas, there will be conflict. This isn't bad; it just comes with the territory. Without conflict, group members cannot create the solutions their problems require. Like labor pains during childbirth, there is no creation without some suffering. The group must experience conflict to be successful.

Myth 5: I Must Like and Be Liked by Everyone

A tremendous amount of emotional energy is spent on the belief that you should like each group member and that each member should like you. When interpersonal conflict arises within a group, remember the one-third rule. My theory is that in any group of people, one-third of them will like you, no matter what you do. One-third of the people will not like you, no matter what you do. And one-third of the people don't care about you either way, no matter what you do. It would be nice if everyone liked everyone else in the group, but unfortunately such a mutual admiration society doesn't happen often. So don't lose sleep over someone's sneer, snide remark, or personal attack. It comes with the territory. Keep in mind the one-third rule and you'll be easier on yourself and on others. You don't have to be liked or approved of by everyone.

Myth 6: Everything Must Go My Way

There is a subtle, almost unconscious assumption that if things don't go the way you want them to go, you should be disappointed, upset, or angry. One of the important lessons in life is that you don't always get what you want. In fact, you would most likely be in a terrible mess if every one of your wishes, fantasies, and dreams came true. Can you even begin to imagine the hideous life you would have right now if even half of the wishes you dreamed about during your high school years came true?

An important discovery I make about myself each time I work with a problem-solving group is that my ideas aren't always the best, my suggestions aren't always the most insightful, and my intuitions are often proven wrong. What I find refreshing in working with a group is a renewed sense of humility, practice in letting go of what I think is right and good, and a deeper appreciation for the beauty and creativity of others. I discover I am moved by other human beings in ways that are unexpected and sometimes even profound.

Myth 7: Every Problem Has a Solution

Many people believe that if there is a problem, there has to be a workable, acceptable solution floating around somewhere in the universe. But this may not always be the case. Today, some experts have pronounced their somber judgments that there might be no current solutions to such significant problems as the destruction of the ozone layer, the continued pollution of our oceans, and the rise in violent crime. I don't know whether this is true or not, but the possibility remains that there may be no solutions to these particular problems based on our current technology and resources. Likewise, your group may encounter a problem that cannot be solved with the resources, technology, and manpower available.

Psychiatrist Carl Jung had an interesting thought about the nature of problems. He felt that many problems in life may have no solution. "They might never be solved," he cautioned, "but merely outgrown." Maybe some problems cannot be solved. We merely outgrow or lose interest in them.

If you keep challenging these seven myths about small group problem solving, you will be a wiser, more effective group participant.

Decision-Making Techniques

Now that you have the right attitude toward working with others in groups, we can introduce some decision-making techniques.

Each of us makes hundreds of decisions every day. Most of these decisions are relatively insignificant: what shoes to wear, where to go to lunch, and when to go to sleep. Other decisions are more significant: Should I leave this job? Can I afford this home? Should I end this relationship?

When it comes to these more significant life questions, how do you make your decisions? Some people consult horoscopes; others flip a coin. One person will ask the advice of a parent; another person will pray for a sign. Others go to a mountaintop and meditate until a direction becomes clear. But when it comes to small group decision making, we do not always have the luxury to consult these more intimate, idiosyncratic methods of making decisions. The small group decision-making process is less private and more public, and relies on five more widely used decision-making techniques.

Decision by the Leader

The first method for making small group decisions, decision by the leader, calls for the leader to decide for the group, either after discussion with the group or without the group's contributions. Traditionally, many American business corporations have made their decisions in this fashion. The advantages of this method of decision making are that it minimizes wasted time, reinforces the traditional hierarchical business structure, and can be efficient in making administrative decisions. The disadvantages can be a lack of commitment to the solution by the group, superficial or minimal group discussion and analysis, and the development of an adversarial relationship between leader and group members.

A variation of this method includes decisions by a designated authority or expert to whom the group defers decision-making authority because the authority possesses more expertise and experience. Another method is decision by an executive committee or subgroup made up of group members. This method works well if the group is overloaded with work and total group participation is not feasible.

Decision by Majority Rule

The most widely used method of group decision making is majority rule or voting. We've all experienced the final invitation to conflict resolution when someone in the group yells, "Well, let's vote on it! I'm tired of arguing about this topic!" The vote is taken and the matter is settled. Or is it really?

The disadvantages of majority rule are that there are always winners and losers and that majority rule provides no protection for the minority. The losers often suffer because they feel their position was discarded by the majority. Many times, the minority will work to sabotage the implementation of the solution or decision. So the majority should never ignore the minority simply because it lost.

The advantages are that decisions can be made quickly and time can be saved. Majority rule is effective for procedural matters, such as voting on meeting times, placement of items on the agenda, and other administrative issues. But decision making that needs commitment from the entire group requires a different way of deciding.

Decision by Compromise

The decision by compromise method of decision making is a bartering technique: "If you give us this, we'll give you that." Members of one point of view will give up some aspect of their solution in exchange for support from other group members. Compromise combines aspects of the most popular solutions being discussed.

In theory, compromise doesn't sound all that bad. Isn't life compromise? But in reality, compromise often results in low commitment to the solution, because the solution can be so weakened or diluted as to make it ineffective or unacceptable.

Compromise is good when the position of members representing one point of view is incompatible with the position of those representing the other point of view. Compromise will permit the discussion to continue, whereas lack of compromise would have killed discussion long ago.

The disadvantage to compromise is that it is often used too early in discussion and prevents productive exploration of alternatives. It also produces decisions or solutions that are watered down, "averaging out" differences between various points of view.

Decision by Arbitration

Sometimes decision making needs to come from outside the group or groups in conflict. For instance, a dispute between labor and management often requires decisions to be made by a third party, an arbitrator. The arbitrator is an impartial third party whose decision both sides have agreed to be binding. In other words, both groups will accept the arbitrator's decision.

The advantage of this method of decision making is that the arbitrator will break an impasse or stalemate. Arbitration gets the ball rolling again, whereas an impasse between the two sides could polarize them even more, increase tension and hostility, and prevent compromise. The disadvantage is similar to majority rule. The loser in the decision must accept the ruling of the arbitrator and in doing so must also accept the fate of the minority.

Decision by Consensus

A highly effective decision-making method for a small group is consensus. Consensus requires that all group members find the decision acceptable. The decision may not be each member's first choice, but each member regards the decision as acceptable and workable.

Consensus is different from decision by compromise in that the final decision is not an averaged out, hybrid decision between two different points of view. The decision is a new, third point of view that each group member regards as workable and acceptable.

A test for consensus during group discussion is the question "Can you live with it for a period of time?" not "Is this your number one choice?" "Are you happy with this decision?" nor "Is this the perfect solution?" The question "Can you live with it for a period of time?" helps the group determine whether the decision is workable and acceptable.

An advantage of decision by consensus is that it increases member satisfaction with the decision, because all group members must buy into the decision of the group. Any member can prevent or block the acceptance of a decision. So the ultimate decision is the product of thorough discussion, and this process can also promote a stronger social dimension in the group and increase commitment to the implementation of the solution.

> Living is the constant process of deciding what you are going to do.
>
> ✌
>
> JOSÉ ORTEGA Y GASSET

A disadvantage of decision making by consensus is that it requires a tremendous amount of time. Whereas the other four methods of decision making—by leader, majority rule, compromise, and arbitration—can terminate discussion with the imposition of the decision, consensus demands the members talk until they discover a decision that is workable and acceptable to all.

Guidelines for Reaching Consensus

Here are five guidelines for group consensus:

1. Don't argue for your position. Present your views and positions; then listen to the views and positions of the other group members.
2. Don't assume this is a contest. Try not to view the discussion as an activity that someone has to win and someone has to lose. Look for the next acceptable option for all members.
3. Don't avoid conflict. Difference of opinion is natural. Critically listen to and evaluate the arguments and evidence of others. Yield only to the views and opinions that make sense to you. Differences of opinion make for higher-quality decisions.
4. Don't use conflict-reducing techniques. Don't vote, flip coins, compromise, or average. These techniques require someone to win and someone to lose.
5. Include the participation of all members. Make certain all group members are included in the decision-making process. Ask low-verbal members for their opinions, reactions, and feelings.

Discussion Questions

One of the most important tools in decision making and problem solving in small groups is the discussion question. The discussion question helps in problem identification. Problems need to be formulated into a discussion question to help focus the group's thinking, research, and discussion. As you will see, different types of discussion questions reveal and produce entirely different kinds of decisions and solutions to a problem. The three types of discussion questions are questions of fact, value, and policy.

Question of Fact

A question of fact asks if something is true, if something is occurring, or if something has already occurred. Questions of fact involve who, what, when, where, and why questions. Examples of questions of fact are:

> How much money is spent by our competitors on advertising?
> When did production begin to increase by more than ten percent annually?
> Who served as group leader during our last meeting?

Questions of Value

Questions of value ask for a judgment on whether something is good or bad, right or wrong. Such questions involve an individual's subjective opinion regarding matters of taste. These questions are more difficult for a group to agree upon, because the values, tastes, and beliefs of each member can be so different. Examples of questions of value are:

> Is it good public relations to donate our product to charitable causes?
> Is our new design pleasing to the eye?
> Who was the best group leader during the last quarter?

Questions of Policy

A question of policy invites discussion regarding what course of action should be taken. Questions of policy are generally the result of a problem or situation needing change or improvement. To answer a question of policy, the group must also answer many questions of fact and value in its problem-solving deliberations. Examples of questions of policy are:

> A problem well stated
> is half solved.
>
> ∽
>
> CHARLES KETTERING

What should our policy be toward increased competition in advertising?
What should we do if we increase profits by more than thirty percent annually?
What should our policy be if group leaders don't meet minimal standards?

Questions of policy are the beginning focal point of a group's attempts to solve a problem. The question of policy should be as specific as possible. Vague and general terms must be avoided. Limit your question of policy to only one issue at a time. Multiple-issue policy questions tend to scatter your group's research, energy, and focus. "What should be our hospital's policy toward rising surgical costs, malpractice litigation regarding psychiatric care, and custodial demands for pay raises?" is a question of policy that covers too many issues. A more specific question would be "What should our hospital's policy be toward rising surgical costs?"

The Standard Problem-Solving Agenda

The most common response to problems in corporations and organizations is to blame or defend. If there's a problem, many people will immediately look for someone to blame or defend themselves from the blame of others. So, when groups are formed to solve a problem, whether it's in a business, school, or neighborhood, the initial response is often to blame or defend. There is another, more productive approach to solving problems, and that's the standard problem-solving agenda.

Most current problem-solving agendas are based upon John Dewey's reflective-thinking model, whether they include all the steps he provided or some modification of them. Although in his book, *How We Think*, Dewey identified the steps most people use to solve problems, his steps have been followed as a way to organize problem-solving agendas for small groups.

The problem-solving agenda presented here is a modified version of Dewey's model, with the addition of an orientation step at the beginning.

1. Check-in
2. Analyze the problem
3. Brainstorm solutions
4. Evaluate the better solutions
5. Reach consensus on the best solution
6. Implement the solution

Before we look at each step in detail, it's important to mention that the variations in the quality of decisions arrived at by groups can be accounted for by the ability of group members to perform four important decision-making functions. They are the effective assessment and discussion of the problem, the criteria for the solution, the strengths of the proposed solutions, and the weaknesses of the proposed solutions (Hirokawa, 1988). You will notice that these four functions are incorporated into the standard agenda we will now examine.

Step 1: Check-In

The first step the group must take is to provide members with the opportunity to establish a supportive and trusting social dimension. Without a healthy social dimension, the group will not be able to function to maximum effectiveness.

Initially, the check-in period might require a substantial amount of time. Perhaps even the entire meeting. The check-in for the group encourages members to introduce themselves to one another by sharing any pertinent professional and personal information they feel may be helpful in letting other members know who they are. It can also be beneficial for members to share any previous experience, knowledge, or expertise they may have in the area, or related areas, to the problem they will be addressing.

After the group has established a supportive, friendly social dimension, the check-in step of each meeting becomes less involved. Usually, each member will take thirty to sixty seconds to share how things have been going in his or her life since the group last met. Much useful information can be provided during the group's check-in, and I've found these five minutes to be important to maintaining the group's social dimension.

Step 2: Analyze the Problem

Analysis of the problem is the second step the group takes to solve a problem. Fruitful discussion during this stage of the process requires that group members have already researched the problem before coming to the meeting and are ready to share and discuss the following questions:

> If you want to make enemies,
> try to change something.
>
> ⟳
>
> WOODROW WILSON

1. What is the problem?
2. What is the question of policy?
3. What is the nature of the problem?
4. Whom does the problem affect?
5. How serious is the problem?
6. What are causes of the problem?
7. What solutions have been attempted before?
8. What will happen if the problem is not solved?
9. What are the constraints for a workable solution?
10. What are three possible solutions that satisfy your criteria?

These ten questions for problem analysis are the most frequently asked questions of problem-solving groups I have worked with. Feel free to modify, delete, and add to this list as you and your group see fit. The next chapter discusses how to research these questions. But for now, I want to say that the quality of your group's research will determine the quality of the information for the remainder of the group's activities.

Step 3: Brainstorm Solutions

The primary purpose in the brainstorming step is to generate a large number of ideas without evaluation. The most serious threat to a group's attempt to select a workable and acceptable solution to any problem is the group's inability to generate more than two or three solutions to solve the problem.

I believe a group should never stop brainstorming until it has generated at least thirty possible solutions—not two or three, but thirty!

During the brainstorming process, each group member writes down every suggestion made during the session (including his or her own suggestions). Number each suggestion as the group moves from item to item. The primary rule is that no evaluation of any idea during this stage of the problem-solving process is permitted. Members sit in a circle and contribute possible solutions to the problem under study. There is no rationale, explanation, or justification for each suggestion, simply the suggestion. Assign a number to it. Then go to the next suggestion until you reach at least thirty suggestions!

Here are some guidelines for a successful brainstorming session:

1. Devote a specific period of time to brainstorming.
2. Every member must take notes, numbering each item.
3. No evaluation of any idea is permitted.
4. No questions, storytelling, explanations, or tangential talking is permitted.
5. Quantity of ideas, not quality, is desired.
6. The wilder the ideas the better.
7. Combine ideas.

You will discover some group members will enjoy this process of generating ideas without evaluation. It's not what we're accustomed to in our daily lives.

There is a problem-solving process that is a variation of this brainstorming technique called the Nominal Group Technique (NGT). The group members individually generate a list of solutions to a problem, then get together to record their lists on a blackboard for the entire group to consider. The advantages and disadvantages of each solution are not discussed, although clarification of items is permitted. The group members then select their five favorite ideas and rank order them on a card. After collecting the cards, the rankings are averaged and the solution with the highest average is the one the group selects.

The NGT is helpful, especially if the group is limited by time constraints, but its primary weakness is the lack of analysis of the solutions proposed. For the best solutions, the group must invest the time and effort into the discussion of the possible solutions.

Step 4: Evaluate the Better Solutions

Now's the time to slip back into a more critical-thinking frame of mind.

Before you actually evaluate the better solutions against the criteria you've established in the second step, you need to spend some time throwing out the ridiculous, illegal, and impractical suggestions created during the brainstorming session. This is where the numbers come in handy. Instead of reading the entire proposal or idea you want to discard or throw out, you simply announce the number to the group. If they agree, they'll tell you. If not, they'll tell you. Either way, using the number instead of reading off the entire suggestion or idea each time will save you time, energy, and effort.

Once the group has ten to fifteen ideas or solutions worth examining, then the real task of Step 4 begins—discussion of the strengths and weaknesses of the better solutions on the list. Here are some guidelines for a more effective discussion:

1. Discuss one solution at a time.
2. Consider its strengths and weaknesses.
3. Consider how many constraints each solution satisfies.
4. Move to another solution quickly. Don't get stuck.
5. Avoid lumping solutions into one large conglomeration.
6. Don't be afraid to challenge a solution. Now's the time to share your reservations.

Evaluation of the better solutions will take time. Keep the six guidelines in mind when considering the better solutions. Speak your mind. Now's the time to voice your reservations as well as your preferences. Above all, listen for understanding while other members are sharing their reservations and preferences.

Step 5: Reach Consensus on the Best Solution

As the group discusses the better solutions, two or possibly three solutions will keep surfacing during the discussion. When you notice this occurring, mention it to the group. Let the members know the group may be arriving at some agreement or common ground.

As the group narrows the selection to two or three, begin to look for areas of agreement within the group. Try to discover any common ground contained in the remaining solutions. Bring these to the attention of the group.

A second mini-brainstorming session may be appropriate at this time to generate a few related solutions to the two or three remaining in hopes of discovering one solution that is workable and acceptable to all group members. Remember, for consensus to occur, everyone must find the solution workable and acceptable.

To test for consensus, ask group members if they can live with this particular solution. They might object, stating it's not their first choice or they're not overly pleased with the solution. Just smile and repeat the question that tests for consensus: "But can you live with this solution for a period of time?"

After the group has reached consensus on a solution, take a break and celebrate. Remember the reinforcement phase of group development? Call out for pizza and soft drinks. The group deserves it!

Step 6: Implement the Solution

After you've cleaned up the pizza crumbs and empty soft drink cans, the group needs to implement the solution, which involves three steps: planning a timetable, assigning implementation tasks, and evaluating the implementation process. If the group is not required to implement the solution, this final step can be disregarded.

Plan a timetable. The group needs to divide the implementation of the solution into its component objectives and assign dates for the completion of those objectives. Be as specific as possible when you describe the component objectives.

Assign tasks. Assign individual members to complete the various tasks. Make certain each member knows the task and the date by which the task must be accomplished. Everyone should have the phone numbers of all group members, because communication is critical to the success of the project at this stage.

Evaluate implementation. The evaluation of the group's effectiveness in implementing the solution to the problem can be accomplished during a face-to-face meeting or over the telephone. Changes in procedure or approach might need to be made for future groups. Additional resources might need to be secured. And individual members might need to be encouraged, pushed, or congratulated. If the implementation was a success and all members are satisfied with their performance and that of the group, once again, I would suggest a social get-together to celebrate a job well done.

Reanalyze the problem (if necessary). If the solution fails to meet the group's expectations or standards, members might need to return to the beginning of the standard agenda and reanalyze the problem in Step 2. The evaluation of the implementation might have provided valuable information or a new perspective that was not initially available to the group. Many times, it's only after a solution is implemented that incomplete, inaccurate, or faulty analysis of the problem becomes apparent. In any case, the group can return to Step 2 and begin the entire process again.

> It's an ill plan that
> cannot be changed.
>
> ✑
>
> LATIN PROVERB

The Circular Nature of Problem Solving

The standard agenda provides groups with the most complete and time-tested problem-solving method (Wood et al., 1986), but that does not mean groups necessarily follow a linear, step-by-step process when they solve problems in the real world.

That's why I include the reanalysis of the problem in Step 6 (as described in the previous paragraph). It enables a group to return to the beginning of the agenda and begin the process again with additional information and new insight.

This circular approach to problem solving is supported by the research of Marshall Poole (1981), who discovered that twenty-three percent of the decisions in problem-solving groups resulted from a strictly linear, decision-making sequence of phases, while approximately forty-seven percent of the decisions were made in repeated cycles of focusing on the problem, then the solution, then back to the problem. Thirty percent of the decisions were made by the groups focusing their discussion only on solutions with little or no attention given to the analysis of the problem.

These findings are helpful when you use the standard agenda because they serve as a reminder that group problem solving is not always a linear, step-by-step process, but more often is circular and dynamic, not following clear-cut divisions. Your group might begin with the analysis of the prob-

> Arriving at one goal is the starting point of another.
>
> ℂℂ
>
> JOHN DEWEY

lem, then skip to a discussion of a solution, and return to problem analysis. Or, as I mentioned earlier, the group might actually implement a solution, only to discover that it needs to return to the beginning of the agenda and begin again with additional information and insight. Don't get upset when these things occur. That's simply the circular nature of problem solving.

Don't take this, however, as license to disregard the standard agenda and engage in a nonstructured approach to solving problems. Research repeatedly reminds us that a systematic approach to solving problems will help increase a group's effectiveness in the analysis of the problem, generation of possible solutions, and decision quality (Hirokawa, 1985). Your goal is to give the group the flexibility to engage in a dynamic, circular decision-making process, within a systematic approach to solving problems.

The standard agenda will provide you and your group with a time-tested systematic approach to problem solving. The group's flexibility in its application will ensure that group members will be given the freedom to do their best work.

Being More Creative

Even though you can approach any problem using the standard problem-solving agenda, your group's success will be determined to a large extent by the creativity each member brings to the process. The problem-solving process will not work if the group doesn't generate creative solutions to the problems. All the researched information, skillfully guided discussion, and eloquently expressed opinions will ultimately fall flat if the group members lack the creativity to produce solutions and adapt to the changing demands of the group process. Here are some specific things you can do to increase your creativity in your group.

Going for the second right answer. One of the most helpful habits you can get into for increasing your creativity is to think in terms of multiple solutions to questions or problems. Our educational experiences from kindergarten to college usually focus on the student finding the one right answer to the question posed by the teacher. With years of trying to find the "right" answer, we are generally satisfied when our group proposes an answer to a question or a solution to a problem and we stop the process at that moment. To encourage creativity, go for the second "right" answer, and the third, and the fourth, and the fifth "right" answer. The brainstorming process in the problem-solving agenda requires us to generate many possible solutions to a problem, but you need to extend that mind-set of looking for many answers to questions and multiple solutions to problems during all the phases of problem solving. Go for the second right answer.

Seeing it from a different angle. Another helpful habit that encourages creativity is seeing events, people, and things from a different perspective. We normally hold one predominant perception, interpretation, idea, or belief about most things in our lives. When working with others in groups, it's best if you can be open and flexible as you listen to the thoughts and opinions of others. Put some effort into seeing the world through the eyes of others. More important, if you can, offer different interpretations of events, people, and things that might not normally be held by the group.

One simple technique that encourages different perceptions is the reframing technique, which begins with the phrase "Another way of looking at it is . . ." Let's say the group feels that a certain solution is not feasible. You can use the reframing technique to help the group see the same solution from a slightly different angle. For instance, your group feels that holding an off-site training seminar at a college campus isn't feasible; it's too much hassle getting there, the classrooms are old-fashioned, and it could evoke bad memories for some workers. Instead of agreeing with this perception, you could reframe the same proposal by saying, "Another way of looking at this is one day in a college classroom might be just what our group needs to stimulate some of the youthful perspective, optimism, and fun we had during our college days."

By seeing something from a slightly different angle, reframing can open up an entirely new way for the group to view an idea, option, or solution. Be a source of creativity by looking at things from different perspectives.

Breaking the rules. A third habit you can acquire to increase your creativity is to break rules occasionally. Nothing illegal, irresponsible, or impolite. But often, creativity can be unleashed when you venture beyond the boundaries of the rules or norms that dictate group behavior. Instead of always following the standard problem-solving agenda, you might want to bend the rules and change the order of the agenda. Start from the last step and work backwards to the first step. Instead of always meeting in the conference room, you might suggest that the group meet at a pizzeria or at a park. You might want to begin the meeting with a compliment session, take twice as many breaks during the meeting for snacks, and maybe even limit every member to only five comments per hour, allowing low-verbal members to participate more. Whatever it is you do, try modifying the rules once in a while to break out of the usual mold of predictable behavior and venture into the unknown. You just might stumble onto something very new, exciting, and worthwhile.

Listening to famous voices. A fun way to increase your creativity and stretch your imagination is to pose your group's question or problem to a famous person, either living or dead. How would Moses, Jesus, Eleanor Roosevelt, Winston Churchill, Mohammed, Abraham Lincoln, Dan Rather, Helen Keller, Albert Einstein, Arnold Schwarzenegger, Bill Gates, Lao Tsu, Leonardo da Vinci, Shakespeare, George Patton, Mother Teresa, or Michael Jordan answer the question or solve the problem your group is considering? By seeing the question or problem from the perspective of these and other famous individuals, you might be opening yourself up to an entirely new

> We all know your idea is crazy. The question is, whether it's crazy enough.
>
> ⌘
>
> NIELS BOHR

and fresh perspective or understanding of your problem. Group members can even role play these famous thinkers and discuss the group's ideas from a very different frame of reference. Try imagining the advice and counsel of different people you admire and respect, and see where it takes you. It just might be what the group needs to get started in a new direction.

Having fun for a change. Another suggestion for increasing your creativity is to have fun. Normally, problem-solving groups are faced with serious issues that require immediate attention. The content and tone of the discussion are often serious, analytical, and urgent. When group members take on this demeanor, their thinking can become much more rigid and unimaginative. Thus, the creativity of the group is thwarted by the ever-increasing seriousness of the group's interactions.

When you're sensing that the group is getting stuck in a serious, inflexible posture that discourages or eliminates creative thinking, you can try having fun by doing some rather outrageous things. You can suggest that the problem really isn't a problem, but it actually prevents worse problems from happening. You can agree that the problem is really a problem, but nothing should be done about it yet because the problem might just solve itself. You can reverse the assumptions of the group. If the group is assuming that solutions that are within the budget are desirable, you can reverse this assumption by suggesting that solutions that exceed the budget are superior because they will force the department to go broke and then upper management will become involved in the problem-solving process. You can find something about the problem to joke about. Or you can joke about the group itself. Sometimes humor and a good laugh can have a healthy effect upon the group.

The successful group must be creative and flexible to succeed. Your willingness and ability to bring some creativity to the group will contribute to the ultimate success of the group's work. Be open to ways that can encourage and develop your creativity as you participate in groups that work.

How you approach the problems that will face you in life will determine, to a great extent, the quality of your life. Will you deny your problems, rushing to the first solution that comes to mind, or will you systematically approach your problems with knowledge, creativity, and thoughtful consideration? In this chapter, you have been given a systematic approach to solving problems—the standard problem-solving agenda. As you work in groups, remember to slow down when addressing problems and devote the time and energy to really understand the problem, to generate a list of many possible solutions, and to allow thorough discussion as the group decides on the best solution. You will discover the best solutions by creating the right circumstances, both in your group work and with yourself.

∽ Individual and Group Exercises ∽

Analyzing a Personal Problem

EXERCISE 5.1 The beauty of the problem-solving agenda is its applicability to your personal life as well as to groups. Examine a problem or conflict you are experiencing (or have experienced) in your personal life. It doesn't matter whether it's a relationship problem, an employment issue, or a living situation. After you've identified a specific problem from your personal life, complete the following questions:

1. Describe in one sentence what specifically is the problem.
2. Whom does the problem affect?
3. How serious is the problem? Circle the appropriate conditions:
   I think about it occasionally. It affects my relationships with others.
   I think about it often. It affects my job/school performance.
   I obsess about the problem. It affects my daily functioning.
4. What are some causes of the problem?
5. What solutions have you already attempted to solve this problem?
6. What do you think will happen if the problem is not solved?
7. What are some constraints to a workable solution?

What did you think about this exercise? Were you honest in your answers to the questions? Were you able to answer all the questions or were there some questions you weren't able to respond to? Does this exercise change or modify how you see your problem? For the better?

Brainstorming Solutions to the Problem

EXERCISE 5.2 Now that you've analyzed this problem of yours, try to brainstorm five possible solutions. I know you've been over this a million times, but most likely you've proposed the same two or three solutions over and over. This time, get crazy. Brainstorm some wild and ridiculous ideas! Give yourself two minutes for this exercise. Here goes! List at least five possible solutions to this problem of yours (I'll supply the other five).

1. _____
2. _____
3. _____
4. _____
5. _____
6. Don't do anything for one year and see what happens.
7. Make the current situation worse by increasing the symptoms.
8. See the problem as an invitation to become a different kind of person.
9. Leave the situation/the state/the country.
10. Lose interest in the problem by creating a more serious problem in your life.

How did the brainstorming session go? Did you refrain from evaluating your solutions? Could you get a little wild and crazy in your suggestions? How did that feel to you? What do you think of your list? What do you think of the five solutions I suggested at the end?

Group Problem-Solving Activity

EXERCISE
5.3

Have your group attempt to proceed through the first three steps of the problem-solving agenda: check-in, problem analysis, and brainstorming. Here's a hypothetical problem that your group can explore using these first three steps: "What should be done about communication studies students who consistently talk in class while the instructor is speaking or students are delivering speeches?" Make sure each group member has a list of the questions in Step 2 and receives instruction on the brainstorming technique. Good luck!

CHAPTER 6

Preparing for Discussion

> The secret to success is to know something
> that everyone else doesn't.
>
> —HENRY FORD

THERE'S a story about a high-rise apartment owner who tried to get his broken furnace to work after it quit for the second time that winter. The owner hired three different furnace technicians to locate the problem. But each time the problem could not be solved. Finally, the owner phoned a fourth technician, who listened to his problem. The old technician guaranteed he could solve the problem.

"Are you sure?" demanded the young apartment owner.
"I think I've seen this problem before," assured the technician. "Most mechanics wouldn't know where to look, but I'm certain I can help you."

Later that day, the mechanic met the owner at the apartment high-rise. The owner led the old man down to the basement where the furnace was located. The furnace was a complicated maze of pipes, wires, and odd-shaped contraptions. The old man walked deeper into this jungle of sheet metal and piping. Eventually, the mechanic stopped, felt the metal above his head, then selected a rubber hammer from his tool pouch. He gently tapped once on a small cylindrical box located above one of the thermostats.

Immediately, the giant heater grunted twice, then coughed up a deep roar of massive flames within the once-dark interior of the furnace. The fans began to swirl, pushing the heat up into the building. Within a minute, cheers could be heard from the tenants on the lowest floors, as the warm air flowed for the first time in days.

"You're a genius!" shouted the young apartment owner. "What will this minor miracle cost me?"
"The bill is $500," replied the mechanic.

"That's outrageous! You're charging me $500 for tapping a metal box just one
   time?" he screamed.

"Oh, no. The tap of my hammer was only $1," smiled the old man. "Knowing
   where to tap cost you $499."

Knowledge is power. The effectiveness of your group is determined to a large
extent by the information it has at its disposal. The combined knowledge of the
group is the material with which it will generate solutions that will solve the problems it faces. You have no control over the information and knowledge the other
group members bring to each meeting. Many people will make no special effort to
educate themselves about the problem their group is attempting to solve. But you
can determine the amount of information you possess and contribute. This chapter
will show you how to research for your group discussions and contribute information that will help you create a more effective group.

You Don't Know Everything

The meaning of this section title is obvious—we don't know everything. If we did,
we wouldn't need the help of others to solve problems in the real world. But we
don't know everything.

The furnace technician knew how to fix the furnace, but he might not know
how to balance the books. The apartment owner might know how to balance the
books, but he didn't know how to fix the furnace. In fact, the first three mechanics
didn't know how to locate the problem. Each person knows some things, but not
everything about everything. You don't, and I don't.

Yet people like you and I will participate in a
problem-solving group without ever once researching the problem, interviewing experts in the field,
or even giving the issue any prior consideration or
thought before taking our seat at the meeting.

> What we prepare for is usually
> what we get.
>
> ⁜
>
> WILLIAM SUMNER

Many times, we simply show up at the meeting, glance at the material sent to us by the chairperson, grab a cup of coffee, and settle down in our
chair for another long discussion. I know this happens often. I've been guilty of it
more than I'd care to admit.

Our lack of preparation is a result of many factors. We're too busy with other
matters to devote any time to research. We might never have learned how to
conduct library research or interview an expert. Many of us don't prepare for a
problem-solving discussion because of laziness. A million other things seem more
appealing, like skiing, shopping, visiting, eating, gossiping, and sleeping. Even
staring at the walls of our office with our feet on the desk would be better than
researching.

We Can Always Know More

Ideally, a problem-solving group would be made up of individuals who are experts in the problem area they are examining. But that is not practical. The majority of problem-solving groups are made up of interested and concerned people like you and me. We want to get a candidate elected. We want to put a stop sign at the end of our street. We want to raise funds for a favorite charity. Or we might just want to make our neighborhoods safer from crime.

No matter what we're trying to accomplish as a group, research can help us in our attempt to achieve the best solution for our problem. You won't necessarily have to make a trip to the city library, but you could phone around to see what other cities have done to reduce crime in their neighborhoods. You might conduct a series of brief interviews with a police officer, a Neighborhood Watch coordinator, a locksmith, and even a former thief to collect information and ideas that will benefit your group's attempts to make your neighborhood safer from crime.

Research is not only looking up information in your local library. Research is any activity that broadens or increases your information base on any topic or subject. In fact, some of your most helpful information will come from experts who deal with your group's problem every day.

No matter how much you know about the specific problem or issue confronting your group, you can always know more. I believe the more information and evidence a group has at its disposal, the greater the probability its efforts will produce a solution that is workable and acceptable to all group members.

Where to Research

The five primary sources for information about your group's topics are your own knowledge and experience, library research, the Internet, interviews, and surveys.

Tapping Your Personal Knowledge and Experience

One of the most neglected areas of research is your own knowledge of and experience in the problem. Take a moment to sit in a quiet part of your house and close your eyes. Imagine a scene from the problem your group is researching. In the case of bicycle theft, what experiences have you had in this area? Has a bicycle of yours ever been stolen? Have your neighbors, friends, or relatives had their bikes stolen? What was experienced? What was learned? What precautions are currently taken to reduce the chances of future theft? Do any books, television documentaries, magazine articles, or lectures related to this topic come to mind? Do any people having special expertise or interest in this topic come to mind?

As you reflect on your experience and knowledge of the problem, keep notes. Jot down any idea, thought, experience, or feeling that may provide information to the group's discussion. You'll be surprised by the amount of knowledge and experience you might already possess about the problem.

> Often the most creative people are the most prepared.
>
> ❧
>
> LEE IACOCCA

This activity of surveying your own knowledge and experience can also generate ideas on where to look for information and whom to seek for expert testimony. Let your mind wander as you research your own experience. Keep your mind open to discovering forgotten experiences and bits of information in the corners of your mind.

Using Library Resources

Any library, regardless of size, usually provides the following sources of information that you will need to research your topic.

The card catalog indexes all the library's books by author, title, and subject. This catalog is your primary guide to the books in the library. If you are unfamiliar with its operation, ask for assistance.

Periodicals (magazines, journals, and newspapers) are another source of information for your research efforts. *The Reader's Guide to Periodical Literature* will be your most valuable resource for locating periodical articles related to your topic. Periodical information is generally more current than information provided by books and encyclopedias. *The Reader's Guide* indexes the articles of more than 130 American periodicals on a wide range of topics.

Your library should have your local daily newspaper indexes in addition to the *New York Times Index.* Local newspapers will often provide the most valuable information concerning problems specific to your area. (You might also consider contacting the local newspaper and explaining your research project. Newspaper folks are often helpful in assisting you in any way they can.)

Most libraries utilize computer technology to make your research easier, faster, and more comprehensive. Computers speed up your survey of books and periodicals. CD-ROM technology gives you access to vast quantities of information available from encyclopedias, periodicals, and newspaper indexes. If you are already familiar with computers, you know the speed, power, and enjoyment this technology provides. If you are not, don't be afraid to ask the librarian for some basic instruction on their use. A few minutes of computer instruction will open up a new world of information to you.

Internet

One of the most powerful tools you have to access information from all over the world is the Internet. The Internet is a collection of computer networks that link computers from around the world. You literally have the collective knowledge of millions of organizations, groups, and people at your fingertips.

You have probably already used, or will use, the Internet to research a paper, check the stock market, or make reservations to a concert. The Internet can also be a fabulous source of information for researching your discussion topics. If you are unfamiliar with using the Internet, you might ask a librarian for help or even consider enrolling in an Internet class at your college. The few hours you invest learning how to use the Internet will produce countless benefits in the coming years.

Keep these two facts in mind when using the Internet. First, much of the information on the Internet lacks authority. Anyone with a computer and Internet access can post information, so some of the information you get is outdated, misleading, or false. You will need to evaluate the information with care. Some of the critical-thinking skills discussed later in this chapter will be helpful in analyzing what you find on the Internet. Second, many valuable sources of information are not available on the Internet, such as copyrighted books, encyclopedias, index and abstract services, and scholarly journals. Given this fact, you will still need to make a trip to the library when researching a discussion topic.

You will want to keep these four questions in mind as you access and evaluate information from the Internet:

1. Is the author of the information a qualified expert in the field? What are the credentials of the author, the organization, or agency posting the information?
2. Is the information accurate? Is the information consistent with your library research?
3. Is the information current? Are the sources up-to-date? If no date is given, the information may be old.
4. Is the information objective? Are sources cited? Are the conclusions based on fact? Are personal opinions and bias clearly stated?

Whatever Internet information you consider, you owe it to your work group to present data that is from reliable, objective, and current sources. Subject your Internet information to the same standards you would library information. You don't want to share false or misleading information with the other group members.

Conducting Interviews

Although you may be reluctant to ask for an interview from a local expert, the rewards of doing so can go beyond that of gaining valuable information. Many a friendship, both professional and personal, and many a job have blossomed because of a fifteen-minute interview. Not only will you be gathering expert opinion regarding your topic of discussion; you will be given the opportunity to connect with another human being you would have otherwise been a stranger to.

The first step in conducting an interview is to decide with whom you want to talk. If your problem is neighborhood crime, you might want to speak with the local police chief. If your topic deals with electing a local candidate, you might want to talk with a political campaign director.

After you decide on one or two experts to interview, the second step is to request an interview. Whether you request an interview in person, over the telephone, or in a formal letter, keep your request brief and friendly. Let the person know you would like to spend only fifteen minutes interviewing him at his convenience (not yours). If he cannot grant an interview, thank him for his time and try the next candidate. If he agrees to the interview, great!

The third step is to write a list of questions for the interview itself. This should be done only after you have researched the topic from your own knowledge and experience and in the library. This preparation will enable you to ask more enlightened, specific, and articulate questions.

> Is there anyone so wise
> as to learn from the
> experience of others?
>
> ✑
>
> VOLTAIRE

The fourth step is the interview itself. Be punctual. Nothing is more annoying to your interviewee than your arriving late to a meeting you requested. Dress up for the interview. Don't arrive in your T-shirt and old jeans. Stick to your time limit of fifteen minutes. At the end, thank the interviewee.

Finally, after you've returned from the interview, take a moment to write a brief thank-you card or letter to the interviewee. The few minutes and the cost of the stamp will add a touch of class that few interviewers ever consider.

Taking Surveys

For some problem-solving topics, the attitudes and opinions of a group of individuals might provide valuable information and help in your decision-making efforts. A survey can gather information about the seriousness and nature of the problem, generate a list of potential solutions, or provide you with an idea of the support or opposition your solution will receive if proposed. These and many other uses suggest that surveys are a rich source of information for your group.

Whether it's randomly surveying twenty employees concerning their feelings on reducing medical coverage rather than cutting wages, or polling the neighbors on their feelings about lowering the speed limit in the neighborhood, the opinions of a group of people can be extremely informative.

If you decide to include a survey in your research, keep these five suggestions in mind. First, develop a clear idea of what you are trying to achieve in your survey. Second, select a large enough population to be representative of the entire population being sampled. In some cases, the number of people affected by the problem is small so that all of them can be polled. Third, decide whether to interview people face-to-face, over the phone, or by mail. Fourth, construct a questionnaire that is to the point, clearly written, and asks only what needs to be addressed. And finally, test the clarity of your survey in a pilot study or mini-survey.

For most problem-solving efforts, your survey doesn't need to be too elaborate or statistically perfect. A simple polling of neighbors' attitudes or the collection of coworkers' opinions will be adequate. If a more complicated or involved survey is necessary, you may want to consult a book on survey methods or ask someone who has had previous experience in conducting surveys.

What to Research

Next, we should consider what to look for when you research. The items you want to seek information and evidence about are the questions from Step 2 of your standard agenda—analyzing the problem (Chapter 5).

These questions focus on your research efforts. You should try to gather as much information as you can regarding these questions. These are merely suggestions. Feel free to add, modify, and delete from this list as you see fit.

1. What is the problem?

The group should agree on what the problem is and define it. Avoid vague, general descriptions of the problem. Be as specific as possible. Instead of "crime," your group might want to focus more specifically on "department store shoplifting by pre-teenage children in the Santa Clara County." This definition will focus the group's research and discussion much more than a general description.

2. What is the question of policy?

The group should agree on the question of policy before you begin researching the topic. Remember to begin the question of policy with "What should be done about . . . ?"

3. What is the nature of the problem?

Find information describing the specific nature of the problem you are investigating. What exactly is the problem? What are the parameters of the problem? Are there any limitations or special conditions presented by the problem? How long has the problem existed? What is the history of the problem?

4. Whom does the problem affect?

Does the problem affect primarily men, women, or children? Young or old people? Does the problem affect a specific subgroup? Try to get as much information about those affected by the problem as possible.

5. How serious is the problem?

This is a question of value. Not all individuals will perceive the problem as being serious, but you need to establish some measurement of its magnitude, scope, and significance. Try to obtain statistical information describing the size and seriousness of the problem. Expert testimony on its seriousness is also helpful in determining how the group should address the problem.

6. What causes the problem?

This can be a question of fact and a question of value. It's a question of value because experts may hold differing beliefs on the probable cause or causes of the problem. Your task is to obtain information on the problem's original cause or causes. Get as much information as possible, citing how and why the problem came into existence.

7. What solutions were tried already?

In your research, be on the lookout for solutions that have been attempted already to reduce or eliminate the current problem. Be as specific as possible when you describe solutions that have been previously attempted. Also list organiza-

> It isn't that they can't see the solution, it's that they can't see the problem.
>
> ∽
>
> G. K. CHESTERTON

tions and individuals who attempted a solution. Describe the effectiveness of their attempts and discuss any suggestions the organizations and individuals may have for future attempts.

8. What will happen if the problem isn't solved?

What do experts or the literature say will happen if this problem is not solved? Once again, this is primarily a question of value, because experts will have differing views. Describe as specifically as you can the situation or conditions that will result if the problem is not solved or its effects reduced.

9. What are the constraints for a workable solution?

Suggest at least three specific constraints for a workable solution to this problem. For instance, three criteria for a solution to the problem of reducing neighborhood theft may be that the solution must cost less than $500 to implement, be implemented within sixty days, and involve participation by all residents. These constraints will help determine the merit of the solutions the group considers.

10. What are five solutions that satisfy your criteria?

After you have completed researching the problem (Questions 3 through 9), brainstorm five solutions. You might want to brainstorm more, but try to keep it manageable. You will be sharing your ideas during the group's brainstorming session.

Constructing an Information Sheet

An easy method for recording all your research data is to use an information sheet, which contains the ten questions from your problem analysis and the evidence you gathered for each question. You should cite the author, source, and date for each piece of information you include, in case another group member questions your data. For an interview, cite the expert's name, qualifications, and date of the interview. Here's an example of a question and the corresponding evidence and documentation for an information sheet.

6. What are the causes of the problem?
   A. "Increased drug use is the primary cause of increased home robberies." Police Chief Mark Henson, San Rafael Police. Interview, 8/26/01.
   B. "The increase in home robberies is due to the increase in drug use." Article by Sheila Graves, *San Rafael Times*, 8/18/01.

When you research the answers to the questions in Step 2 of the standard agenda, you may need to refer to more than one kind of research source. Don't limit yourself to magazines, newspapers, books, or expert opinions. Use as many sources of information as you can discover.

Using Visual Aids

Important information and research can be more effectively and persuasively presented to your group with the help of visual aids. In addition to talking about the information, you can also show them with a visual aid. There are many kinds of visual aids you might consider.

The chalkboard or flipchart is one of the most readily accessible visual aids that can help you communicate your point. Chalkboard use is best for a brief impromptu presentation, when you have no preparation time to construct a drawing, chart, or PowerPoint presentation. The disadvantages of chalkboard or flipchart use are many. Often the speaker will speak to the chalkboard or flipchart and not to the group. And the speaker's body can obscure much of what is being put up on the board. One advantage of a flipchart is that you can save the sheets of paper you've written on and have a record of the items or topics discussed.

Drawings and sketches are perhaps the easiest of all visual aids to construct. Your drawing or sketch doesn't have to be a work of art. With a few felt pens, a compass, a straightedge, and some patience, you can create a drawing or sketch that will add clarity and dimension to your presentation. Keep your drawings simple. Don't overload the other members of your group with unnecessary details when a stick figure sketch would suffice. Make your drawings, sketches, and lettering large enough to be seen by the group and no bigger. Keep it simple.

Charts let you present a wealth of information in very little space. Word charts, number charts, steps in a process, and organizational flow charts add important visual dimensions to any presentation. Line graphs, pie graphs, and bar graphs can also be utilized to present statistics in a fashion in which large amounts of data can be seen at one glance.

If you decide to use visual aids in your discussion, here are some recommendations you may find helpful:

1. Make sure the visual aid is large enough to be seen.
2. Keep your visual aids simple. The other group members must be able to grasp their meaning quickly.
3. Use visual aids only if they clarify or reinforce a point you are trying to make. Don't overdo the use of visual aids.
4. Show your visual aids only when you are presenting them.
5. Don't talk to your visual aid. Talk to the group.

Computerized Presentational Programs

There are many computerized presentational programs, like Microsoft's Power-Point, that offer simple yet impressive ways of designing and constructing much more elaborate visual aids and multimedia presentations for your discussions. Most folks know the basics of putting a PowerPoint presentation together, but if you don't, you can learn the fundamentals online, through your local community college, or at a large computer outlet. If you own a laptop computer, even a very simple or brief PowerPoint presentation can add a professional touch to your discussion contributions. When using any computer-generated presentational program, keep these guidelines in mind:

1. Be brief. Computer-generated presentational programs should be used to enhance your group contribution, not replace it. A helpful rule of thumb is to present one slide for every one minute of speaking time.
2. Keep your presentations simple. Allow your program's design wizards to help you select the designs, colors, and print type. Don't reinvent the wheel each time you speak.
3. Be consistent. Use consistent lettering, transitions, and bullets throughout your presentation. Too much variety can be distracting to the audience.
4. Use one to three words per bullet. Don't use more than five or six bullets per slide or you'll lose the group's attention.
5. Be prepared. Practice with your computerized presentation.
6. Set up any equipment you'll need well before your discussion time. Test the computer program, check the room lighting, and test anything else you might be using during the discussion.
7. Remember that you can print out graphs, tables, lists, outlines, etc., from your computerized program for distribution to the members of your group.

Testing Evidence and Reasoning

The purpose of researching the problem is to broaden the information base available to your group. Each piece of information or evidence added to the discussion increases the group's chances of discovering a workable and acceptable solution to the problem. Without the research of each group member, the probability of discovering a viable solution is decreased. Information is power.

During the group's problem-solving discussions, members share information, especially during Step 2 (analysis of the problem) and Step 4 (discussion of the strengths and weaknesses of the better solutions). It is for the benefit of the group that members carefully examine the evidence, proposals, and reasoning supporting the proposals. Critical thinking is the process of analyzing and evaluating information and ideas in order to reach sound judgments. Only with critical thinking can the group select the best solutions.

> Reason for most people means their own opinions.
>
> ✑
>
> WILLIAM HAZLITT

Three categories of research contributions require examination: opinions, evidence, and proposals. These are the three most prevalent contributions of researched information to group discussion. We will now examine what each category is and how to evaluate it.

Testing Opinions

Although personal opinions of group members are not technically a documented piece of information or evidence, they can often be presented as such without the expert testimony or evidence to support them. Examples of personal opinions are:

"The rise in crime is due to the influx of minorities into our area."
"Juveniles are the cause of the increase in crime."
"The solution is more state and federal laws against drug addiction."

In each example, the personal opinion was stated not as an I-statement, but rather as a statement of fact or expert testimony. When you hear statements such as these in a discussion, you can force the speaker to own his statements simply by asking, "Is this your personal opinion?" Most of the time, the speaker will qualify his personal opinion by rephrasing his opinion, such as:

"I think the rise in crime is due to the influx of minorities into our area."
"It's my opinion that juveniles are the cause of the increase in crime."
"I believe the solution is more state and federal laws against drug addiction."

The importance of forcing I-statements is that the speaker cannot subtly persuade or influence the group with more credibility than his own opinion should carry. It also separates personal opinion from expert opinion during discussion.

If the speaker doesn't own his opinion, but instead says, "It's my opinion and the opinion of others," or "Experts say the same thing," then ask, "What evidence do you have to support your last statement?" The purpose of asking for evidence is to examine the support for the speaker's statements.

The sharing of opinions is important to group discussion. With them, the group gets a feel for the attitudes and positions of each member. However, opinions need to be posed as I-statements. If members don't own their opinions, their statements can be mistaken for expert testimony or research findings, which can lend unwarranted weight to their statements.

Testing Evidence

In the course of discussion, especially during problem analysis, group members may present documented evidence. Most of the time, you'll jot down the information in your notes if you think it's important, thereby adding to the group's information base. But on some occasions, a piece of evidence might sound contradictory to the rest of the information presented on the problem. The evidence might sound old, or not as recent as you would like. Or you might want to know more about the author of the research, publication, or source. If this is the case, then testing evidence is required. Testing the quantity, quality, recency, and relevancy of research presented during discussion is not only your right as a group member, it is also your responsibility. Let's briefly examine the four tests of evidence.

1. **Testing quantity**. The evidence or information a group member presents may be documented fully, with author, source, and date, but you may want to know if there is other supporting evidence. To base decisions solely on one study or one expert testimony may not be the wisest course of action. Other experts who agree with the testimony or research presented lend additional strength to the position. You can test for the quantity of evidence by asking such questions as "Do you have additional evidence to support this point?" "Were there any other studies suggesting the same conclusion?" "Did anyone else find similar evidence?" By asking for supporting evidence, you also encourage low-verbal group members to contribute.

> Question authority.
>
> ❧
>
> BUMPER STICKER

2. **Testing quality**. Group members might present reams of evidence supporting a certain point or position, but the quality of the sources or the qualifications of the authors or experts could be questionable. The second test of evidence is quality. You might need to know the source of the evidence, the qualifications of the author, or the specifics of the design of an experiment.

To test for the quality of evidence, the following questions can be helpful: "What is the source of your evidence?" "Where did you find that information?" "Who is the author of your evidence?" "Describe the qualifications of the author." These and other related questions can test the quality of the evidence presented during discussion. Don't be afraid to ask questions about the quality of evidence. Most people will readily provide the additional information you are seeking. And an unwillingness to do so is also valuable information for the group to consider.

3. **Testing recency**. The more recent the evidence, the more valuable it can be to the group. Outdated or old evidence or information provides questionable value to the discussion. If a member cannot cite the date of an article or research finding, the evidence can be misleading or counterproductive if more recent and contradictory information has been discovered. That's why it's important to know the recency of evidence shared in discussion. Here are some questions that test for recency: "When was that evidence published?" "How recent is your information?" "When was the interview conducted?"

> Many persons of high intelligence have notoriously poor judgment.
>
> ✍
>
> SYDNEY J. HARRIS

4. **Testing relevancy**. Evidence that is irrelevant to the discussion provides no valuable contribution to the discussion. The truth or falsity of irrelevant evidence doesn't concern the group, for it has no bearing on the topic being discussed. Irrelevant evidence or information isn't usually identified as such during discussion, and the discussion can get sidetracked and derailed. Silent group members who are reluctant to challenge the relevancy of such information might feel frustration and hostility. For the sake of the task and social dimensions of the group, test the relevancy of evidence by questioning its bearing on the topic. Here are some ways to pose the question: "How does your evidence relate to our discussion?" "What's the connection between your evidence and the topic?" "What is the relevance of your evidence to our discussion?"

The four tests of evidence will improve the quality of group discussion. Without adequately testing questionable or unclear evidence, the information being considered can be confusing, misleading, and even harmful to the effectiveness and productivity of the discussion.

When testing evidence, keep these four guidelines in mind. First, the purpose of testing information is clarification and thoughtful consideration, not personal attack or assault. Second, your nonverbal communication cues should match this intent of clarification. Be soft in your tone of voice. If the speaker is offended by your question and responds defensively, maintain your gentle nonverbal posture. Third, let the other person "save face." Give the person you are questioning some room to clarify, modify, or withdraw his information. Don't push the speaker. Don't attack the speaker. Simply pose your question and let him respond. Finally, submit your own evidence to the four tests before you enter the discussion.

Testing Proposals

The testing of proposals occurs when the group discusses the strengths and weaknesses of the better solutions. A proposal is stated in the form of a solution to the problem the group is considering. During the course of group discussion, many proposals will be presented for consideration. Effective group problem solving requires critical testing of these proposals.

A proposal is any solution the group is asked to accept or support. The reason is the rationale for accepting the proposal. And the inference connects or links a particular reason to the proposal. These inferences can be either valid or invalid. The logical structure of any argument would look like this:

Because (reason) and (reason), therefore, (proposal).

Here is an example of a proposal you might encounter in your group's problem-solving discussions:

We should adopt a salary freeze if profits drop by ten percent (proposal) because it has been successful in other companies (reason) and it involves the participation of all employees (reason).

Or stated in logical structure form:

Because it has been successful in other companies (reason), and because it involves the participation of all employees (reason), we should therefore adopt a salary freeze if profits drop by ten percent (proposal).

Very rarely will a proposal be stated with all its reasons. Usually someone will say, "I think we should freeze salaries if profits drop by ten percent."

At this point in the discussion it's important to test the reasons supporting a particular proposal. The way you test is to ask for the reason or reasons supporting the proposal—"Let's examine the reasons supporting this solution." The inferences that link the reasons to the proposal are rarely stated; they are usually implied or suggested. Therefore, it is important to examine and test the validity of these inferences.

Inferences are either deductive or inductive. With a deductive inference, you begin with a generally accepted fact or belief and connect it to a specific issue to draw a specific conclusion or proposal. If the reasons are true, the proposal must be true. For example:

Because all prison inmates must be at least eighteen years old (reason), and Bob is a prison inmate (reason), therefore, Bob is at least eighteen years old (proposal).

A deductive inference forces us to accept the conclusion. If the reasons are true, there is no chance of the conclusion being false.

An inductive inference, on the other hand, is one in which we project a likely or probable outcome or conclusion based on one or more known facts or experiences. The inductive inference does not force or guarantee the truth of the conclusion or proposal; it merely speaks to the probability of it being true. For example:

> Because Bob has already served his prison term (reason), and Bob has obeyed all the regulations of his probation (reason), and Bob has been attending church regularly (reason), therefore, Bob will never commit a crime again (proposal).

The important thing to remember about inductive inferences is that they cannot guarantee 100 percent the conclusion they suggest. They can suggest only a high probability of correctness or truth. In the example above, we cannot be 100 percent certain Bob will never commit a crime again, even though he served his time, obeyed the probation rules, and attends church.

Most inferences suggested in your group discussions will be inductive. In other words, you must test the validity and soundness of the reasons supporting each proposal. Here are some questions you can ask when testing inductive inferences:

> Are there sufficient reasons to accept the proposal?
> Are the reasons directly relevant to the proposal?
> Do we have sufficient evidence to support each reason?
> Is the evidence supporting each reason acceptable, recent, and relevant?

Recognizing Logical Fallacies

In addition to testing the reasons supporting a proposal, you should be alert to any logical fallacies contained in the inferences suggested by each proposal. A logical fallacy is a mistake in logic or a mistaken or false belief. Here are five of the most common logical fallacies you will encounter in your discussions:

1. Overgeneralizing

An overgeneralization is a conclusion based on insufficient evidence. For instance, if there are two reports of car stereo thefts in your neighborhood during the past month, you might conclude that the rate of car stereo thefts is on the increase nationwide. This conclusion is not supported by the data. Two reports of car stereo thefts in your neighborhood is insufficient evidence to make generalizations about the nation. When this happens in a group, you should inquire about additional evidence to support the conclusion or suggest that there is insufficient evidence to support the proposal or conclusion.

2. Causal Fallacy

A causal fallacy is an argument that suggests two events are causally connected, though no such relationship is established. This is one of the most common fallacies made in discussion. Someone says, "We've never had a problem with car stereo thefts until you moved into the neighborhood." The speaker has assumed that the presence of the new neighbor is the cause of the problem, which may or may not be true. But a causal link has not been established. The speaker has provided no evidence showing the new neighbor is the cause of the problem.

If a causal fallacy is made, one approach you can take is to suggest additional causes or causal relationships that may explain the event. You can also mention that simply because these two events occur at the same time, it doesn't necessarily follow that one causes the other.

3. False Analogy

A false analogy assumes that because two things are alike in one or more respects, they are necessarily alike in some other respect. In group discussion, a solution to a problem is suggested because that solution worked somewhere else. Let's say someone draws the analogy between eating and marriage. Eating the same food day after day would quickly become boring, he argues. Therefore variety in food selection is desirable. Similarly, he concludes, having only one girlfriend can also become boring, so maintaining relationships with three women at the same time would eliminate such boredom.

Do you see the fallacy of this analogy? What works under one circumstance does not always work under another. If you believe a false analogy is being used, question the strength of the similarities of the two circumstances or situations. After careful examination, are you convinced the two situations are similar enough to warrant comparison?

4. Either-Or Thinking

The either-or fallacy supposes that only two options are available for consideration and that one of them must be accepted by the group. "Either we do it this way or we do it that way." "Either you support the solution or you don't." "Either you are with the group or against the group." Each statement gives only two positions for consideration, when in reality, many positions are possible.

When either-or thinking happens, don't let your group be fooled into believing they can take or consider only two positions. There are always more. Challenge either-or thinking in your group by suggesting other options. Or speak in terms of more and less. For instance, instead of describing a proposal as good or bad, you can point out it is less expensive than some and more practical than others. Don't let the group's thinking become too rigid or limited.

5. Ad Hominem Argument

The ad hominem argument consists of attacking the opponent in a personal way as a means of ignoring or discrediting her evidence or position, instead of focusing debate on the evidence or issue under examination. An example would be to say, "Your view of gun control can't have validity because you're a Democrat." The attack is leveled against the person's character, beliefs, or behavior as a means of diverting attention from the strength of her arguments and reasoning. When this occurs in a group, try to direct the discussion back to the issue or bring the attacker's behavior to the attention of the group.

Ethical Communication

The primary goal of any small group is to complete the group's tasks while maintaining a reasonable social dimension among the group members. The manner in which the group members satisfy these two dimensions of group process is rarely discussed openly by the individuals in the group. Will they be honest in their communications with one another? Will they be respectful of the group's diversity? Will they behave with integrity? Will they be fair in their dealings with one another? Will they keep promises? These and other questions involve the ethical variables that need to be considered if the group is to function in an ethical and honorable way.

Ethics in small group work refers to the moral aspects of group interaction. Does the speech, behavior, and impact of the group members help or harm others? Group members have a moral obligation to be honest, respectful, fair, and responsible in their personal and interpersonal interactions within the group. And the impact of the group upon the world at large should be positive, constructive, and fair. Ethical communication is the foundation upon which all small group interaction should be judged.

The importance of ethical communication was emphasized by the National Communication Association recently in their adoption of The Credo for Ethical Communication. Here is a summary of their credo:

1. We advocate truthfulness, accuracy, honesty, and reason as essential to the integrity of communication.
2. We endorse freedom of expression, diversity of perspective, and tolerance of dissent to achieve the informed and responsible decision making fundamental to a civil society.
3. We strive to understand and respect other communicators before evaluating and responding to their messages.
4. We promote access to communication resources and opportunities as necessary to fulfill human potential and contribute to the well-being of families, communities, and society.
5. We promote communication climates of caring and mutual understanding that respect the unique needs and characteristics of individual communicators.

6. We condemn communication that degrades individuals and humanity through distortion, intimidation, coercion, and violence and through the expression of intolerance and hatred.
7. We are committed to the courageous expression of personal convictions in pursuit of fairness and justice.
8. We advocate sharing information, opinions, and feelings when facing significant choices while also respecting privacy and confidentiality.
9. We accept responsibility for the short- and long-term consequences for our own communication and expect the same of others.

These nine statements articulate the principles by which ethical communication should be evaluated. The themes of honesty, respect, fairness, choice, and responsibility are clearly identified and encouraged.

There are three areas ethical communication should be considered in all group work. Let's take a look at each one of these three areas and suggest specific ways you can consider implementing ethical communication.

Individual Ethical Considerations

To be an ethical group member you have the responsibility to uphold the highest standards of truthfulness, honesty, and respect as you research and prepare to participate in your group.

Perhaps the most important guideline you can follow is truthfulness. You have the ethical responsibility to tell the truth when talking with your group. Though you might be tempted to exaggerate information to impress your colleagues or make up evidence because you didn't want to invest the time to research, the result is the same—you are lying. And if the other group members discover that you are exaggerating or lying, your credibility is forever tainted and held in question. Even if your lies are never discovered, you will always know.

You also have an ethical responsibility to select discussion topics that will benefit others; not insult, take advantage, or harm them in any way. Select topics that will improve the lives of others.

Your ethical responsibilities also include any research the discussion topic may require. Many people are satisfied by just collecting the minimal amount of content material or none at all. But as an ethical group member, you have the responsibility to research your topic as completely as you can. Your group deserves the most relevant, accurate, and recent information you can provide. You don't want your group members to listen to misinformation, information that is inaccurate or false, or information that is out-of-date. As an ethical group member, give your group the best information available.

In addition to thoroughly researching your subject, you have the ethical responsibility to present your ideas in a fair and unbiased fashion. A person can get so excited about the information she finds that she can exaggerate its importance. This distortion of the evidence is unethical. Your group deserves to hear a fair and balanced presentation of your information. Be fair when you present your material and give credit where credit is due. Cite the source of any information or evidence you present during the discussion. When you quote someone directly, you must provide the name of the person you are quoting.

Avoid plagiarism in reporting any relevant research to the group. Plagiarism occurs when you present the ideas or words of others as if they were your own. The temptation to save some time and steal the words and ideas of others is unethical and in some instances illegal. So always give credit where credit is due.

Group Ethical Considerations

When you discuss a topic with your group, you have a number of ethical responsibilities to consider. First, strive to promote an open and supportive group climate. Seek and respect the opinions and feelings of your fellow group members. Listen with an open mind and try to understand the content and the intent of what other group members are communicating before you evaluate or respond to their messages.

Encourage freedom of expression and tolerance for those who dissent against the majority opinion. Avoid communication behaviors that degrade others by distorting information, intimidating participation, or coercing agreement. Be willing to see issues and positions from the perspectives of others. Be fair in your analysis of the information. And above all, strive to help and not hurt, to build up and not tear down the opinions, feelings, and integrity of others, always considering what is best for the group rather than for yourself.

Your ethical communication during your group discussions can have an enlarging effect, not only upon your fellow members, but ultimately upon you and how you develop and mature as a human being.

Group Environment Considerations

Finally, your group has an ethical obligation to the people and environment outside of the group itself. The group's decisions, the solutions proposed, and the implementation of those solutions should benefit the people involved and the environment in a positive way. The impact of your group should help and never harm. The goal of your group's efforts is always to make the world a better place.

During the course of your group's research, discussion, and decision-making, the ethical responsibilities you have to the people who will be affected by your decisions and solutions should be kept in the forefront of all your thinking and behavior. The purpose of your group's existence is predicated upon the assumption that you will do good and not bring harm. That your efforts and energy are directed at improving the world in some small way honors the rights of others, promotes the healthy development of society, and considers the long-term impact upon the environment.

Your Time Management

Are you the kind of person who manages your time well? Do you set personal goals and prioritize your tasks for the month, the week, and the day? Do you keep a daily calendar of things to do and check them off with satisfaction as you complete them? Are you punctual or even arrive a few minutes early to your scheduled appointments and meetings? And are you organized, dependable in completing assignments on time, and able to say "No" to distractions? Are you a person who keeps promises to others?

Or are you the kind of person who doesn't set personal goals, avoids prioritizing tasks, or doesn't keep track of tasks at all? Are you late to appointments or even fail to show? Are you disorganized, unwilling to say "No" to distractions, and continually asking for extensions on your assignment deadlines? Are you a person who breaks promises to others?

Your answers to these questions reveal a great deal about you as a person. Your ability to manage your time effectively affects almost every aspect of your life, the perceptions people have of you, and ultimately, how you see yourself. Time is not only money, as the saying goes, it is life. Your life.

Now, I'm not saying you have to be organized, punctual, and responsible in your personal life. That's your business. But I am saying that your ability to manage your time effectively and keep your promises is fundamental to your effectiveness and success when working in groups. When you're participating in a group, you are no longer afforded the luxury of being a lone cowboy or cowgirl on your horse in Montana cattle country. You are now a member of a group, a team of people who depend upon one another. They depend upon your willingness and ability to manage your time effectively. Here are seven suggestions that will help you become more effective in managing your time.

1. Prepare Ahead of Time

Even before you attend your group's first meeting, prepare mentally ahead of time. You need to realize that your involvement and participation in the group will require a certain amount of time—time that you would otherwise be spending in different activities. That's the commitment you make when you join a work group. So take responsibility for your decision to participate in the group and accept your obligation to manage your time effectively and wisely.

2. Identify Your Assignment

There's an old saying that, "If you don't know where you're going any road will do." That is especially true when working in a group. Know what your group goals are and specifically, what your specific assignment is in achieving those goals. What particular tasks and responsibilities are required of you? If you don't know what's expected, you'll soon discover yourself wandering aimlessly without a clear idea of where you're going.

As the group decides on a course of action or a set of implementation objectives, make certain you know what part you play in achieving those goals. Write them down. If you're uncertain or confused about your exact task or tasks, ask the group. Clarify your assignment. Be certain you understand what the group wants from you and the due dates for your assignments.

3. Decide On Your Incremental Goals

Once you know what your specific goal is, break it down into its incremental or smaller goals. Don't just write down, "I'm in charge of planning a luncheon with the City Council Members and our group." Instead, divide that goal into its incremental elements or mini-goals, such as (1) exploring possible dates for the luncheon that are convenient for both City Council members and your group, (2) setting a date for the luncheon, (3) deciding on a restaurant, (4) making the reservation with the restaurant, and (5) sending written invitations to all attendees.

4. Establish Due Dates for Your Incremental Goals

By dividing your goal into incremental goals you are in a better position to accomplish those goals by establishing due dates for their completion. By doing this, you have now spread out your task into a more manageable approach to achieve your goal. In the example of the City Council luncheon, by assigning five due dates for your incremental goals you have organized your time more efficiently and this actually makes your task easier. Remember to write the due dates on your desk calendar or enter them into your mobile device.

5. Just Do It

Like the Nike slogan says, "Just Do It." The single most difficult requirement for effective time management is the actual physical accomplishment of your tasks. Whether it's getting up in the morning when the alarm sounds, writing a report, cooking dinner, or purchasing a car, there comes a time when you simply have to do it. Don't procrastinate. Just do it.

In our example, you'll actually need to make that phone call to the City Council secretary and request possible luncheon dates. You'll need to actually visit the restaurant and decide upon the menu and the room. And you'll need to actually write and mail or e-mail the invitations to the luncheon. There comes a time when you'll actually have to do something. This separates those who do from those who don't. And don't wait until the last minute. Psychologically, the unfinished task or assignment hangs over your head like a dark cloud until it is completed. So decide to manage your time wisely and keep checking off your "to do list" day by day, week by week, and month by month. You'll be happy you did.

6. Say No to Distractions

In your efforts to manage your time effectively, a hundred distractions will seem to appear and attempt to pull you away from accomplishing the first five steps. There will always be e-mail to peruse, Netflix to scan, snacks in the refrigerator to gobble up, or a drive in the country to enjoy. These and a hundred other distractions will tempt you as your tasks and responsibilities get closer to their due dates. That's life.

But say "No" to these distractions. Realize that to manage your time effectively, especially when the other group members are depending upon you, you must sooner or later defeat that enemy of "The Distraction." It will attempt to derail your best efforts to accomplish your goals. But this is your time to take a stand, to be a responsible group member, and say "NO" to those distractions.

All this afternoon, as I've been writing this section on time management, I've been tempted to go for a motorcycle ride. It's been raining for the past three days and this is the first day it's been sunny. But I said "NO" to the temptation and sat here all morning to work on this task, since this is my due date for this section. It's on my calendar. I'm managing my time effectively by just saying "NO" to my BMW motorcycle all morning as I type. But now my assignment is almost done and I'm ready to celebrate with a motorcycle ride in the country.

7. Celebrate Your Completed Tasks

One way to reinforce your time management victories is to take time out and celebrate your completed task. That's right, actually doing something fun or rewarding for yourself to acknowledge your accomplishment no matter how big or small it might be.

We can go through our lives dutifully fulfilling the many responsibilities and obligations on our to do lists without stopping for a moment and really appreciating the time, effort, and discipline we exerted to get the task accomplished. That feeling of a job well done is one of the true joys of life. And by celebrating, you strengthen your resolve to repeat the process in the future. Not everyone manages their time well, accomplishes the goals they set out to achieve, and keeps their promises to others. You do.

So remember to take the time and celebrate, whether it's a special cup of coffee, a lunch out, a movie, a new book, or even a motorcycle ride in the country. My motorcycle is warming up in the driveway right now as I finish this section, on time I might add. Life is good.

This chapter explored ways to increase and use your knowledge about a specific topic. When you work in groups, your knowledge base and ability to critically examine the information and reasoning employed by the group will determine the quality of your decisions and create a more productive group. Whether you are sharing information with your group or examining and analyzing the information of others, remember to do so slowly, respectfully, ethically, and punctually because your communication behavior influences and shapes the behavior of others.

❧ Individual and Group Exercises ❧

Interviewing an Expert

EXERCISE 6.1 Select a problem of at least statewide importance that you feel strongly about, such as the rising cost of education, air pollution, hate groups on the Internet, child abuse, or rising gas prices. Construct a question of policy for the problem you have selected and brainstorm five possible experts who have specialized training and/or experience with this problem. Choose one of the five individuals and schedule a twenty-minute interview with him or her. Interview this expert, using Questions 3–9 from the information sheet outlined in this chapter.

Whom did you select for your interview? Why did you select this person? How do you feel about the questions you asked? Discuss your overall effectiveness as an interviewer. What did you learn about the problem? What did you discover about yourself in this assignment?

Group Research

EXERCISE 6.2 Have your group select one communication behavior that all group members feel they should improve. Listening, clarifying messages, summarizing ideas, resolving conflicts, and encouraging low-verbal members to contribute are some examples of these behaviors. Once a topic is selected, have each member independently research two library resources and interview one expert in an effort to gather information about this particular communication behavior. Meet as a group and have each individual share the information he or she gathered from the two library sources and interview. Also have the members share what they learned from their research experience.

Being an Ethical Group Member

EXERCISE 6.3 Have the members of your group take twenty to thirty minutes to discuss what it means to be an ethical group member. Begin by having each group member share a personal experience when he or she was not entirely ethical in a work, school, or family situation, and to briefly describe the outcome of the unethical behavior. After all the group members have shared one brief incident of questionable or unethical behavior, discuss the advantages of being an ethical group member using the suggestions given in this chapter.

Research Time Management Skills Online

EXERCISE 6.4 Go online and type in "Small Group Time Management Skills." You'll find scores of web articles on how to manage your time more effectively in a small group. Select one of the articles that appeals to you and read it, right now. Might as well make good use of your time. Anyway, see if the article has two or three suggestions on managing your time more efficiently and envision where you might put those suggestions to use in the future. You can always take a nap later. But for now, go online and learn a new thing or two. Just do it.

CHAPTER 7

Guiding Discussion

If you don't know where you're going,
any road will do.

—Basho

HANSEN is a speck on the map about thirty miles southeast of Twin Falls, Idaho. My wife's uncle runs a cattle ranch just outside Hansen, right at the foot of the Sawtooth Mountains. Uncle Chuck's house is nestled in a sleepy little hollow, flanked on both sides by a year-round creek and shaded by a grove of willows.

Several years ago, my family and I spent four days at Uncle Chuck's. Time stands still at his ranch. It takes me two days just to unwind and slip into country time. Schedules there are governed by the rising and the setting of the sun. Folks there talk slow, with a deep richness, unhurried, and seemingly unaffected by this century. I like all this, up at Hansen.

But what I like best is watching Sheila and Ted, Uncle Chuck's two spirited border collies, keeping a hundred head of cattle moving straight on course during a cattle drive.

Border collies, I'm told, are the smartest cattle dogs in the world. A hundred cows can be packed into a tightly stuffed orb by one dog and moved almost effortlessly, like the shadow of a cloud rolling silently over the flowing landscape. The dogs dodge, dart, shove, and pack the cows into one obedient, single-minded mass of livestock, headed for a yet unseen destination.

One rancher down the road from Chuck's went into a three-month depression when his border collie, Nick, died of old age. The rancher shed more tears over Nick's death than he did when his wife left him. At least that's what Uncle Chuck says, and Uncle Chuck doesn't exaggerate. In fact, he doesn't say much at all. And that's why the last night we were in Hansen, Uncle Chuck surprised me with something he shared.

"Too bad our cattlemen's association didn't have some border collies to keep us in line," he lamented, as we sat on the back porch steps. "Seems like our association can't ever seem to agree on anything because we don't stick to the topic."

"Like those cows, maybe you need some help staying on track," I suggested.

"Yeah. And we might be dumber than cows. At least cows don't fight with one another." He smiled.

I smiled too as we listened to the water in the creek begin its journey to the sea.

This chapter will show you specific ways to guide the discussion of a group in the task and social dimensions of interaction. Strangely enough, your influence and impact on the discussion of a group is initiated more through asking questions than making statements, or through stating your opinions and feelings. You can have a more positive and productive impact on your group by encouraging others to participate and contribute, rather than always focusing on sharing your ideas and opinions. In addition to learning specific ways to guide the group's discussion, you will be introduced to some guidelines on being a more effective follower in group work. Without the willingness and ability to follow, there can be no effective leadership. Create more effective groups by learning to guide and follow.

Guiding Discussion to a Shared Path

The funny thing about trying to keep five or six people on track during a discussion is that it's not as easy as you might think. One person will start the discussion with one idea only to be interrupted by someone else, who begins to weave a second, unrelated thought or idea into the discussion, while two people chuckle at a humorous remark made by a third speaker. And the sixth member of the group is staring out the window, oblivious to the other three conversations.

Each person, it seems, has a different idea of where to go, what to do, and how to do it. Some members talk a lot; others don't. At times, each group member seems to be taking a separate path.

The initial task during any discussion is not solving a problem. That will come in its own time, if it is to come at all. The initial task of the group is to keep the discussion focused, coordinated, and on track in a supportive, open atmosphere. No matter how well

> One question, one gentle word, can change the course of a conversation and a life.
>
> ∽
>
> ALFRED ADLER

informed, committed, and articulate each member might be, the group can wander aimlessly, like cattle without those border collies, if it cannot stay focused.

This chapter will show you specific ways to guide the discussion of the group to a shared path. Like border collie training, but with a higher calling in mind. You won't be as pushy and controlling as a border collie, but you will know the moves to keep the group on track during your discussions.

The communication behaviors you will learn are called guiding behaviors because they keep the discussion focused and coordinate the participation and contributions of the individual members in the most productive manner possible.

You will learn two categories of guiding behaviors. First, task-guiding behaviors are intended to keep the discussion productive, participatory, and on track. The second, social-guiding behaviors are designed to establish and maintain healthy interpersonal relationships between group members. The goal is for each group member to discover a wide array of guiding behaviors he or she can put to use during a discussion, depending on the situation, the mood of the group, and his or her particular inclination at that given moment.

Task-Guiding Behaviors

Kenneth Benne and Paul Sheats have proposed a list of task and social roles that have enabled us to get a clearer idea of what specific behaviors individuals can perform in groups. The following is a modified list of these behaviors sets. Task-guiding behaviors are those behaviors that initiate and maintain a productive task dimension during the group's discussions. The six task-guiding behaviors are requesting information, providing information, clarifying information, guiding/summarizing discussion, analyzing, and negotiating.

Requesting Information

Requesting information from the group is an important function of every group member. It serves to broaden the information base of the group, initiate interaction when the discussion lulls, and encourage low-verbal members to contribute. Requesting information is a basic communication skill that invites others to communicate, participate, and contribute. Here are some examples of requesting information:

"What do we think about . . . ?" "How do we feel about . . . ?" "Does anyone have any information dealing with . . . ?" "Does anyone have any evidence concerning . . . ?" "Did anyone interview an expert about . . . ?" "What information haven't we shared yet?"

The important thing to remember about requesting information is that you are opening up the discussion to everyone again. This behavior can often have an invigorating effect on a discussion that is needlessly stuck on an overworked item. It can also serve to discourage a high-verbal member from monopolizing a discussion.

Providing Information

Sharing evidence, information, or personal opinion is a vital behavior each group member is expected to perform. Without the sharing of information, there can be no discussion. You have thought about and researched the topic before attending the meeting, so you are prepared to provide the group with the fruits of your labor. Here are some ways to begin:

(Providing evidence/information)

"In my research I discovered . . . ," "I read that . . . ," "One study suggested . . . ," "During my interview with _____ I learned that . . . ," "According to . . . ," "A recent poll concluded that . . ."

(Providing opinion)

"I think . . . ," "It's my opinion that . . . ," "I believe . . . ," "I feel . . . ," "It's my understanding that . . ."

If you research the topic, you owe it to the group to share or provide as much relevant information to the discussion as possible. By withholding or failing to share your information, you can prevent the group from arriving at the wisest decisions and proposing the best solutions. You could be holding the one piece of information the group needs to succeed!

Clarifying Information

After a group member shares information, some confusion or question might arise about the content or meaning of the statement. This is when you need to clarify any ambiguous information. Here are some ways you can initiate that process:

"Are you saying . . . ?" "Do you mean . . . ?" "Do I understand your research to suggest that . . . ?" "So this tells us that . . . ?" "Another way to say this may be . . . ?" "Can we interpret the evidence to suggest . . . ?" "Could you repeat it?"

The purpose of clarifying information is to ensure that the picture in the speaker's head is the same as or similar to the one you intended. Clarify any ambiguous information presented to the group. Take the time to ask questions. This is true for group discussion work as well as for your personal life.

Guiding/Summarizing Discussion

Guiding/summarizing discussion behaviors keep the discussion on the agenda, regulate participation, and announce time limits. Without these behaviors the group loses direction. Notice how powerful each of these behaviors is in guiding the group:

> In dealing with others
> be gentle and kind.
>
> ✑
>
> LAO TSU

(Initiating the agenda)

"Let's define the problem."

"Can we move on to brainstorming solutions?"

"I think we can move to the next step of. . . ."

(Maintaining the agenda)
"I think we need to return to the agenda."
"We need to return to the topic of . . ."
"How does this relate to our agenda item?"
"We're off track. Can we get back to . . . ?"

(Regulating participation)
"So, what you're telling us is . . . ?" (regulate high-verbal)
"Can you summarize your point?" (regulate high-verbal)
"What is your opinion, Mary?" (encourage low-verbal)

(Announcing time limits)
"Our meeting should last one hour. It will end at 2:30."
"We have ten minutes left. Do we want to go to the next agenda item?"
"Our time is up; shall we table this until next time?"

(Summarizing discussion)
"So far, we've heard three explanations. They are . . ."
"The brainstorming list of solutions is. . . ."
"I'm hearing two schools of thought on this. First . . . and second. . . ."

Analyzing Evidence and Testing Reasoning

As mentioned earlier, the need for careful and thoughtful analysis of evidence and reasoning is crucial in the problem-solving process. You need to be able and willing to analyze the evidence presented and test the reasoning of the proposals set forth. Here are ways you can analyze evidence and test reasoning:

Analyzing evidence
"Do you have additional evidence for this position?" (testing quantity)
"What makes this researcher qualified?" (testing quality)
"When was the article published?" (testing recency)
"How does this relate to our topic?" (testing relevancy)

Testing reasoning
"Have we looked at enough examples to explain this event?" (testing over-generalization)
"Are there other causes that would explain this event?" (testing causal fallacy)
"Are these two situations similar enough to warrant comparison?" (testing false analogy)
"Could there be other positions?" (testing either-or thinking)
"Are we analyzing issues or attacking personalities?" (testing ad hominem attack)

Analysis of evidence and reasoning is the hallmark of critical thinking. I cannot overstate your responsibility to test the thinking and information of your group. Without diligent effort on your part in analyzing evidence and testing the reasoning of arguments, the group's effectiveness will be compromised. Discover the detective within you.

Negotiating

We all possess the capacity to suspend personal judgment and appreciate the benefits of different points of view. Negotiating is the skill of bringing differing parties to mutual agreement, and you'll find this skill particularly valuable as the group gets closer to consensus. These negotiating skills are also helpful in settling minor conflicts and differences throughout the course of discussion. Here are some ways you can help in the negotiating process:

"Can we all agree that . . . ?" "Do we all think/feel . . . ?" "Is anyone opposed to . . . ?"

"What things can we all agree to?" "Can we combine the strengths of these two proposals?" "Is this solution workable and acceptable to all of us?" "Can we all live with this solution for a period of time?"

Your ability and willingness to negotiate and serve as a consensus builder will be one of the most important contributions to the success of the group. Try to see the beauty and strengths in all the ideas and proposals presented to the group. Be positive and constantly alert to any common ground—areas of agreement, common ideas, and similar beliefs—where your group can meet as one.

Social-Guiding Behaviors

Social-guiding behaviors encourage and maintain a healthy social dimension during group discussion. They include encouraging, expressing feelings, harmonizing, and energizing. Each behavior is designed to ensure a friendly, supportive, and trusting atmosphere within the group.

Encouraging

Many times group members need encouragement to continue speaking, participating, or even remaining in the group. Encouragement fosters a caring, supportive group atmosphere. You can be encouraging to others by acknowledging their presence, agreeing with their statements, complimenting their behaviors, or reframing negatives into positives. Some things you can say to encourage others are:

(Acknowledging)
"I'm glad you're here today, Ingrid!" "I see your point, Seth!"

(Agreeing)
"I agree with you, Frank." "Your comment makes sense to me."

(Complimenting)
"I appreciate the handouts you prepared for us, Sarah." "Your idea is wonderful!"

(Reframing negatives into positives)
"Another way of looking at this is _____." (positive interpretation)
"By pointing this out, you showed me some positive aspects, such as _____."

When you participate in a discussion, look for ways to encourage others. We all need encouragement and compliments. Discover the part of you that nurtures, cares, and supports others. It can also be an enriching experience for you, the encourager.

Expressing Feelings

Although your problem-solving group is not a therapy group, the expression of feelings and the acknowledgment of those feelings are essential to a healthy social dimension of any group. Whether it's to congratulate the group's successes or explore the group's interpersonal conflicts, the expression of feelings is crucial to the health and maintenance of the group. Here are some ways to encourage the expression of emotions:

> Helping others to express their feelings is an act of liberation, a freeing of the soul.
>
> ✐
>
> STEPHEN LEVINE

"How are we feeling right now?"
"Are you guys feeling as frustrated as I am? Maybe we need a break."
"I love being in this group."

Many groups avoid expressing any emotion. They incorrectly believe such disclosure is inappropriate to the group process or a sign of weakness. Nothing could be further from the truth.

Without some gauge to measure the social dimension of the members, the group will not know when to devote attention to resolving an interpersonal conflict, celebrate a task success, or merely take a much-needed five-minute break. Do what you can to encourage the expression of feelings within the group.

Harmonizing

Occasionally a disruption appears in an otherwise supportive and friendly group atmosphere. The tension or conflict between two or more members rises to a level that affects the group's task dimension effectiveness. Whether it's a disagreement over a substantive issue, hurt feelings because of an insensitive remark, or a minor feud between two individuals, the social dimension of the group is negatively affected. You should make some attempt to bring harmony back to the group. Here are some things you can say to reestablish harmony:

> "Maybe the two of you can discuss this matter after the meeting."
> "Let's not allow our feelings to get the best of us."
> "Can you two disagree without disliking one another?"
> "We need to focus on the issues, not personalities."

Continued conflict needs to be brought to the attention of the group. To ignore or deny its existence would give the conflict more power to disrupt the social dimension. Therefore, the initial intervention is to bring the tension or conflict to the conscious awareness of the group. Then the individuals involved can strive to discover some way to disagree without disliking, punishing, or hurting one another. We will cover specific ways to deal with this in greater detail in a later chapter. For now, however, you might want to try some harmonizing behavior when there is tension or conflict within the group.

Energizing

Working with other people in a small group can be psychologically, emotionally, and physically draining. Extended periods of time spent discussing, debating, and deliberating are taxing and can quickly deplete our energy levels and exhaust our enthusiasm. When you sense that the vitality of the group is slipping, you can try to energize the group by saying:

> "We've done well so far and we only have a little ways to go!"
> "I think we're doing a great job!"
> "I know we can accomplish what we've set out to do!"

There are no magic words you can chant or somersaults you can perform that guarantee bringing a group to life. But your attempt at energizing the group can be inspiring in and of itself. Enthusiasm is contagious! Choose to be the source of energy when the rest of the group is ready for a nap—you might be surprised at your impact on the group's enthusiasm.

Being an Effective Follower

The emphasis of this chapter has been on taking an active role in guiding the task and social dimensions of group discussion. But you have to know how to be an effective follower also. Every member of the group cannot be guiding and leading the others all of the time. Chaos would result if everyone was trying to lead and no one was willing to follow. The purpose of this chapter is to provide you with the skills to guide and direct the flow of discussion when appropriate opportunities arise, not all of the time. What specific attitudes and behaviors can help you be an effective follower?

Putting the group first. The focus of most people is on the self. How am I feeling? What am I thinking? How does that affect me? What do I want? What can I get? To be an effective follower, you must be willing to put the group first and yourself second. This is not forever, just for a period of time. If the individual members do not subordinate their personal goals and needs to those of the group, there is no effective group.

So the first question you might want to ask yourself is "What's good for the group?" instead of "What's best for me?" This subtle shift in focus and emphasis might be your first step toward being an effective follower.

> Why is the sea the king
> of a hundred streams?
> Because it lies below them.
> Therefore it is the king
> of a hundred streams.
>
> ∽
>
> LAO TSU

Listening to others. After you have made the decision to put the group first, you should know what the desires and needs of the group are. Pay attention to the discussion of the other members of your group. In other words, keep quiet and listen. My father always used to tell me that "you never learn anything new when you're talking," so one very obvious way to follow the discussion is to listen. You might just learn some new things. Be a receptive follower.

Discovering things to agree with. I have the hardest time working with the chronically disagreeable person, that individual who must disagree with everything everyone says. He constantly searches for weaknesses in your ideas, flaws in your thinking, and objections to your proposals. He is the opposite of the team player. He's not only out for himself; he is against everyone else as well. He helps create groups that experience strife, exhaustion, and often failure.

You can be an effective follower by being on the lookout for ideas and suggestions that you can agree with and support. Look for those aspects of the discussion that are going well, those things you can agree with and support. Don't always focus on the weaknesses and flaws of everything you hear. Discover things to which you can agree. Be a positive follower.

Whenever someone shares an opinion or suggestion that you strongly agree with, don't just sit there in silence; say something. Something simple like "I like that idea," "I think that's a good point," or "I agree with your idea 100 percent!" You might even want to compliment the individual whose idea or opinion you agree with by saying, "Barbara, I think you have a wonderful idea," or, "Congratulations, Tim! That's the best suggestion I've heard this entire meeting!" People need to hear confirmation and affirmation that their ideas or suggestions are shared by others. You can follow their lead by simply agreeing with the ideas and opinions of others. Be a verbal follower.

Volunteering to support the suggestions of others. In addition to voicing your agreement with the ideas and suggestions of others, you can venture forth and commit to supporting them in tangible ways. Not only can you agree with them; you can volunteer to "put your money where your mouth is" and help in some physical way to bring their idea, opinion, or suggestion to fruition. You can volunteer to do something to support their idea or suggestion by stating that "I'll do some of your research on the Internet," "I'll make the arrangements for the luncheon," "I can call those four managers and get their opinions if you'd like me to," or, "Let me contact the personnel office and see what the policy is regarding your wonderful suggestion." Talk is cheap; volunteer your time and effort to support the ideas and suggestions of others. Be a helpful follower.

Rather than suggesting specific ways you can show your physical support of someone's idea or suggestion, you can ask what is the most helpful or effective way you can be of help to advance his or her idea or suggestion. You can simply inquire, "What can I do to support your suggestion?" "How can I help you advance this idea to management?" or "Count me in on implementing this solution." Many times the author of an idea or suggestion will know best as to the process or procedure to implement his or her idea or suggestion. Let him or her tell you how you can best serve. Let him or her be the boss and you concentrate on being the follower who asks helpful questions.

Following through. Once you've been assigned a responsibility or given a task to support someone's idea or suggestion, follow through. Be good on your word. Keep your promises. If you say you will do something, just do it. If you don't keep your promises, you not only let down the group; you can jeopardize or destroy your reputation in the group as someone who can be trusted. Once you've agreed to something, complete the task. Your good name is at stake.

Being cheerful. Above all else, choose to be cheerful as you follow others. Don't go about your tasks and responsibilities with a grudging attitude or negative spirit. This type of behavior will harm the group's spirit and effort. It's better that you withdraw from the group than be a source of resentment and ill will. Take your pity party somewhere else and sulk. So you promise to be cheerful following the ideas and suggestions of others? Good! A happy, cheerful attitude will bring joy and productivity wherever it goes. Be a cheerful follower, above all else.

> Choose to be happy.
> It's one way to be wise.
>
> ∽
>
> COLETTE

This chapter shows you specific ways to guide group discussion in the task and social dimensions of interaction. By asking guiding questions and making guiding statements, you can have a more effective and productive effect upon the group. Being a willing follower is just as essential to creating an effective group as guiding the group, so realize that leading and following are simply two sides of the same process—creating an effective group.

Individual and Group Exercises

Guiding Behavior in Your Personal Life

Use one or two of the task-guiding behaviors from this chapter and implement them in your relationships with others. For instance, you might want to ask people more questions (requesting or clarifying information), compromise your positions (negotiating), or think more critically (analyzing). How does using these guiding behaviors feel in your daily interactions with those individuals in your life?

Guiding Behaviors in a Small Group Meeting

Form groups of five in class and hold a twenty-minute meeting to plan a hypothetical class picnic. During the meeting, decide on where the picnic will be held, how long the picnic will last, what to bring, who is to bring what, a list of six fun class activities or games, who is to lead each game, prizes that should be awarded, and who will clean up. Your group is to perform all of these functions and the rest of the class will simply come and enjoy the event your group has planned.

During the twenty-minute planning meeting, each of the five group members will take a turn at guiding the task dimension of the discussion for four minutes. After all five members have led the discussion, take a few minutes to share your reactions to the exercise and give feedback to one another regarding their strengths and weaknesses.

Learning to Be a Follower

EXERCISE 7.3

This exercise will teach your body (not your mind) how to follow another person. The exercise will require another person to provide the finger your finger will follow for three minutes. You and your partner are to sit comfortably in chairs facing one another, close enough so your knees can touch. Your partner is to raise her right pointing finger about eye level and point it in your direction. Her finger should be above her knees. You are to raise your left pointing finger so it is within one or two inches of her finger.

The object of the exercise is for you to simply follow her finger with yours for a period of three minutes. No matter where she goes with her finger, you simply follow it as best you can. Your partner is to keep her finger in the two dimensional plane that separates your knees. Pretend a sheet of glass is separating you and your partner extending from the floor, between your knees, and above your heads. Your partner is not to move her finger so quickly that it's impossible for you to follow.

And neither of you are allowed to talk during the three minutes. Just see what it's like to simply follow her finger.

What was this experience like for you? Do your responses to this exercise give you any insight into your willingness and ability to be a follower in your group work? How might you modify or change your attitudes and behaviors to be a more effective follower in the future?

Leading a Group

> A good leader makes opportunities
> for others to succeed.
>
> —MAXWELL JOHNSTON

FRAN didn't look like a leader to me. She was petite, about five feet tall, and weighed maybe ninety-five pounds. Her voice was soft, and when she took her seat at the conference table during the group's initial meeting, she appeared to be a head lower than the rest of us.

Fran was a new faculty member, clearly one of the youngest in our group. She looked almost like a student sitting at that oversized, wooden table in the president's conference room. The seven of us had been appointed by the president of our college to propose ways to market our institution to the local community.

There was no proposed agenda and no designated leader. Only the seven of us scheduled to meet eight times during the semester. Six of us knew each other from years past, but we didn't know Fran. However, during the following decade, Fran was going to become very well known to us—she would become our college president.

What makes an effective leader? Well, it depends. Each task and every group are different. And what works in one setting may not work in another. But there are some common denominators that are characteristic of an effective small group leader. And I observed them in Fran's interactions with us in that committee many years ago.

Fran's foremost purpose in every meeting was to serve the committee, not further her own agenda, ideas, or proposals. She brought out the best in each of us by consistently demonstrating those guiding skills and behaviors discussed in Chapter 7. Fran would gently guide us back on track when we wandered, summarize the various points when we got long-winded, and negotiate consensus when we hovered near agreement. She prepared handouts and visual aids for the group and even brought donuts to a meeting or two.

All these things she did without fanfare—without requiring the limelight or special thanks, without our becoming jealous of her skills, without really anything. Although other members brainstormed better ideas or debated with greater skill, it was Fran who consistently and unselfishly brought out the best in each of us. She sincerely and deeply wanted the best for the group. The effective leader is the one who serves the group well—to help the group realize its goal.

The theme of this chapter is that you can participate in the leadership of any problem-solving group. Leadership is not relegated to only one individual in a group; the functions of leadership can often be shared by all the members of a group. You can create a productive and successful meeting by using the suggestions outlined in this chapter and you can really enable the group to be effective by assuming the role of servant leader. The leadership skills you develop in this chapter will help you create effective groups.

What Is Leadership?

Since the beginning of time, people in groups have listened to the counsel, followed the suggestions, and even looked up to specific individuals within the tribe, hamlet, community, or organization. These individuals are the leaders of the group. Whether inherited, won by battle or election, or arrived at by group consensus, leadership has been a focus of attention and interest throughout history. For the purposes of this book, however, we will limit our discussion to the leadership of small groups assigned to solve a problem.

First, what is a leader? A leader is an individual who is perceived by group members as having a legitimate position of power or influence in the group. The leader can be assigned or designated to that position. Or the leader may emerge from within the group's interactive process or even by group election.

Leadership, however, is different. Leadership is the process of influencing the task and social dimensions of a group to help it reach its goal. By this definition, leadership can involve more than one individual. All group members can share leadership.

Each individual in the group has the potential and opportunity to participate in the leadership functions of the group. Although this chapter provides specific and practical suggestions for a designated leader to more effectively run a meeting or manage a small group, it emphasizes ways each group member can help the group reach its goal.

Approaches to Leadership

To enhance your ability and willingness to participate in the leadership of problem-solving groups, it will be helpful to examine the primary perspectives on leadership. The four most prevalent approaches to studying leadership are the trait, styles, situational, and functional approaches to leadership.

Trait Approach

The trait approach suggests that individuals are born with certain personality traits that make them good leaders. In the past, physical traits such as attractiveness, height, a deep voice, and a full head of hair were linked or perceived as predictors or requirements for leadership. Personality traits such as achievement orientation, self-confidence, intelligence, enthusiasm, adaptability, sociability, and responsibility were also perceived as required traits for leaders. The trait approach implicitly suggests that most of these traits are characteristics an individual is born with. Thus, the "born leader" illustrates the trait approach to understanding why certain individuals become leaders. Television, movies, and the media often portray corporate and national leaders as individuals who possess these physical and personality traits, but in reality, there are scores of famous leaders, and I'm sure you have experienced leaders in your personal life, who do not possess all the physical and psychological requirements set forth by the trait approach. Group process is too intricate and diverse, and personality too complex, to be so easily explained.

> Everyone leads. Leadership is action, not position.
>
> ✺
>
> DONALD MCGANNON

Styles Approach

The second approach to understanding leadership is the styles approach, which examines how an individual leads rather than why a certain individual becomes the leader. The three styles of leadership are autocratic, democratic, and laissez-faire.

Autocratic leader. The autocratic leader rules with firm control over the group process. She generally sees herself as the leader and the rest of the group as followers. Often, the autocratic leader will listen to the ideas and suggestions of the other group members or subordinates, but the ultimate decision-making process rests more with her than with the group. She believes she knows what's best for the group and expects the others to follow and support what she feels is the wisest course of action. The autocratic leader will often use a variety of methods to enforce her decisions and establish compliance within the group.

Democratic leader. The democratic leader encourages the full participation of group members in discussion and decision making. The democratic leader recognizes the value of group input and participation, and seeks the majority opinion, or consensus. Emphasis is placed on the group and the democratic leader leads by example, not by force.

Laissez-faire leader. The laissez-faire leader lets the group lead itself. Whether the leader selects this style because she is uncomfortable leading others or believes that her leadership will have counterproductive effects on the group, she chooses to operate from a "hands-off" approach. She will generally see herself as just another group member and will not attempt to enforce or exercise her position as leader. Instead, she will let the members engage in the work themselves.

These three styles of leadership have advantages and disadvantages. Research has shown the most productive styles can be the autocratic and democratic approaches to leadership. The autocratic style produces more efficiently run groups, which complete tasks in less time. The democratic style generally produces the greatest member satisfaction, but requires more time to complete tasks. The laissez-faire style is effective with groups of extremely independent or creative members who require a great deal of freedom and latitude in performance.

Current research on group productivity and member satisfaction confirms the notion that the democratic style of leadership appears to be the most effective approach to leading a group (Schultz, 1996). I've found from my personal experience that a democratic style of leadership usually produces higher member satisfaction and productivity than do the autocratic and laissez-faire styles. Keep in mind that the leader's communication skills and relationship with group members are important determinants of group success, regardless of leadership style.

Situational Approach

The third approach to leadership study is the situational approach, which stresses that the requirements for effective leadership depend upon the situation. In the situational approach, groups locate the relevant characteristics of the situation and determine what kind of leadership style and personality would be the most effective in achieving the specific goals.

Hersey and Blanchard (1988) have proposed a very useful situational model for understanding leadership. They consider three very important variables:

1. The amount of guidance and direction (task dimension) the leader provides.
2. The amount of interpersonal support (social dimension) the leader provides.
3. The readiness level in performing the tasks that followers demonstrate.

The interaction between these three variables will determine which style of leadership would be most effective for a given situation with a particular group of people.

Hersey and Blanchard describe four leadership styles that are most effective for various situations. The telling style (high task/low social emphasis) is authoritarian and directive in nature. This leader provides specific directions, close supervision, and relatively little effort into developing the social dimension of the group. The selling style (high task/high social emphasis) stresses an authoritarian leadership style with attention to the social dimension of the group. This leader attempts to convince the group that his decision or plan is the best, but it is still his decision, not theirs. The delegating style (low task/low social emphasis) is laissez-faire or nondirective in nature. The leader lets the group direct itself by giving the members the responsibility to make decisions and implement the solutions to problems. The participating style (low task/high social emphasis) is also laissez-faire. The leader lets the group make its own decisions and implement solutions, but she will actively encourage the development of the group's social dimension.

The readiness level of the group members is an essential factor in determining which style of leadership would be most effective. Readiness is determined by the ability and willingness of the group members to perform the tasks needed to create and implement solutions. The ability is the knowledge and skills that the group members bring to a particular task. The willingness is the group's motivation and commitment to accomplish the task.

When the group members are at lower levels of task readiness or willingness to perform the required tasks, the group is most effective when decisions are leader directed. When the group members are at higher levels of task readiness or willingness to perform the required tasks, the group decisions can be member directed. The general rule is that the higher level of group readiness, the lower level of leader-directed decision making.

Functional Approach

Whereas the situational approach stresses the readiness levels of the group members in skill and willingness, the functional approach offers a different perspective on leadership. It examines the communication behaviors of any group member that helps the group achieve its goal. Beatrice Schultz defines functional leadership as "a process in which a leader engages in many behaviors, both verbal and nonverbal, to help a group achieve a goal." Rather than pay attention to the characteristics of the leader, the style of leadership, or the situation within which the leader must emerge, the functional approach focuses on the individual acts that influence the task and social dimensions of the group and move the group toward its goal.

William Schutz has proposed the "leader as completer" perspective on functional leadership. When the group members fail to perform the various duties or behaviors necessary to get the job done, the elected or designated leader will complete the job. The duties or behaviors are usually task dimension behaviors such as giving information, asking for information, guiding discussion, arranging for meeting times, or calling group members, but they can also include social dimension behaviors such as encouraging or relieving tension. The leader does whatever it takes to complete the job.

The functional approach to leadership I would like to propose is the school of thought that "every group member can help lead." Although there can be an elected or designated leader who arranges the meeting dates and times, plans the agenda, and initiates the discussion, the task and social dimension behaviors of leadership are carried out by all the members of the group.

During the problem-solving discussion itself, the most vital behaviors that all group members can perform were highlighted in Chapter 7, the task- and social-guiding behaviors:

1. Requesting information
2. Providing information
3. Clarifying information
4. Guiding/summarizing
5. Analyzing
6. Negotiating
7. Encouraging
8. Expressing feelings
9. Harmonizing
10. Energizing

Every member of the group can perform these ten guiding behaviors. During the meeting, the responsibility of participating in and guiding the direction of the discussion is not limited to the elected or designated leader. It can be shared by all the members of the group. This modified perspective of the functional approach— every group member can help lead—is one that greatly enhances and encourages the participation of each member of the group. It also takes much of the pressure off the designated leader, since every member of the group is now encouraged to perform these vital tasks. Perhaps the most important advantage to this perspective is that it empowers each member to see the entire process of group discussion in an entirely new light, one of greater ownership in the process and the outcomes. There is no longer just one individual who is able and willing to participate and guide the group at the leader level, but every group member is capable of completing the task.

The Attitude of the Servant Leader

As you use these ten leadership skills, it's important to develop the attitude of the servant leader. Just like Fran in our opening story, the most effective leader is not the individual who sits back and barks out orders and commands, but rather, she is the person who participates and serves others. Rather than looking down from some glass and steel corner office watching the members of her group labor, the effective leader is one of the group, participating equally with the other members and volunteering to do the humble and menial tasks as well.

Like Fran, the servant leader will not only guide the actual meeting, but is also willing to buy the donuts on the way to the meeting and set up the chairs before the others arrive. There's a famous story about the chairman of Toyota Motor

> Leading well means serving well.
>
> ∽
>
> VAN CUMMINGS

Company, whose desk was just one of many desks in the accountants' division office and he always emptied his own wastebasket at the end of the day, just like the other workers in the area.

To be an effective leader, you must assume the attitude of a servant, one who creates opportunities for others to work well and realize their potential as human beings. It is a higher calling than that of the traditional model of the leader as an individual who receives preferential treatment and respect, and has others serve him.

For thirty years, Robert Greenleaf was the director of management research for AT&T. He studied thousands of managers and corporate leaders in America and discovered that the most effective leaders were the ones who "put serving others, including employees, customers, and community, first." It was Greenleaf, in his book *The Power of Servant-Leadership*, who coined the term servant leadership, which stressed the "leader's desire to serve first" as the most essential element in effective leadership.

Rather than the leader who expected special treatment from his subordinates, Greenleaf discovered that the most effective managers and leaders gave special treatment to their workers and subordinates. He found that the most effective leaders were those "who helped consensus evolve within the group," rather than shaping or directing it. More striking, Greenleaf discovered that the most effective leaders were those who "were sensitive to and encouraged the personal growth of their workers," and not always focused on productivity, efficiency, and profits. Here are some suggestions that Greenleaf encouraged leaders to consider as they prepared to lead.

Be aware. The fundamental requirement for a leader is to be aware—to be awake and sensitive to the people with whom you are involved and to yourself. Many leaders are so self-absorbed with their own needs and desires that they fail to be aware of the needs and desires of others. You should observe others, ask questions, open up to others, and be sensitive to others. This requires that you pay attention to what they do, what they say, and what they don't say. Equally important, you need to be aware of yourself. Not just to your conscious needs and desires, but to those voices within you that are often drowned out by the noises and distractions of everyday living. To sit silently each day for five or ten minutes can do wonders for increasing your awareness of yourself. This increased awareness will enable you to better serve others.

Listen. The most important communication skill a servant leader can use is that of listening. Not only is listening essential to the receiving of messages; it acknowledges and honors the person speaking. There is no more powerful way to communicate respect for another person than to keep your mouth shut and truly listen to his or her ideas, opinions, and feelings. The servant leader, above all else, is someone who will listen to what others have to say. How can you ever know how to serve and lead others if you don't know what they need?

Be empathetic. The servant leader must be a person who feels what others feel. She must be able to move beyond her own ego and see and feel the world through the eyes of others. Without the willingness and ability to be empathetic, the leader will lack the sensitivity and awareness to experience her group members in a more full, three-dimensional way. The process of maturity, not only for the leader but for all people, is to move from self to others—the willingness and ability to get out of your own head and heart and experience the world from the vantage point of others.

Encourage the growth of others. The ability to communicate with others, to work with others, to resolve differences and conflicts with others, to compromise with others, to forgive others, and to celebrate with others are all activities of the small group.

But they are also the important activities of personal growth. What group members learn and practice in the group also influences, shapes, and determines how they will live their lives when they get home. As a servant leader, you need to be sensitive to and encourage each member's personal journey to wholeness, to a life in which they can communicate and experience their lives to the fullest. That is one of your most sacred responsibilities as a leader, to encourage each member's personal growth and development.

> Character is formed
> primarily by one's work.
>
> ✐
>
> E. F. SCHUMACHER

Use your servant leadership to lead a meeting in a way that creates effective and productive outcomes.

Leading an Effective Meeting

One of the most important functional skills of any leader is to lead an effective meeting. Many specific skills and behaviors go into running a meeting that is productive, organized, and even enjoyable. Here are suggestions for you to run an effective meeting as the leader of these groups.

Deciding to Lead a Group

Clarify the leader's job description. Before you volunteer, are appointed, or are elected as the leader of a group, you need to clarify the duties and responsibilities of the position. Consult your boss, supervisor, group, or an appropriate source to review what is expected of you in this leadership role. Get the job description in writing if possible. What are the expected timelines for projects? When does this position end? Under what circumstances can you be replaced? What special things should you know about the duties, the group members, or the project you will be in charge of?

Consider if you want to be the leader. Take the next two days and weigh the pros and cons of being the leader of this specific group. After considering the duties, responsibilities, and time expected of you, be honest with yourself. Is this something you really want to do? Is this something you really need to do? Is this a way to receive recognition or exercise power? Honestly consider your motives. You should ask yourself whether this is a position in which you would want to serve others—the group members and the organization.

If you've never led a group before, don't be afraid to accept the position or nomination. Every great leader had a first leadership position. This could be yours! If you decide to accept the position, you will discover many wonderful things about yourself and others. You might also experience moments of disappointment, stress, failure, and disillusionment. All this comes with the territory.

Preparing for the Meeting

Determine to meet or not to meet. Once you are in a position of leadership in a problem-solving group, have your group meet. Most of the time, the meeting times and dates are determined for you. But if they're not, you will need to contact your group members and negotiate meeting times and dates.

After the scheduled meetings have begun, you might occasionally determine that certain future meetings do not require members' physical presence, and the information or business can be communicated or conducted by phone, memo, or e-mail. Take every opportunity to conduct the group's business in the most expedient fashion possible. Use the phone, e-mail, and inter-office mail to your advantage. If you decide not to convene a meeting, your group members will love you for it.

Prepare and send the agenda before the meeting. If possible, prepare and send a copy of the meeting's agenda (and any pertinent reading material) to each group member one week before the meeting. This gives ample time for group members to read, consider, and even research appropriate material before you meet. I usually have a rule when I chair a group that members cannot verbally participate in discussions if they haven't read the agenda and other material before the meeting. This prevents members from shuffling paper and reading material during discussion.

The following is an example of a generic meeting agenda. Refer to it when constructing your own agenda:

Agenda

1. Call to order.
2. Approve agenda.
3. Approve minutes from previous meeting.
4. Announcements.
5. Reports (officers and committees).
6. Old (unfinished) business. List all items that will be before the group for discussion or action.
7. New business.
8. Adjournment.

Limit and prioritize the agenda items. When you construct the agenda, limit the number of items you schedule the group to address and discuss. I know a group leader who limits each meeting to just one item or issue. Not two or three. One. He swears by this method. It's a little extreme, but I would rather err in his direction than have too many agenda items. A group needs focus, so limit the number of discussion items in new and old business.

Prioritize your agenda items starting from the most important, in terms of significance and weight, to the least important. That way, if your group doesn't get to the last item or two, you have at least addressed the higher-priority items. You'll have other meetings.

Envision what will happen at the meeting. Take a few moments and try to envision what will happen at the meeting. Close your eyes and visualize each group member at the meeting. See as many details of this mental picture as possible. Keep your eyes closed. Relax. And get a sense of what you want to happen.

Pre-Meeting Procedure

Arrive early. Arrive ten to fifteen minutes early to the meeting. Arrange the chairs in a circle, check the lighting, open windows if it's stuffy, and plug in the coffee-maker. No, an office assistant isn't supposed to do this. Remember, effective leadership means effective service. Get a feel for the atmosphere of the room before people begin arriving.

Mingle with the members. As the group members arrive, mingle, join in, and make them feel welcome. Thank people individually for coming early. Listen to them and be really present in mind and body.

Running the Meeting

Start the meeting on time. About two minutes before the scheduled meeting time, announce to group members the meeting is about to begin. Invite them to get another cup of coffee and move to their seats. After they see you seated, they will usually follow. Begin the meeting exactly on time! This is the first official act you perform each meeting. Don't be sloppy or indecisive with this initial responsibility.

Check-in time. Let each member of the group "check-in" by sharing one good thing that has happened since the group last met. Limit each member's comments to twenty seconds. This "check-in" provides each person with the opportunity to say something positive, to reduce any speaking anxiety, and to let the members know what's going on in his or her life. Don't let members ask questions or comment on one another's check-in statements. This will sidetrack the discussion. Just provide a brief time for the group members to say hello and get comfortable before making your announcements.

Make announcements quickly. After everyone is seated, get any announcements that weren't included in the agenda out of the way as quickly as possible. Announcements are not open to debate or discussion. Briefly answer any questions about the announcements. This is not the time to get bogged down with tangential remarks and off-the-track discussions.

State the meeting objectives and time limits. Thank the group members for attending the meeting and for being punctual. Then state the objective or objectives for the meeting. Provide a tentative time limit for each objective or agenda item, and state the ending time for the meeting. Group members appreciate a leader who will publicly announce the time limits for agenda items and the ending time of the meeting. It gets things out in the open and provides a framework for discussion.

Don't stop the meeting for latecomers. Occasionally, a group member will arrive late to the meeting. Don't recap what's already been covered and don't acknowledge or listen to her excuse for being late. Simply ensure that the discussion continues without giving attention to the latecomer. Chronic tardiness can be a symptom of passive-aggressive behavior (indirect anger directed at you or the group) or a challenge to your power. Don't give the chronic latecomer any power.

Restate objectives and time limits periodically. About every ten minutes, restate the objective the group is currently working on and how many minutes are left in the meeting. If possible, avoid holding any meeting for more than sixty minutes. Human beings get tired and bored after one hour.

Remain impartial. As the leader, your primary goal is to ensure the smooth functioning of the task and social dimensions of the group. Let all group members voice their opinions on a particular issue before you share your thoughts. Your duty is to solicit and guide the group's discussion so it stays on track and on time. Your job is to serve the group.

Guiding the group. The specific guiding behaviors you can draw upon to guide group discussion are discussed in detail in Chapter 7. Keep a note card summary of these guiding behaviors in front of you during each meeting as a reminder.

Seek participation. Even though asking for information is one of the guiding behaviors mentioned in Chapter 7, I want to stress its importance. Ask for the opinions of low-verbal members and summarize the long speeches of high-verbal members. Your group needs to know and experience your control of the group. It needs to see you provide equal (at least not lopsided) group participation. Be sensitive to who's not talking and who's talking too much.

Summarize often. I know I mentioned the guiding behaviors already, but I need to bring this one up again. Occasional summaries can work wonders to focus discussion, to quiet high-verbals, and to keep the group on time. Look for opportune moments to summarize the group's ideas and progress.

Compliment members often. See the positive in the contributions and participation of each member. Verbally compliment individuals during the meeting. Someone once said, "A person can accomplish a great deal if he doesn't worry about who gets the credit." Don't worry about who ultimately gets credit for anything the group does. Give the credit (and compliments) liberally to your group members. You will not only boost their feelings of importance; you will encourage participation and encourage member loyalty to you.

Keep the meeting moving. Don't get bogged down on any one item or issue too long. Table items to the next meeting if additional information is required or if the tension in the group is getting too great. Remember to summarize and state the time remaining in the meeting. During the last ten minutes of the meeting, I usually give time-remaining announcements a couple of times: "We've got nine minutes left," "We've got six minutes left," and so on.

Check-out time. During the last two or three minutes of your meeting time, you might want to let the members check out by individually sharing one thing they liked about the meeting and one thing they think might improve the next meeting. Limit each member's remarks to twenty to thirty seconds. This check-out time can be very valuable for letting members compliment one another or the group and to provide specific suggestions for improvement. Remember to record any suggestions for improvement.

End the meeting on time. If you conclude the meeting on time, you will be establishing one of the most powerful norms of group work. That norm is "This leader ends when she says she will end, so I'd better get what I want to say in and accomplish what I intend to accomplish during the time or I'll have to wait until the next meeting." Or stated another way, the norm you establish is "This leader keeps her promises."

End the meeting on time and your group members will love you for it. Each member has a life outside the group (at least you hope that's true). So end on time and let them get on with their lives. During the last minute or so of each meeting, I summarize the objective or objectives we've accomplished and remind the members of the next meeting time and date.

Impromptu Speaking

As the leader of your group or even as a group member you might be called upon to give an impromptu speech. A request for an update on the group's progress to your communication class, a weekly summary of your accomplishments to the other production teams at work, or even an unexpected invitation to speak at a City Council meeting are just a few of the many opportunities you may have to address an audience.

Your ability to speak to an audience with little or no preparation is one of the most valuable skills you can possess. It can also be one of the most frightening. Public speaking is often rated as the one activity we fear most. More than spiders, going bankrupt, and death itself. It's bad enough to have a manuscript speech that has been practiced several times, but an impromptu speech can be even more challenging. And in life, you will more likely be called upon to give an impromptu speech than a formal presentation. So how can you construct a brief, effective talk on the spur of the moment?

Let's look at two different types of impromptu speeches—the One Point Impromptu Speech and the Standard Impromptu Speech.

The One Point Speech

Most of the impromptu speeches you will deliver in your lifetime will be very brief, usually less than one minute in length and the focus of your remarks will involve only one specific thought, idea, or opinion. There is no need to develop a fully developed introduction, body with three points, and an inspiring conclusion. These brief, spur-of-the-moment responses to questions, inquiries, or requests can be covered in a short one-minute talk—the One Point Impromptu Speech. The One Point Impromptu Speech has three parts—the statement of the point, development of the point, and the restatement of the point.

Your primary goal in your One Point Impromptu Speech is just that, to present only one point to your audience. Not two points, not three points, not a history lesson of the United States. Just one point. Here are the three steps:

Step 1: State Your Point.

First, decide quickly on the one point statement you wish to make to the audience. Not two or three. Just one statement. "I believe addition funding is necessary for the project," "I disagree with the marketing team's decision," or "Overtime pay is a powerful incentive to employee satisfaction." These are all examples of a one point statement.

Before you state your point, smile to your audience, take a moment to breathe, and then make your statement slowly and clearly. Don't open with a funny story, a touching anecdote, or a long-winded history of the topic. If you do, the audience might expect you to give a much more developed speech. Just make your statement and remember that brevity is your goal.

Step 2: Develop Your Point.

Once you've stated your point, you move on to the second step of developing your point. When you're asked to speak on the spur of the moment, you will most likely not have access to statistics, expert testimony, or an excerpt from a magazine article, but you can provide an example, illustration, or story from your personal life or work experience to develop your point.

Person experience illustrations can be the most powerful and persuasive source of developmental material for your One Point Impromptu Speech. "I'd like to develop my point with a *brief story* about how my department has had to sacrifice due to the project's funding cuts …," "Let me share *my experience* with a similar setback caused by the marketing team's decision-making approach …," and "I'd like to *remind you* of the positive employee responses and increased cohesion that the temporary overtime pay last summer …" are the beginnings of anecdotes or illustrations that support the point the speaker is trying to make.

If you don't have a personal experience to support your point, you can also use examples or illustrations you've read about, heard of, or even saw in a movie. The important point is to develop your statement in a way that will have a favorable impact upon your listeners. This second step should constitute about 90 percent of your One Point Impromptu Speech.

Step 3: Restate Your Point.

End your speech with a simple restatement of your original point. This is not the time to introduce new information or try to drag things out. Just remind your audience of your one point. "I believe addition funding is necessary for the project," "I disagree with the marketing team's decision," or "Overtime pay is a powerful incentive to employee satisfaction." Keep your One Point Impromptu Speech simple.

The Standard Impromptu Speech

There are occasions when you might be required or desire to develop your impromptu remarks in a more developed and structured fashion of more than a minute or two. That's when you would use the Standard Impromptu Speech, a more developed and detailed approach to speaking on the spur of the moment.

This Standard Impromptu Speech has an introduction, body, and conclusion. The speech length is generally two or three minutes and it provides you with the opportunity to present two or three points in a more developed fashion. There are five steps involved in preparing the Standard Impromptu Speech.

1. Select One Thought.

The first step is to select one thought, idea, or theme. You'll divide this thought into two or three points later. Before you do, however, select one thought you wish to communicate to your audience. For example, "I believe additional funding is necessary for the project." Keep your thought, idea, or theme brief.

2. Organize Your Thought into a Pattern.

Once you have selected your one thought, you can organize that thought or idea into a pattern that develops and supports your two or three sub points. Here are four ways you can arrange your main thought:

Topical Order: two characteristics about… , two reasons we should…
Chronological Order: past / present / future
Spatial Order: near / far, up / down, offices / reception area / kitchen
Problem/Solution: crime / education, divorce / communication workshops

Here is an example of how these patterns might be used to develop the statement, "I believe additional funding is necessary for the project:"

Topic Order:

I.   Funding would sustain current research.
II. Funding would increase research efforts.
III. Funding would increase team morale.

Chronological Order

I.   Funding in the past.
II. Current funding.
III. Future funding desired.

Spatial:

I.   Funding on the East Coast.
II. Funding on the West Coast.
III Funding in Asia.

Problem/Solution: I.   Lack of department funding.

                               II.   Provide additional funding from marketing fund.

3. Support Your Sub Points with Specifics.

Now that you've decided upon your organizational pattern, you are ready to move to the third step of supporting your sub points with definitions, comparisons, examples, anecdotes, statistics, facts, or quotations. Since an impromptu speech doesn't provide you with the time to research, the supporting material you use will have to be those bits of information you carry around in your head. One of the easiest methods of support is to reach back into your own life experience and share anecdotes or illustrations that support your sub points. Your stories and illustrations will also help the audience feel more involved with you as the speaker. This portion of your two-minute impromptu speech should take about ninety seconds or roughly thirty seconds for each sub point.

4. Constructing an Introduction.

After selecting your topic, choosing an organizational pattern, and developing your two or three sub points, you are now ready to plan your introduction. Your introduction consists of an attention getter and preview of your sub points and should take about ten to fifteen seconds of a two-minute impromptu speech.

The attention getter can be an audience question, personal statement of belief, or a brief anecdote. A one sentence preview of sub points should follow your attention getter. Your preview is a one sentence statement of your two or three sub points. An example would be, "The two reasons for our need for additional funding are (1) rising material costs and (2) increased number of development projects."

5. Constructing a Conclusion.

The conclusion should contain a review of your sub points and a final thought. For a two-minute Standard Impromptu Speech, your conclusion should be about ten to fifteen seconds in length. Your review should remind the audience of your two or three sub points. Keep it brief. One sentence is all you need. "The two reasons we explored for our need for additional funding were (1) rising material costs and (2) increased number of development projects."

Your final thought is the last thing you say to your audience. Make it memorable. End with a quotation, appeal, or challenge. This is not the time to introduce new information or ramble on and on. Just end with a statement that is memorable and maybe even inspiring.

The Standard Impromptu Speech Outline

This outline will help you visualize the components of a two-minute Standard Impromptu Speech. It can also be used as a template for a speech or presentation of any length.

INTRODUCTION (fifteen percent of speech time)
    Attention Getter (ten seconds)
    Preview of Sub Points (five seconds)
BODY (seventy to eighty percent of speech time)
    I.   Sub Point (forty-five seconds)
    II. Sub Point (forty-five seconds)
CONCLUSION (fifteen percent of speech time)
    Review of Sub Points (five seconds)
    Final Thought (ten seconds)

Whether you use the One-Point Impromptu Speech or the Standard Impromptu Speech, your ability to speak to an audience without prior preparation or practice will serve you well in all your group communication experiences. Be willing to address an audience, even when you're least expecting it.

Taking Care of Yourself as the Leader

The duties and responsibilities of a leadership position can be psychologically taxing, emotionally fatiguing, and physically draining. Whether you're the president of a large corporation or the head of the Little League pancake breakfast, the job of leading a group of people can push you to the limits of your capabilities and patience.

To avoid leader burnout, I'd like to suggest some ways to take good care of yourself when you're the leader of a problem-solving group. These are attitudes you can adopt and things you can do to remain centered, open, and productive in your role as leader.

Leave some things to others. My first suggestion is to volunteer or accept a position of leadership only for a group whose purpose you believe in deep in your heart. Life will go on without you as the leader, so don't feel obligated to volunteer for a leadership position you don't believe in.

> Your number one responsibility is to take good care of yourself.
>
> ✇
>
> SHELDON KOPP

If you really don't believe in and support the functions and purpose of the local Little League Organization, don't volunteer to chair the pancake breakfast committee. You can serve as a member of the committee out of a sense of obligation if your child or little brother is on a team, but don't volunteer to chair the committee if your heart's not in it.

I realize there are some situations where you might not have a choice, such as in your job, where a boss or supervisor assigns the responsibilities of leadership to you. In those instances, you can still choose to discuss your concerns or misgivings with your boss. Maybe you will be successful in changing your boss's mind. If not, you can choose to utilize the skills and understanding you've gained from this book and lead with a positive attitude.

Leave your ego at the door. As the leader of a group, you will often be the target of criticism when things go wrong, the butt of jokes behind your back, and the last one to know if members are dissatisfied with your performance. In extreme instances, individuals and coalitions within your group can assail your recommendations, find fault with your style of leading, and attack your character. The price of leadership can be high.

You will need to discover ways to detach from your ego if you are to be an effective leader. Once you enter the meeting room, you will have to leave your ego at the door, or forever be pulled and tugged, hurt and angered by every questioning remark and critical suggestion directed toward you during the heat of discussion. Remember that you're not paid to be their friend. Your role is to lead.

Leave time for other things. Obsession is one of the most common mistakes leaders make. They do nothing but eat, think, and sleep their role as leader. The leadership position consumes their days and haunts their nights. To avoid this, make sure you leave time in your daily life for other things. Talk with loved ones and friends about anything other than your problem-solving task. Take up a new sport or hobby. Spend more time with your spouse or children doing things you meant to do last summer. See more matinee movies during the week. Take walks around the neighborhood and make some new acquaintances. Teach your dog new tricks. Do things to balance your life.

Leave the paddle at home. Self-doubt, self-criticism, and self-punishment can cripple and immobilize even the best of leaders. No one is perfect. We all make mistakes. No leader is blameless or beyond error. We need to accept our faults and weaknesses, as well as our strengths. When you become a leader of a group, don't be too demanding on yourself. Don't beat yourself up after every minor mistake. Be gentler on yourself. Leave the paddle at home.

Leave room to learn. One marvelous way to look at all problems and conflicts with others is to see them as an opportunity to learn a lesson about you.

Suppose some jerk tries to push into your lane during a traffic jam. Cars are at a standstill and she aims her front bumper toward your car and creeps in your direction. She doesn't smile at you or even make any eye contact to acknowledge her intentions. She thinks she owns the road. Well, you could pull up to prevent her entry into that tiny space between you and the car in front of you. You could honk and communicate your annoyance. You could yell something really terrible to her. You could even aim your car in her direction and play a little two-mile-per-hour chicken. You could do all kinds of terrible things in this difficult situation.

But another way you can look at it is as a lesson to learn something wonderful about yourself. I know this may sound a little corny, but it can work wonders. You can see this situation as an opportunity to learn unselfish, altruistic courtesy and kindness. You can let the jerk (I mean person) into the space in front of you.

This used to sound unthinkable to me a few years ago, but since I've been trying to take this new approach to driving and actually let people pull in front of me, I've changed a little. I have learned I'm capable of being kind in a situation when I could be rude and vindictive. I've learned to be courteous and not even expect a brief wave of thanks from the driver. I've learned to let people have the space I once occupied. I've learned to let go a little more. And it's made all the difference in the world.

I've taken an old problem and chosen to see it as a way to learn to be a little kinder to others, without expecting anything in return. This is how you can also choose to view the problems and conflicts you may experience as the leader of a group. During your tenure as leader, people will aim their cars at you, wanting things you might not want to give up. But choose not to see it always as a challenge to fight, or an opportunity to assert your power. See it as an invitation to learn some new things about yourself.

As the group leader, be open to discovering the many untapped skills, characteristics, and talents that still lay hidden from your conscious mind. You are much more complicated, competent, and caring than you think. Be open to discovering more and more about yourself as you lead others.

One important assumption presented in this chapter is that any member of the group can participate in leadership functions—those behaviors that help the group reach its goal. As you assume leadership functions and responsibilities, it is my hope that you will also assume the attitude of a servant as you create opportunities for your group to be productive and successful. You can encourage the personal growth of your group members as you band together to solve the problems that bring you together.

❧ Individual and Group Exercises ❧

Interview a Leader

EXERCISE
8.1

Select a leader you have worked with in the past or present who you feel is an effective leader. This individual could be a project manager, a committee chairperson, a supervisor at work, a coach, a personnel director, a scoutmaster, the president of your PTA, and so on. Arrange for a fifteen-minute interview to gather his or her insights concerning leadership. Review the suggestions for interviewing presented in Chapter 6 before you request the interview. Here are some possible questions:

What is the single most important lesson you learned from leading others?
What do you like best about leadership?
What do you like least about leadership?
What do you do to increase the group's task effectiveness?
What do you do to increase the group's social effectiveness?
What specific suggestions could you give for becoming an effective leader?

How did your interview go? Did you remember to send a thank-you card? What things did you learn about leadership from your interview? Are there any suggestions or insights you could incorporate into your leadership skills or knowledge? Did your perceptions or feelings about this individual change after the interview? How? What is the most important lesson you learned from interviewing this individual?

Leadership Role Play

EXERCISE 8.2 Have your group work on a simple problem-solving task (such as planning a group picnic or constructing a midterm exam) and select one group member to role play an autocratic leader for ten minutes. Then have the same individual role play a laissez-faire leader during the next ten minutes. For the final ten minutes, have the individual role play a democratic leader. How did the group members feel about each leadership style? How did the role player feel about playing each leadership style? What did the group learn about leadership during this exercise?

Leading an Out-of-Class Problem Analysis Meeting

EXERCISE 8.3 It's time to put all those neat leadership skills to some practical use. In this exercise, you are to actually lead a small group meeting of at least twenty minutes in length using the suggestions presented in this chapter. Find a very small, specific problem-solving task at your work, place of worship, school, or community that you can lead a group of four or five people to discuss (not solve). If you cannot locate a group outside of class, you can also use a group of four or five students in class to discuss some minor campus problem for twenty minutes. Once you have the group formed, agree on a meeting time and place, construct a five-point agenda that analyzes the problem, and review the suggestions for holding an effective meeting presented in this chapter. Lead the group. After the meeting, have the group members give you feedback on what they liked and didn't like about your meeting. Remember, be a servant leader!

CHAPTER 9

Building a Cohesive Group

Be kind, for everyone you meet
is fighting a hard battle.

—PHILO

EVERY quality control meeting began the same way—a magical way—with each group member sharing one new or significant thing that had happened since the group last met. Barbara, the team leader, had learned about this process during a workshop she had attended some years ago. Every person spoke for only thirty seconds as the members went around the table to "check in," but this brief activity let them touch base with one another, to connect at the human level before conducting their regular business.

Occasionally these "check-ins" would elevate the group to another level of seeing, understanding, and caring for one another. Once, one woman shared that her high school daughter's leukemia was in remission. One man revealed that he was afraid to propose to his girlfriend. And another woman proudly announced to the group that she had parachuted from 9,000 feet the previous weekend. These and a hundred other little bits of individually experienced life were shared collectively during the sixteen months this group met at Zytech Computers, and each sharing brought these people closer together as a team.

After meeting each week for six months, their leader missed four consecutive meetings because of a business trip. Barbara was temporarily replaced by Doug, a second-level production manager, who began the first meeting with a nervously delivered joke, then proceeded with the agenda. Toward the end of that meeting, Carlos, one of the group members, asked Doug if they could "check in" at the next meeting.

After explaining to Doug what a "check-in" was, Carlos added that he missed hearing what the others had been up to during the past week. The members of the group quickly agreed.

"I miss the check-in," added JoAnn. "It's one of the few times that we get to really connect during our hectic schedules."

"Plus, it makes me like you guys, which is a miracle in itself," joked Tim.

"I like the way it helps me be more patient and understanding," said Vaveck, "and most important, I think it makes our meetings much more productive, too!"

"I agree," chimed Tim.

"Okay, whatever you guys want," said Doug with a smile. "Maybe this check-in will help me, too."

At the beginning of the second meeting, the group spent the first few minutes checking in, with Doug concluding the process by sharing that he liked hearing their "new and goods," as he referred to the check-in. The next two meetings began with the check-ins and Doug felt a real connection with these people who were strangers just days before. He also observed a positive difference in his own attitude and behavior during those meetings.

At the fourth meeting check-in, Doug shared that he believed that the group's connection at this personal level helped them weather some difficult disagreements. He also told them that he not only appreciated how productive the group was, but how close he had grown to feel about it, too. Doug admitted that he had never experienced anything quite like this before and wished that he could join the members for their remaining nine months. And he did.

This chapter examines ways you can create caring and build a social dimension within your problem-solving group that encourages cooperation and productivity. If group members discover some level of personal success, connection, value, support, and trust during the process of working with one another, they will more likely experience a social dimension that produces a cohesive group.

The Social Dimension

The social dimension of a group lives on long after the task has been completed. An individual's feelings of successful cooperation, connection, appreciation, support, and trust derived from the group experience can play a significant role in shaping and strengthening his or her self-concept. If the social dimension, however, is characterized by competition, apprehension, and mistrust, the group experience can impact the individual's self-concept and attitude in a negative way for years to come.

> Work can provide one with a shared smile, a friend for life, and the liberation of the soul.
>
> ✑
>
> THOMAS MOORE

The significance of the social dimension cannot be overstated. Without a healthy, supportive social climate in which to conduct the work of the group, task effectiveness can be compromised (Fisher and Ellis, 1990; Shaw, 1981).

Whereas the goal of the group's task dimension is productivity, the goal of the social dimension is cohesion, the attraction and connection of group members to one another and to the group.

Feeling Successful

The primary reason for the problem-solving group's existence is to solve a problem. To experience success in problem solving can contribute to building a cohesive group. Members of an athletic team who win all their games during a season will more likely feel connected to one another than will members of a team who lose every game. Successful goal attainment plays a significant role in how members feel about one another and themselves. Without experiencing some level of goal achievement, a problem-solving group often deteriorates into a collection of frustrated, disconnected, and disappointed individuals.

Here are four steps you can take to bring success to your group: agreement on the group's goal, formulation of mini-goals, emphasis on group cooperation, and achievement of personal goals.

Agreeing on the Group's Goal

The first step you can take toward success is to make certain that each group member agrees on the group's goal. A group cannot be successful in achieving a goal if there is confusion or disagreement about what that goal is.

In a technical way, this step is accomplished during the second step of the problem-solving agenda, analysis of the problem. During this phase, the group formulates the question of policy ("What should be done about . . . ?" or "What should our policy be toward . . . ?"). This step provides the group with its task goal. Without a clearly defined and agreed-upon goal, the group can drift aimlessly.

Formulating Mini-Goals

A simple technique you can use to make your group experience successful more often is to formulate mini-goals—breaking down the larger goal into its smaller or component parts. For instance, instead of focusing on eliminating neighborhood theft, the group may want to break down this larger goal into its incremental parts. Smaller goals can include gathering information from law enforcement agencies, conducting an attitude survey of neighbors, holding an informational meeting for the neighborhood, and distributing a list of possible solutions to neighbors for their input.

When I chair a problem-solving group, I construct a list of mini-goals with suggested completion dates and the name of the individual responsible for each goal. I distribute this list to group members at the beginning of each meeting, and group members announce the progress of their particular mini-goal for that session. I've found that people enjoy bragging about their mini-goal achievement and appreciate the compliments from group members.

Another advantage to formulating mini-goals is that it divides the labor among the group. No individual is stuck doing all the work. When one group member, through choice or circumstance, is left with an inordinate amount of responsibility, the social dimension can suffer. It's more effective from a task point of view to utilize this division of labor and assign mini-goals to each member. Most important, it provides each individual with added opportunities to experience success during the process of attempting to achieve the larger group goal.

> A great cathedral is built
> one brick at a time.
>
> ɷ
>
> DALE CARNEGIE

Emphasizing Group Cooperation

A third step you can take toward group success is to emphasize group cooperation rather than competition. A group that encourages competition among its members will often experience a social dimension characterized by mistrust, selfishness, and rivalry. When members attempt to outdo one another, or to win at the expense of someone else's loss, they threaten the group's cohesiveness. Competition creates a win-lose atmosphere. And where there are losers, there are individuals who don't feel good about themselves.

Here are two ways to emphasize cooperation within your group. First, divide the group into subgroups of two or three individuals and make each subgroup responsible for a mini-goal. This will provide members with the opportunity to work together in a smaller group setting, helping to build teamwork and intimacy. Second, hold what I refer to as an "expert session," in which group members share a problem they might be experiencing with their mini-goal and the other group members try to provide helpful or "expert" information or advice. This also emphasizes cooperation between members.

Achieving Personal Goals

Although the primary function of each group member is to participate and contribute toward the achievement of the group goal, there are also concurrent personal needs each individual hopes to satisfy while participating in the group. Many times these personal needs are minor and incidental, such as the need to investigate a new topic, use a new communication skill, or brag about an interview. Other times, they can serve as the primary motivation or reason for seeking group membership. Loneliness, underappreciation, and a desire for control are some examples of why an individual seeks group membership to satisfy personal needs.

You can make it possible to satisfy these needs by having group members state any personal needs they may be conscious of during the orientation phase. After group members introduce themselves, I also have them state one or two personal goals they'd like to achieve during the course of our group work.

Most of the time, individuals share personal goals that can be easily achieved during the course of the group's life. I will occasionally begin a meeting with a check-in. At that time group members are given an opportunity to share any progress they made toward one or more personal goals. During the course of an hour meeting, I devote three to five minutes to this activity every third meeting. This can do wonders for building a cohesive group.

Feeling Connected

A second way to build a cohesive group is to make each member feel connected to the other members. Some groups are characterized by an atmosphere of distance, coolness, and indifference, whereas other groups enjoy an atmosphere of connection, inclusion, and trust. Here are some ways you can make your group members feel connected and included in the group setting: acknowledging others, structuring an all-channel network, being interested in others, and socializing as a group.

Acknowledging Others

Do not forget to welcome group members as they arrive to the meeting before it begins. Greet them with a smile and use their first names. It's amazing what a smile, a handshake, and a first name will do to make someone feel welcomed and included. If a group member is not included in some of the pre-meeting chitchat, go over and say hello. Offer that person a cup of coffee. Ask how his or her day went. These simple acts of acknowledging someone's presence can determine the emotional experience for an individual's entire meeting. If in doubt, smile and do your best to make someone feel included and connected to the group. That can be your most important act of the entire meeting.

Structuring an All-Channel Network

Another way to make group members feel connected to the group is to structure an all-channel network system for the group process. A communication network is the arrangement of communication flow within a system. With an all-channel network group members have access to all the other members without having to go through the

> In healthy groups, everyone gets to talk to everyone.
>
> ❧
>
> SALVADOR MINUCHIN

leader or a central gatekeeper. Each member is free to speak and listen directly to every other group member.

There are a number of specific steps you can take to ensure an all-channel network in your group. First, from a purely physical point of view, have the group always sit in a circle. Move the chairs or desks into a circle before the meeting begins. Request that latecomers join the circle upon arrival. A circle configuration permits contact among all members. It discourages members from feeling left out, as might be the case if the group sat in rows or at a long table. Second, have group members exchange phone numbers and e-mail addresses. This enables everyone to have access to each group member. Everyone can speak directly to everyone else. Third, discourage dialogues between two individuals during a group discussion. Whenever two members begin to conduct an extended dialogue, interrupt them and bring the discussion back to the group. Often, two powerful group members will dominate discussion, and the group process will begin to resemble dialogue between two people rather than group communication. Don't permit this to occur. For a group to be cohesive, provide open and equal access to communication.

Being Interested in Others

Our lives are busy, and we may find ourselves left with little time to become acquainted with even those we work with. Feeling connected to others can also be achieved by taking a moment or two to show an interest in another group member.

Rather than seeing others as merely cogs in the machinery, you can devote a brief period of time before and after each meeting to initiate a more personal discussion with another group member. Nothing too deep and heavy. But you can show an interest in another person by simply asking questions about family, hobbies, sports, interests, and so on. Don't force anything. Be gentle and friendly. Remember, the point is to connect with another person. The actual content of your after-meeting conversation is not nearly as important as your showing interest in another person by asking questions and listening attentively.

> Practice being
> interested in others.
>
> ∾
>
> WILLIAM FORESTER

Socializing as a Group

Some of the most famous electronic companies in the world owe a large part of their accomplishments to their legendary Friday gatherings. Companies like Apple Computer, Tandem, National Semiconductor, and Rolm are famous for their socializing on Friday afternoons. Over food, drink, and music, employees from every level of the corporation get together informally to talk shop, socialize, and get better acquainted. They've discovered this is a wonderfully enjoyable way to have fun, become better acquainted, and solve work-related problems.

You might want to do something along these lines with your own problem-solving group. It's not necessary to throw a $5,000 bash on a Friday afternoon for the six members of your group, but you might offer to treat the group to pizza and soft drinks after the next meeting or bring refreshments to the meeting. You can offer your home for a potluck dinner/meeting the next time your group is scheduled to meet.

Whatever you try, look for ways to occasionally socialize with your group, after or even during the meeting. When we socialize, we change our demeanor and the group has a new frame of reference from which to work. Socializing with the group members is one of the most enjoyable and powerful ways to enhance the social dimension of any collection of people.

Feeling Valued

In addition to experiencing task success and feeling connected to the group, members need to feel valued for their effort and contributions. Expressions of appreciation and compliments contribute to a strong social dimension in any group, and serve an especially vital function in building a cohesive group. When group members feel valued for their effort, their loyalty and commitment to the group are strengthened. Here are three ways you can make people feel valued in your group: seeing the best in others, communicating appreciation, and sharing compliments.

Seeing the Best in Others

When was the last time you told someone you appreciated them? Have you communicated appreciation to someone in the last day? How about the past week? We are often so busy, so preoccupied, and so involved with our own lives, we neglect to notice and appreciate others. In your problem-solving group, you can become more appreciative by seeing the best in others and communicating your appreciation to them.

I have a theory about life: On any given day, eighty percent of our life is working well and twenty percent of our life is not working at an acceptable level. I call it my eighty/twenty rule.

Roughly eighty percent of your work life, your personal relationships, your body, your automobile, your yard tools, and so on are working or performing at an acceptable level. The other twenty percent is not. Yet, when you stop and think about it, we often give that twenty percent of our lives 100 percent of our attention. We become fixated on a critical remark from our boss. We obsess about someone else getting a raise. We worry about an overdrawn check. We spend a great deal of time and effort fretting about twenty percent of those things that aren't going well, while we ignore the eighty percent of our lives that is functioning well.

The eighty/twenty rule also operates in our problem-solving groups. We often tend to focus our attention on the twenty percent of frustrations, disappointments, and failures experienced by the group, and neglect the eighty percent that is successful.

In order to appreciate others, we need to wear new glasses. We need to look for those things, big and little, that are working. We need to notice that everyone arrived to the meeting on time. We need to see that everyone contributed something to the discussion. We need to recognize that we made some progress on reaching consensus. We need to be aware of the subtle attempts of some members to improve how they interact during discussion. We need to see the best, not the worst, of what is happening in this moment.

> The deepest principle in human nature is the craving to be appreciated.
>
> ᥣ᧞
>
> WILLIAM JAMES

Communicating Appreciation

Once you've decided to see the best in every situation—to concentrate on the eighty percent of the group process that is working well—you need to verbally communicate your appreciation. Simply make an I-statement of appreciation: "Yung, I appreciated your efforts in having us reach consensus this morning," "Alison, I appreciated the questions you asked that helped me clarify my thoughts during the meeting," and "Victor, I thank you for letting me put my report on the agenda today."

These aren't long, involved statements, just short messages of appreciation and thanks. They take only a moment or two of your time, but can remain with the recipient for a lifetime. Try to communicate the appreciation you feel inside. It will be worth your effort.

Sharing Compliments

Everyone appreciates a compliment. During the course of your group work, you can compliment someone's effort, achievements, and character.

Complimenting effort. One area we neglect to compliment others on is effort. We usually reserve our compliments for those moments when the first-place trophy is awarded, when the final problem is solved, or when the last obstacle is overcome. But those moments are few and far between. We need to notice and compliment the effort our fellow group members are putting forth right now, long before any problem is solved or any trophies are awarded. A simple statement complimenting someone's effort can really encourage an individual who may feel his efforts are going unnoticed. Compliment a person's efforts and you'll take another step toward building a cohesive group. You might make a friend, too!

Complimenting achievement. Whenever a group member achieves some task or personal goal, verbally compliment the individual in front of the group (and personally after the meeting). Public complimenting of task or personal achievements builds solidarity and goodwill within the group. It communicates an unselfish, appreciative attitude on your part, and models complimentary behavior to other group members. Remember, your own behavior can have a ripple effect on the entire group. Compliment the achievement of others. It's amazing how productive a group can be when its members applaud the achievements of one another.

Complimenting character. Who a person is, not what they've achieved, can be the focus of your compliment. Honesty, integrity, patience, understanding, caring, kindness, compassion, and humor are just some of the components of character you may want to compliment.

Rarely are individuals complimented on their character strengths. They might not even be aware of a particular facet of their character until you bring it to their attention. Complimenting character publicly in the group can also serve to draw attention and focus to a certain kind of behavior or attitude you want reinforced within the group. Show your appreciation for them by complimenting their character.

Feeling Supported

A fourth way to build a cohesive group is to make the members feel supported. During our lives we may feel no one understands us, no one cares, and no one is there to lend a helping hand. I think we've all felt this way a time or two. Whether it's showing understanding for someone who is frustrated with a group task or experiencing the pain of a recent divorce, these acts of support can deepen the social dimension of a group. A problem-solving group can do a great deal to provide support for its members by communicating empathy, communicating caring, and giving assistance.

Communicating Empathy

Empathy is the ability to take the perspective of the other and feel what the other is experiencing. This doesn't mean you need to assist, correct, or rescue the other person. It means you can understand or feel what the other person is feeling. An empathic response is often the only thing an individual wants, to feel someone understands. No desire for evaluation, advice, or even assistance. Just someone who understands.

Earlier we discussed listening for the speaker's feelings and ways to reflect those feelings back to the speaker. This is the primary way you can demonstrate empathy, to mirror feelings.

If you feel a group member could use the support that empathy provides, try listening for that person's emotional messages. Listen to how he or she might be feeling. Then reflect those feelings with active listening: "Sounds like you're really frustrated about . . . ," "You're feeling upset about . . . ," or "Sounds as if you're really happy about . . ."

Merely reflecting what you think the speaker is feeling and experiencing is a powerful way to demonstrate empathy. Notice that some of the statements dealt with positive feelings also. Empathy involves positive and negative feelings. So be open and sensitive to reflecting both. Let him or her feel understood.

Communicating Caring

The second way you can communicate support to a group member is to tell him or her so. Once you understand what an individual is experiencing and you've demonstrated empathy, you can go the next step and communicate your concern. Nothing heavy. Just a word or two expressing concern or caring. Statements of caring and support can be very encouraging and uplifting. Here are some ways to communicate this form of support: "I hope things work out for you . . . ," "I know you'll be fine . . . ," and "I support your decision to . . ."

When a fellow group member experiences frustration with a task, is in conflict with another member, or falls behind on his group assignment, a word of encouragement or concern can make a difference in his attitude and resolve. We all need to know others care about what is going on with us. A brief sentence or two communicating caring can raise the spirits of a disappointed or discouraged individual.

Giving Assistance

In addition to demonstrating empathy and communicating caring, you should offer your assistance to other group members if you have an inclination to help and are in a position to do so. Most of the time such assistance will include making a copy of a report, helping with the overhead projector, or distributing written material. Sometimes your assistance might require more involvement, such as making a visual aid, typing a report, or giving a ride to the airport.

> We cannot live for only ourselves, a thousand fibers connect us with our fellow men.
>
> ❧
>
> HERMAN MELVILLE

Take the opportunity to lend a helping hand. I know you have a million things to do yourself, but your assistance can be of tremendous support to another member and will nurture a cooperative spirit within the group. Don't be selfish with your time and energy if you see an opportunity to lend some help. The recipient of your help will remember your gesture, and the relationship between the two of you will be changed for the better.

Someone once said, "The purpose of life is to help others make it through." You can make the problem-solving group experience truly meaningful and significant if you help others. Your willingness to put your caring into action will do more to improve cohesion and commitment toward one another than any other act I know. It proves your support.

Trusting Others

Although a person may feel included, acknowledged, valued, and supported in a group, the experience can be diluted and even negated if he or she senses an intentional manipulation or deception.

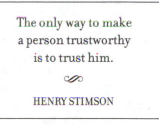

A furniture salesman can make us feel acknowledged and included. In fact, he can complement, praise, and flatter us with expert mastery, but deep down we realize this is his job. He wants to manipulate and control us. To sell us. To get something from us. But in the end, do we really believe his compliments, warmth, and friendliness? Most likely not.

For the social dimension of a problem-solving group to achieve true cohesiveness, group members must trust one another. We need to trust that what they're saying is honest and true. We need to trust that their support and assistance are sincere. We need to trust that their warmth and friendship are genuine and heartfelt. Without this trust, all the other components necessary to building a cohesive group are suspect.

> The only way to make
> a person trustworthy
> is to trust him.
>
> HENRY STIMSON

What indicators of trustworthiness are there? What clues can we search for in determining the level of trust we can give a particular individual? How do we know we can believe what someone is telling us?

The answer is we can't. No one can measure or predict with 100 percent accuracy the truthfulness of another individual's statement or behavior. There are no fail-proof tests, no totally accurate examinations. The best we can do is to assign probabilities to another person's honesty based on our past experiences with this individual. Oftentimes we are 99.99 percent certain that a person's statements are true or his behavior is sincerely motivated. But we are occasionally shocked by that 0.01 percent of the time when our predictions are wrong, and a trusted friend, colleague, or acquaintance lies or behaves in a dishonest way.

For the group to experience a high degree of cohesiveness, its members must have a certain level of trust in one another. A basic trust that what an individual member says is true. That the person's behavior accurately portrays his or her internal feelings and intentions. Without this trust, there can be no extended cooperation within the group, because communication would be doubted and behavior would be suspect.

Although there are no fail-proof tests for trusting others, there are two things you can ask to improve your decision to trust a certain individual. Does that person keep his or her word? How does that person treat others?

Does That Person Keep His Word?

Does an individual arrive at meetings on time? Can he keep his promise to show up on time or even show up at all? Does he complete assigned tasks? Or does he make up excuses or blame others for failure to finish a job? When someone makes you a promise to do something, does he actually follow through and make good on the promise? After a time, do you continue to believe or do you disregard his commitments to you?

If an individual keeps his word, you should be more likely to believe what he says is true. This doesn't work all the time. And there are exceptions to every rule. But a person who keeps promises is a better risk, as far as trusting is concerned, than someone who does not keep promises. Who keeps promises in your group?

How Does That Person Treat Others?

An individual's conduct with others is important to observe when determining whether to trust or distrust someone. How does this individual treat others? Does she gossip about others when the target of the gossip is absent? Does she lie or exaggerate the truth when she communicates with others? Do you sense manipulation or calculation in her actions and dealings with others? Is she inordinately complimentary or flattering to others in the group? In general, do you trust the way she treats others?

These two methods for determining the trustworthiness of an individual are helpful; but in the end, you must decide for yourself. For the purposes of decision making and problem solving in small groups, I assume the best and trust each group member will participate in an open, honest, and responsible manner. From this frame of reference, I can begin the group experience positively and optimistically.

Groupthink: When Groups Are Too Cohesive

Making group members feel successful, included, acknowledged, supported, and trusted are five ingredients that make group members feel committed and dedicated to one another. The social climate of the group will determine its task effectiveness. And it is the social dimension experience that lives on in the memories and hearts of group members long after the task has been completed.

But you must be careful that your group does not become too cohesive. The primary threat to sound decision making and problem solving with a group that experiences extreme cohesiveness is a phenomenon called groupthink.

Sociologist Irving Janis coined the term groupthink to describe the situation when a group departs from rational, reality-based decision making to irrational, nonreality-based decision making, because they are too cohesive. Although groupthink doesn't manifest itself very often in problem-solving groups at work or school, it is important to understand the factors that move a group to think it can do no wrong.

You can recognize groupthink when a group believes it is invulnerable and no harm can come to it. This perception is not based in reality, but is due to the extreme cohesiveness of the group. Once the group perceives itself as invulnerable, its decisions can involve more risk than the group would normally accept. The second way to recognize groupthink is by observing unusual pressure toward conformity. Dissension is discouraged and the group moves toward the majority view. Even if their ideas and proposals appear extreme to the group members themselves, they feel morally justified to pursue their objectives. Closed-mindedness is the final way you can recognize groupthink. The group will rationalize its decisions, even when the evidence points to contrary conclusions or a group member raises objections to their course of action.

It's important for you to be aware of these signs of groupthink and occasionally measure the behavior of your group against them. Does your group think no harm can come to it? Does it pressure its members toward conformity? Is it closed-minded?

If you answer yes to any of these questions, you need to consider the extent to which it is true. Simply because a group is occasionally closed-minded does not necessarily mean it is experiencing groupthink. But if your group experiences some of these telltale signs for an extended period of time, you would be wise to bring them to the group's attention.

No rock group is bigger than us. We can do anything we want.

⟋

KEITH RICHARDS,
The Rolling Stones

The best way to avoid groupthink is to take precautionary steps. It's much better to avoid the development of groupthink from the beginning than attempt to eliminate it once it's established. Here are four ways you can prevent groupthink from developing in your group. First, the leader should stress critical evaluation. From the very first meeting, the group leader should emphasize the role each group member is required to play in critically evaluating and analyzing the decision-making process of the group. Second, seek outside feedback. Each group member should discuss the decision-making processes with trusted colleagues outside the group and report these outside perceptions with the group. Third, assign a devil's advocate within the group. The leader can assign one group member to play the role of devil's advocate to challenge the prevailing ideas and proposals of the majority. The role of devil's advocate should be given to a different group member for each meeting. Finally, invite outside observation. The group can occasionally invite a qualified individual from outside to observe the decision-making process of the group.

Use these techniques to keep the decision-making process in your group open, subject to critical analysis, and reality based. Everything you do in your group affects each member in some way. A smile, a compliment, or an invitation for coffee can change a life. You might never fully realize your effect on the group members, but I would encourage you to discover the caring, sensitive, and loving aspects of who you are. Perhaps it will be in a problem-solving group that you discover many beautiful things about yourself.

This chapter examines five ways you can create a cohesive problem-solving group. Remember, each group member has personal needs and desires that transcend the goals and needs of the group. Rather than deny or ignore this personal dimension of each group member, you can implement many of the suggestions outlined in this chapter to create a sensitive, caring, and cohesive group. It is this group cohesiveness that will enhance their ability to solve the problems brought before them.

～ Individual and Group Exercises ～

Sharing Appreciation

| EXERCISE 9.1 | Reflect on your personal life and notice the eighty percent that is working well. From the list of things in your life that are going smoothly, select one individual who is currently contributing to this process. Per- |

haps it's a friend who occasionally calls just to see how you're doing. Maybe it's a coworker who gave you a hand on a project the other day. And possibly your spouse was especially thoughtful or concerned this morning. After you've selected an individual who is contributing to your well-being, thank her with some home-baked cookies, a bouquet of flowers from your backyard, or a gift certificate to your favorite restaurant. Let this person know you appreciate her role in your life.

Personal Goals for New Groups

| EXERCISE 9.2 | When the members of a new problem-solving group meet for the first time and chart out their initial plans and agendas for the work that lies ahead, they often neglect the social dimension of the group. They will |

fail to consider and become aware of the personal needs and goals of the individual members of the group.

One exercise your new group can do is called "personal goals for new groups." During your first meeting, share one personal goal you would like to accomplish during your time with the group. Goals such as improving listening, being more punctual, handling conflict more constructively, receiving criticism, being more caring, and becoming more assertive are common aspirations. Invite the other members to also describe a personal goal they would like to achieve. If each group member shares one goal, the awareness of all the group members will be greatly increased in terms of what people are trying to accomplish. The group members can devote a few minutes at the beginning or end of each discussion to review their individual progress on their personal goals and receive the kind of acknowledgment, encouragement, and thanks they desire. Give this a try. It will help you create a caring, sensitive group.

Devil's Advocate in the Group

| EXERCISE 9.3 | Have your group attempt to solve a mini-problem, and once the group begins to reach consensus on a proposed solution, have one of the members play the role of devil's advocate. The role player should question |

the reasoning and opinions of the majority membership. The devil's advocate should raise objections to the proposed solution and continue to object for at least ten minutes. How did the devil's advocate influence the group? How did the role player feel? What positive contributions to group problem solving can a devil's advocate have on the group process?

CHAPTER 10

Managing Conflict

No fight. No blame.

—Lao Tsu

THE refrigerator light cast a white glow on the two young boys as they sat on the kitchen floor, bickering with one another.

Between the two brothers was a plate containing the last slice of apple pie, which they were going to share. Holding the butter knife in one hand, the seven-year-old was trying to cut the piece in two, while the younger brother was grabbing at the knife, complaining he always got the smaller piece when his brother was in charge of dividing the remains of a dessert. Back and forth they bickered as they tugged on the butter knife. Then their mom entered the scene of the conflict.

"What are you kids fighting about now?" asked the mother.

"When Tyler cuts the pie, he always gives me the smallest piece," complained the younger brother.

"I do not," Tyler shot back.

"You do, too," yelled Jared.

"Do not."

"Do, too."

"Okay, you guys. Settle down. I've got an idea," suggested the mother. "How about one of you cuts the pie and the other gets to select the first piece."

Smiles slowly broke out on both the young boys' faces.

"All right, I'll still cut the pie," said Tyler. And he did. But Tyler never measured, eyed, and remeasured a piece of pie so carefully as he did this one, because he knew Jared got to choose. So he cut the piece perfectly in half.

Jared got to select the piece he wanted, but Tyler didn't mind because each piece was exactly the same size. Both parties agreed to a solution they found acceptable. The conflict was peacefully resolved, but it wouldn't be the last before they went to sleep.

"And shut that refrigerator door!" the mother said as she winked at the boys.

This chapter will present three step-by-step processes designed to resolve procedural, interpersonal, and substantive conflict within a group. You will also be given a variety of specific interventions you can use for each of the five dysfunctional communication styles that might arise in your group work with others. By using these approaches to resolve differences, you can create an atmosphere in which conflict can be dealt with in a healthy, productive fashion.

A Different Approach to Conflict

The mother in the opening story could have settled the conflict in many ways. She could have ignored the battle and walked past the skirmish. She could have punished both boys for fighting. She could have eaten the pie herself to teach the boys a lesson.

But she didn't. She flowed with their conflict. She joined with their little clash and suggested an alternative that required their cooperation and produced an acceptable solution they were both happy with. If only the rest of our conflicts could be so easily resolved.

In your small group work, you and the other members will occasionally experience conflict. A struggle over the placement of an item on the agenda. An argument over the merits of a proposed solution. Or feuding between two members of the group. These and other situations can reduce the group's task effectiveness and strain the relationships of its members.

Group members can ignore or deny conflict. They can address it indirectly through innuendo and insinuation. They can be more direct and blame and punish. They can even expel the member causing conflict. They, like the mother of the two boys, have many methods at their disposal for dealing with conflict.

Problem-solving groups often employ counterproductive approaches in dealing with conflict. Members close their eyes. They blame. They hit. And they hurt. Yet such approaches do very little to resolve conflict. And in many instances they serve to escalate differences, increase tension, and sever relationships within the group.

> The art of living lies less in eliminating conflicts than in growing with them.
>
> ∞
>
> BERNARD BARUCH

There's an old Zen saying that suggests another approach to dealing with conflict: "Hug your problem and it may disappear." This might sound paradoxical. Hug your problem? Aren't we trained to run from conflict? Or at least find someone to blame for the mess to distance us from responsibility? "It's not my fault," we say.

I think the hugging suggestion is actually an invitation to get closer to conflict rather than further away. It suggests a direct and open exploration of conflict, without blame or punishment. Conflict can be a wonderful teacher. It can teach us valuable lessons about others and ourselves. Instead of always trying to ignore, deny, blame, or fight during conflict, we can choose to join with it. Acknowledge its presence openly in the group. Explore rather than blame. Loosen rather than tighten. We need to flow with our conflict.

Myths of Conflict

Conflict is a struggle or disagreement between two or more options or people. This struggle or disagreement can be over differences of opinions, beliefs, or values in the task dimension of the group. Conflict can also be experienced in the social dimension between two or more people having differences in feelings, perceptions, and behaviors. Three commonly held myths concerning conflict are conflict should be avoided at all cost, conflict is always someone else's fault, and all conflict can be resolved.

> The resistance to the unpleasant situation is the root of suffering.
>
> ✎
>
> RAM DASS

Myth 1: Avoid Conflict at All Costs

One of the most common ways to deal with conflict is to avoid it. Now this is good advice if you're walking down a dark alley and you see three figures lurking behind the garbage bins. You should turn and walk the other way. Sometimes conflict, or possible conflict, can and should be avoided.

But in your small group problem-solving efforts, don't avoid conflict at all costs. Conflict can often benefit the task and social dimensions of the group. In fact, conflict can be an opportunity to listen to differences, discover new common ground, and uncover more effective ways to interact together as a group. It's out of the differences of group members that strength is built and wiser decisions are made.

Myth 2: Conflict Is Always Someone Else's Fault

Frequently, our first response when conflict occurs is to find someone to blame. It's what I call the "blame first, explore later" syndrome. We blame first; then we may examine what the problem really was. Many times we fail to explore the various factors of a disagreement or dispute. We want to blame—maybe because if someone else is to blame, we can't be at fault. In the complexity of group work, there might not be someone at fault or someone to blame. Maybe we're barking up the wrong tree when we automatically look for a culprit rather than examine the disagreement at hand. Any time you have five or six people working together, there will be, and should be, differences of opinion. When these differences surface, instead of finding someone to blame or fault, you may want to first explore and examine. Your group will function better when you do.

Myth 3: All Conflict Can Be Resolved

The final myth is that all conflict can be resolved. The belief that if we try hard enough, if we talk long enough, and if we compromise well enough, we will eventually resolve whatever conflict is before us. This is not always the case.

Not all substantive or idea conflicts can be resolved in a manner acceptable to all parties—especially those issues concerning questions of value. Conflicts centered on what is morally, ethically, and theologically correct and true might never be satisfactorily resolved in the group. Deep-seated personality conflicts between two group members might never be adequately resolved and healed during the life of the group.

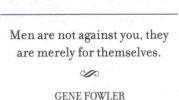

> Men are not against you, they are merely for themselves.
>
> ✐
>
> GENE FOWLER

Some conflicts might never be resolved. And that's okay. That's life. Not every relationship works. Not every dream is realized. Not every desire is satisfied. Our lesson can be to learn to let go in situations like this, give in to another individual's wishes, and accommodate others for the sake of the group. Not all conflict can be resolved. It might ultimately involve our departure from the group.

Advantages of Conflict

Any time conflict exists within a group, there is always the potential for growth for each group member. This growth can take the form of expanded awareness, improved participation, increased productivity, greater cohesiveness, and developed maturity.

Expanded Awareness

Many times when a group is running smoothly, its members working together cooperatively, there is a sense of satisfaction, a feeling of well-being. Complacency can often result. And a deadening of the senses can occur, which may cause a trancelike state. If you've ever ridden on a train across flatland for an extended period of time, you know how quickly the monotony of the ride can lull you to sleep.

When conflict is brought out into the open it can have an arousing effect upon group members. They are awakened from the productive hum of their routines. They are called to process, interact, and behave in a different, more focused manner. They are now in the midst of a conflict! The shift in focus from the mundane to the exceptional can be stimulating. It can wake us from our sleep.

Improved Participation

Just as the mere introduction of open conflict to the group process can foster expanded awareness, it can also encourage increased participation from group members. Many times, members will spring to action and participate with greater frequency and enthusiasm when the discussion turns to matters of dispute and struggle. In fact, many a relationship has been based upon this one variable: conflict.

Increased Productivity

The results of disagreement over substantive and procedural conflicts can benefit the productivity of the group. When the group resolves conflict and discovers new solutions, ideas, and procedures, the productivity can be greater than before the conflict. The labor pains brought about by conflict might also signal the birth of fresh ideas, better solutions, and improved relationships.

Greater Cohesiveness

After the group deals with interpersonal conflict in a productive and healthy manner, the cohesiveness of the group can be greatly enhanced. A better understanding and working relationship often results from interpersonal conflicts between group members if the group handles the conflict positively and maturely. Once the group members share perceptions, air differences, and establish new common ground for interacting and relating to one another, they can share more intimate feelings of connection.

Cohesion within the group frequently occurs when the group resolves substantive conflicts regarding the task dimension also. With the struggle over a specific task successfully negotiated and put behind them, the group can experience a feeling of achievement and intimacy. Good work often fosters good feelings.

Developed Maturity

Conflict within a group can help an individual increase in maturity. By that I mean, grow up. Each one of us is childish and infantile in certain areas of our lives. Having to butt heads and hearts with other human beings in our group can provide us with a rich, growing environment from which we can develop our abilities to disengage our egos, practice empathy, exercise patience, respond non-defensively, demonstrate compromise, and ask for

> I have had more trouble
> with myself than with
> any other person.
>
> ❧
>
> DWIGHT MOODY

forgiveness. These and many other activities brought about by conflict can tremendously benefit our personal growth and development as human beings.

Three Types of Group Conflict

When you consider the enormous potential for conflict within any problem-solving group, it's amazing any collection of individuals can work together in relative harmony and reach agreement on any matter. Literally thousands upon thousands of minor and major task and social dimension issues can ignite disagreement and struggle.

Every group experiences conflicts. Each conflict centers on a different issue. Each conflict focuses on differences, yet requires distinctly unique perceptions, approaches, and interventions on the part of group members to address the conflict successfully. No matter what conflict you face, it will fall into one of three categories: procedural conflict, substantive conflict, and interpersonal conflict.

Procedural Conflict (Structure)

A procedural conflict deals with the structure or procedures the group follows during discussion. These procedures outline how the meeting will be run, the order of the agenda, how disagreement will be handled, and how decisions will be made. A procedural conflict involves disagreement or struggle over the mechanics of the group's operation.

Substantive Conflict (Issues)

A substantive conflict involves disagreement or struggle over the substance or issues of discussion. This type of conflict centers around the task dimension of the group. Substantive conflict can involve disagreement or arguments over the tests of evidence, analysis of reasoning, proposed solutions, or any matter that deals with the content of discussion. Whereas a procedural conflict debates the mechanics of how something will be done or conducted within the group, a substantive conflict struggles with the ideas, opinions, beliefs, and values of group members themselves.

Interpersonal Conflict (People)

Tension or conflict between individual members of the group is called interpersonal conflict because it involves the feelings and behaviors of individuals. Although interpersonal conflict can often present itself as a procedural or substantive conflict initially, stronger feelings and statements attacking the person (ad hominem attack) can result, unmasking conflict between people.

Now that you know the basic differences between procedural, substantive, and interpersonal conflicts, I'll present some specific ways to deal with each category of conflict.

Dealing with Procedural Conflict

Any conflict or struggle aimed at the process or method by which the group works is called a procedural conflict. These types of conflicts often involve:

- Changes in the frequency, times, and locations of meetings.
- Changes in the agenda format.
- Changes in the structure of the meeting itself.

- Extending debate on a controversial issue.
- Terminating debate on a controversial issue.
- Modification of decision-making procedures.
- Modification of speaking rights/time limits.

How to Resolve Procedural Conflict

The group leader or chairperson needs to identify these conflicts, bring them to the group's attention, and act on them. Normally, the leader will have the power to accept or reject a proposed change in the procedures of the group. And the leader's decision is final.

But if there is no designated leader, or the leader wants to employ a more democratic method for discussing and structuring the procedures of the group, the leader can adopt a more open process. This process involves the basic parliamentary procedure steps:

1. Have a proposal (motion) stated to the group.
2. Ask if there is a second (a second member supporting the motion).
3. If there isn't a second, the proposal is rejected.
4. If there is a second, the group discusses the proposal.
5. A vote is taken when the discussion is completed.
6. The proposal is either accepted or rejected based upon the vote.

I prefer this method when faced with a procedural conflict because it directs the question back to group members, it opens discussion to all, and the decision is based on the majority vote. If the majority of the group votes to accept or reject the proposal, there is usually majority support to enforce the old or new procedure.

Dealing with Substantive Conflict

The second category of conflict experienced in groups involves ideas and issues. The focus of substantive conflict is what the group is discussing, not how it is being discussed. These content issues can include disagreement concerning the:

- reliability of information or evidence.
- reasoning supporting a proposal or idea.
- acceptability of an opinion or idea.
- acceptability of a specific proposal.
- acceptability of a goal or objective of the group.

When a group experiences substantive conflict, the leader or the group might attempt to resolve the conflict by avoidance. The group can drop the issue and move to another topic. The leader can force a decision upon group members, thus eliminating the substantive debate. The leader or group can also try to please members of both sides by using compromise and having both sides give a little ground. Finally, the group can vote to determine what idea will prevail. Each strategy for dealing with substantive conflict reduces the group's effectiveness by prematurely eliminating open and honest discussion of the issue, forcing compromise, and imposing a win-lose atmosphere on the group's social dimension.

How to Resolve Substantive Conflict

An open discussion of the issue is required with all substantive conflict. Whether group members vigorously debate the admissibility of evidence to the discussion and the reasoning of a proposal, or modify the primary purpose of the group, these steps will contribute to a more positive, productive, and successful approach to substantive conflict:

1. **Identify the conflict**. State the substantive conflict in specific terms. Summarize the differences of opinion or sides to the debate.

2. **Share perceptions**. Once you've brought the conflict out for discussion, ask the other members for their perceptions of the conflict and the seriousness of the conflict.

3. **Share opinions**. Group members can voice their opinions about the issue, but should refrain from verbally attacking members with the opposing viewpoint. Remind the group that it's possible to disagree with another person without having to dislike him or her. Focus on issues, not personalities.

4. **Listen actively**. Whenever an individual has made a statement, have the opposition restate the idea or feeling to the satisfaction of the speaker. This listening for understanding will promote more accurate communication and prevent emotions from escalating during discussion.

5. **State the opposition's strengths**. Have the opposing sides point out the strengths in the other's arguments or opinions. This is the difficult one. They won't normally want to state the other's strengths, but if you can get them to participate in this fifth step, you've come a long way to bringing about agreement.

6. **Discover common ground**. Try to have the opposing sides discover something they can both agree on. It doesn't necessarily have to be a major point of agreement, just some common ground both sides can agree to. Perhaps both sides can only agree that a conflict exists and they will work to resolve the conflict. That's a beginning. From this point of common ground, the two sides can hopefully discover more points of agreement as the discussion continues.

7. **Take a break**. After heated and often draining debate, a break is in order for the group. Take a five- or ten-minute break to stretch the legs, talk about something else, and get something to drink.

8. **Continue the discussion or move on**. After the break, continue the process of Steps 3 to 6 until the sides reach some sort of consensus on how they see the issue, proposal, or group goal. Or, after extended discussion, the group might feel that no common ground or consensus can be reached and will need to discuss how to move

on despite difference of opinion. Remind the group of all the things that are working and going well, and that this particular issue is just one of many the group will face in its life.

You probably recognized that this eight-step process is a modification of the consensus decision-making technique presented in Chapter 5. It should be, because the purpose of consensus is to discover a proposal, decision, or solution to some problem (or conflict) that is workable and acceptable to all group members.

> To every disadvantage there is a corresponding advantage.
>
> ∽
>
> W. CLEMENT STONE

In your dealings with substantive conflicts, keep in mind that the reason we work in small groups is to utilize the best each member is willing and able to contribute to achieve the group's goal. Differences of ideas will inevitably surface, but those differences also constitute the strength of the discussion process. It's the discarding of those ideas the group decides are unnecessary and the retaining of those ideas it feels are valuable that makes the group's product superior to the best individual's product.

Dealing with Interpersonal Conflict

Sometimes there might be conflict between two group members. The interpersonal conflict can be minor and fleeting. Examples of this are inappropriate remarks directed at an individual or a rude comment spoken in frustration, where in each instance, someone was upset or hurt by the comment. The interpersonal conflict can also be major and sustained, as in the case of aggressive and open feuding between two or more group members. Here are some causes of interpersonal conflict:

- Residual emotional injury from substantive or procedural conflict.
- Different values and beliefs.
- Cultural or racial differences.
- Different personalities.
- Different communication styles (dysfunctional roles).

No matter what causes the interpersonal conflict, it negatively affects the social dimension of the group because one or more members experience conflict at the personal level with another individual or individuals within the group.

Often interpersonal conflict can be disguised as a procedural or substantive conflict, but the real cause of the dispute is a concealed interpersonal conflict between two or more members. Even during legitimate procedural or substantive conflicts, tempers may flair and feelings get hurt, which can invite retaliation and attack at the personal level. It's often difficult to prevent sustained substantive conflict from developing into interpersonal conflict. Our hearts are connected to our heads in ways we don't yet fully understand.

How to Resolve Interpersonal Conflict
Caused by Normal Differences

Most of your interpersonal conflict in the group can be dealt with using the steps suggested here:

1. **Self-check-in**. Before you do anything, just sit and breathe. Don't say anything to the individual you're experiencing difficulty with. Just sit and breathe for now. After the meeting, go home and conduct a five-minute check-in with yourself about this conflict. Ask yourself, What specifically did this individual say or do to upset me? Did I overreact? Am I overly sensitive today? How am I doing in other aspects of my life? Am I still upset about what this person said or did? Before you do anything, sleep on it. Do you feel the same after you awaken? If you're feeling better, good. Give the individual another chance. If not, go to Step 2.

2. **Ask for third-person perception check**. Share your perception and discuss this matter with another group member who is not involved in the conflict. Briefly share your basic perceptions of the conflict; then ask this third party for her perceptions of the remark, behavior, or event. Did that person share your perceptions? If not, consider the feedback of this individual and put the matter on hold for a while. If the conflict recurs, then start over at Step 1. If the third party confirms your perceptions, go to Step 3.

3. **Decide what you want**. Once you've received some confirmation from a third party regarding the conflict, decide what you want to do. Do you want to let the incident go? Do you want to share your perceptions with the individual? Do you want to retaliate in kind? Do you want to punish the person? Do you want an apology? What do you really want? Think long and hard about this one. Most of the time, if the conflict was a brief, one-time event (a remark, a joke, an accusation, a slur), you'll let it go and see if it happens again. If you won't let it go, don't consider retaliation, punishment, or even getting an apology. Go to Step 4.

4. **Conduct perception check-in with the individual**. Ask the individual if you can meet for two or three minutes after the next meeting. If she asks what you want to discuss, explain that you want to share your perceptions of a recent event involving her. If she refuses, let it go. Then go back to Step 1. Don't push the matter. If you can meet, ask for her perceptions of the event. In most instances, the individual will either defend the behavior, back off and modify her position, or apologize. If she apologizes, accept the apology, shake hands, and let go of it. If the person backs off and modifies her position, support that position in whatever way you're comfortable and go to Step 5. If the person attacks you, disagrees with your perception, or defends her position, remain calm and breathe. Then go to Step 5.

5. **State your boundary**. A boundary is an imaginary line that separates what is acceptable to you from what is not acceptable to you. If the individual disagreed with your perception or defended or modified her position, state your boundary regarding future behavior. A boundary statement is not a blaming, accusing, or

punishing statement. It is an informational statement. Its basic structure is: If you _____, then I am prepared to _____.

For example:

"If you continue to criticize me in front of the group, then I am prepared to leave the room."

"If you don't bring the video camera to our meeting, then I am prepared to purchase one for the group and bill it to your department."

6. **Enforce your boundary statement**. The very next time the individual repeats the unacceptable behavior, enforce your boundary response. Whether that means identifying the interaction, leaving the meeting room, or bringing the matter to the attention of the group, you enforce your boundary statement, immediately.

This six-step interpersonal conflict resolution model is just that, a model. It's one way to manage interpersonal conflict. There are other methods you might want to learn about in the future, but this approach is simple and direct. Regardless of your strategy, however, remember that a gentle, open, and sincere attitude on your part will help create an atmosphere in which you can invite the others into dialogue.

Specific Interventions for Dysfunctional Behavior

In addition to the six-step interpersonal conflict resolution process, specific interventions for dysfunctional behavior of group members in any one of the three areas of conflict are helpful to know. A dysfunctional behavior is any habitual behavior that disrupts the task and/or social functioning of the group.

Generally, you cannot deal effectively with dysfunctional behaviors using the harmonizing behaviors mentioned in Chapter 7. The causes of dysfunctional behavior are more deeply ingrained and beyond the scope of this book. Yet you can try to bring the behavior to the attention of the individual or use some interventions that can help correct the dysfunctional behavior. Here are some interventions you might want to try when you discover mild forms of dysfunctional communication behavior in your group.

Controller

The controller tries to dominate, regulate, and manipulate group interaction. His verbal communication patterns are usually issuing orders and directives. He tends to give directions and explain the superiority of his ideas and solutions over all others presented. The controller often uses logical appeals and intricate reasoning to get his way. He can be a master of words and persuasion. He blocks and redirects discussion for his own purposes. His nonverbal posture is often rigid, tight, and stern.

Level 1 controller intervention. The controller tries to dominate the discussion by speaking at length, interrupting others, and repeatedly bringing the discussion back to his point of view. If you notice a member displaying this type of characteristic behavior, you can:

> Summarize what the controller has said.
> State your own opinion when the controller pauses for breath.
> Ask the other group members for their input or feedback.
> Respond to his interrupting by saying, "Were you aware I was speaking?"

Level 2 controller intervention. If the controller reacts in a hostile fashion to Level 1 interventions or continues to exhibit controlling behavior, you might use Level 2 interventions. The purpose of Level 2 interventions is to confront the controller directly. Don't call him names or blame him directly. Your best strategy is to confront the controller personally, away from the group, and share your perceptions of his behavior. Ask him for his feedback on your perceptions to initiate a dialogue so that you can request him to give more speaking time to the other group members and actively listen to them. A controller will not readily give up his attempts at control, however. Be prepared to confront him again at future discussions. The important point is to label his controlling transactions while he is performing them. Here are some ways you can confront the controller:

> You've been talking about your idea for eight minutes and I'm concerned that other points of view aren't being expressed.
> When I'm (or another member is) talking you seem to be interrupting.
> You're interrupting . . .
> You're bringing the discussion back to your idea. Have we discussed this enough, group?

Blamer

The blamer usually finds fault with others and their ideas and suggestions, although she won't usually offer suggestions of her own. She generally blames others for the shortcomings and failures of the group. She will cast a shadow of doubt and gloom upon the solutions proposed and will be the first to say "I told you so" when a solution fails. Although she will rarely admit a mistake or failure, the blamer almost relishes casting fault on others. She'll slouch in her chair and throw her arms in the air. Everyone's to blame but her! And she told you so.

Level 1 blamer intervention. If a group member constantly blames or complains, the first intervention is to have her provide more information to support her point. Second, ask other group members for their perceptions. Present your perceptions of the event or person being discussed. Have the group discuss one specific issue at a time. Don't let the blamer scatter the focus of the group by changing the subject with a different complaint or individual to blame. Keep the discussion focused.

Level 2 blamer intervention. If the blamer continues to blame and complain, even relishing the additional time and attention the group has provided her with Level 1 interventions, you need to change your strategy. Call attention to her blaming behavior by directly labeling her transactions: "You're blaming again," or "You're complaining again," and notice if this changes her behavior. If not, you can confront the blamer as a group and share your feelings about her behavior.

It is never easy to correct blaming behavior. The best you can do for the group is to bring the behavior out in the open by labeling the blaming transactions. There's something about bringing behaviors into the open that can help to modify the blamer's behavior.

Pleaser

The pleaser attempts to avoid conflict and confrontation by giving in to the wishes of the others. He agrees to just about anything the others ask or require. When a conflict begins to surface, the pleaser does whatever it takes to dissolve or neutralize the disagreement. The pleaser is generally uncomfortable asserting his own opinion, defending his position, and sharing his feelings. He backs down rather than fight. He agrees to just about anything for the sake of peace and tranquility.

Level 1 pleaser intervention. When an individual constantly placates and attempts to please other group members (usually the controller), you can modify his behavior by playing the "heavy." Normally, when a pleaser pleases or placates, no one intervenes and the cycle is reinforced. You can challenge the pleaser by stating positions and making demands that are the opposite of what the pleaser is agreeing to. No matter what the pleaser is agreeing to, take the opposite position (generally against the controller) and see what the rest of the group does with your intervention. Your goal is to throw the pleaser off balance by not agreeing too quickly with his or her characteristic behavior. Continue this intervention when the pleaser tries to please.

Level 2 pleaser intervention. If the pleaser continues to please, despite your contrary interventions, you can employ a different strategy. You can label his transaction and invite a different perception by saying, "You're being too agreeable. Are there any weaknesses or disadvantages to this proposal?" Many times, just by saying that someone is "being too agreeable" and asking them to note any weaknesses is enough to cause them to pause and take a second look.

Distractor

The distractor doesn't give in, blame, or control. Her role is to draw or deflect the attention away from the issue at hand. When the group experiences stress or conflict, the distractor will usually joke about the situation or redirect the discussion to an unrelated issue or topic. Often the distractor is just as uncomfortable with conflict as the pleaser, but her method for handling her discomfort is different. Whereas the pleaser will placate or give in, the distractor will utilize some avoidance technique to change the subject. The distractor will attempt to sidetrack the group's work. She will joke, flirt, or question the importance of the task at hand. She is often the court jester, the class clown. For an occasional tension release, she's fine. But as a continual disturbance, her behavior can be frustrating and detrimental to the group's functioning.

Anyone can have
an off decade.

LARRY COLE

Level 1 distractor intervention. The best way to deal with a constant distractor is to ignore her diverting comments and request that the group return to the discussion topic. Remember to label her transactions by saying, "You're distracting us from the topic at hand. Can we return to our discussion?" Be swift in making your request to return to the discussion after the distractor makes her statement, even though she might object to your being "too serious" or "too uptight." Ignore humorous or sarcastic remarks from the distractor; simply make your request to "return to the discussion."

Level 2 distractor intervention. If the distractor refuses to cooperate by continuing her distracting behavior, you should bring the matter to the group for discussion. Share your perceptions of her distracting behavior and how you feel about its dysfunctional effect upon the group. Ask for feedback from the other members of the group. Most likely, the distractor will use humor or divert the attention of the group by shifting blame to something or someone else (namely you for being too serious). Your interventions should be able to modify or eliminate her distracting behavior.

Ghost

The ghost is a group member who is habitually absent or does not participate in the group's discussion. Whether he's sitting with the group or has missed the meeting again, he contributes nothing to the group. Like a silent face in the crowd, the ghost sits there in the group and says nothing. The cause of this behavior may be stage fright, lack of commitment, apathy, or a host of other explanations. But the result is always the same. He's the group member who doesn't participate or show up. The ghost has been called the nonperformer, the low-verbal, and the passive-aggressive personality. I simply refer to him as the ghost, because he's not really there. Yet his impact on the group's task effectiveness and social atmosphere can be devastating.

Level 1 ghost intervention. Of all five dysfunctional behaviors, this one is the most difficult to prescribe an intervention for because of the variety of reasons that might be causing his behavior. Without going into a more involved and detailed discussion of these reasons, I'd like to suggest some simple guidelines for dealing with this behavior:

Encourage the ghost (silent or low-verbal member) to share his opinion.
Compliment the ghost for any contributions.
Take the ghost out for coffee after a meeting. Be friendly.
Confront the ghost for not following through on duties.
Confront the ghost for not attending a meeting.

Level 2 ghost intervention. If the ghost continues to remain a silent (or low-verbal) group member, maybe that's his personal or cultural style of communication. There are individuals who are, by nature or past experience, more reticent than others, and you have to find gentle ways to encourage their participation. There are also individuals whose cultural or ethnic backgrounds differ from ours in terms of interaction expectations. Many cultures regard direct eye contact, personal remarks and requests, and individual achievement as undesirable and objectionable. You should be sensitive to these differences in cultural perspective and still discover ways to invite and promote participation in the group.

Of the five dysfunctional roles, the ghost can be the most difficult individual to accurately and effectively deal with. Be tentative, gentle, supportive, and sensitive with him, but enforce rules that govern completion of tasks and attendance. Neglecting responsibilities and absences from meetings cannot be tolerated indefinitely. If in doubt, be kind but firm.

These five dysfunctional roles may arise occasionally in your group. The behavior of those exhibiting any of these roles will normally be mild and subtle, requiring only one or two interventions on your part to modify or eliminate it. But if the behavior is extreme, exaggerated, or physically threatening, appropriate steps should be taken to release the individual from the group.

The Spirit of Collaboration

The fact that a work group is formed does not necessarily guarantee that all the group members will work together in a constructive, harmonious, and productive way. The assumption or hope is that the members of the group will work together, as a team, using their individual knowledge, skills, and experience to help the group reach its goal by placing the group needs above their own needs.

But this doesn't always happen. Too often individuals in the group will place their personal needs and desires above the needs and requirements of the group. Desiring high status, control, appreciation, prestige, admiration, or avoidance of effort are just a few of the self-centered ways group members can quickly turn the atmosphere of the group into a defensive and destructive climate.

For any work group to perform effectively, it must operate within a climate of collaboration. The Latin word, "colaborare," from which our word collaborate comes, means "to labor together." For our purposes in group work, let's define collaboration as three or more individuals working together towards a common goal with a collective sense of purpose, sharing, and trust.

Under this definition, the group members agree that the goal of the group supersedes their own personal needs and desires. The accomplishment of that goal is the purpose for their existence as a group. Information and resource sharing is fundamental to their collective efforts. And the interactions and activities of the group members are based upon trusting the personal honesty and integrity of each individual. Although these objectives might seem lofty and difficulty to achieve, there are things the group can do to actually develop these elements of a collaborative spirit. Here are seven guidelines that can help you foster a spirit of collaboration within your group.

1. Commit to a Common Purpose

The most important element of developing a collaborative group spirit is to have the individual members agree upon and support the idea that their purpose as a group member is to help the group reach its goal. That defines each individual's purpose and the group's common purpose. The group goal is more important than any individual's personal goals and desires. During the initial meeting of the group, it is important for the group members to discuss their common purpose. It's also helpful to remind the group members that they each share equally in the responsibilities that will be required in achieving their common goal.

2. Respect Differences

A second element of collaboration requires that individuals respect the differences of other group members. Whether it be ethnicity, culture, gender, age, education, experience, or simply taste in clothing, differences should be viewed as strengths, not as reasons to judge, criticize, or condescend. Every effort should be made by group members to identify and appreciate the skills, knowledge, and experience that each person possesses. And above all else, the respecting of opinions and ideas differing from our own, should be encouraged. It is from our differing opinions, ideas, and solutions that the real strength of collaboration surfaces and manifests itself.

3. Open Communication

There should be open communication between all group members. During the meetings, the seating arrangement should encourage equality, accessibility, and comfort. A round table works best since all members are equal distance from one another, as opposed to a long conference table that positions two people in highly visible positions and the rest of the members in less visually prominent positions.

During the discussion, oral contributions should be distributed as evenly as possible, without dominance by one or two members. Seek to encourage participation from the low verbal members, while attempting to limit high verbal dominance. Efforts made to balance the contributions among the members will go a long way to establish a spirit of collaboration, with everyone's opinions being sought and valued.

Communication between group members should also be encouraged outside of the meeting room. Keep each member informed and updated with current information and announcements. The beauty of group text messaging, e-mails, conference calls, and other social media is the simplicity of keeping everyone informed. Always remember to include yourself in every message you send so you have a record of your correspondences.

4. Encouraging Communication

In addition to making every effort to keep group members included, connected, and informed, a spirit of collaboration is fostered by the kind of communication we give. Make an effort to enlarge others with your words. There's an old saying that "We are not only our brother's (and sister's) keeper, we are their maker." In a very real way, the words we speak to others can literally shape their self-concepts. Look for behaviors to compliment in the other group members. Take time to encourage a group member when he or she appears discouraged, fatigued, or disappointed. Your encouraging words will not only lift the spirit of those you speak to, it promotes a spirit of collaboration within the group. Be enlarging and encouraging with your words, for they might just be the highlight of the day for another group member.

5. Shared Resources

Food always tastes better when it's shared and the same holds true for the resources you share with the other members of your group. Rather than keep researched information, equipment, and other resources for yourself, share it with the other group members. "What's mine is yours" is an attitude that can also generate a spirit of collaboration within a group.

One of the easiest ways to share a helpful article you've discovered on the Internet is to simply e-mail the article link to the other group members along with a cheerful message. Another way to share your resources is to invite your group to coffee or lunch, on you. Pick up the tab and see the smiles appear. Good for you. Don't hold on to your money too tightly in this lifetime. Be generous. Your group will love the experience.

6. Trust

Without trust there is little hope for a spirit of collaboration. If a group member pledges allegiance to a common goal, communicates openly, and even shares his resources with you, but you suspect that he is acting insincerely, manipulatively, or deceitfully, you will not give him your full trust. In fact, you might question everything he says and does.

To earn the trust of your fellow group members and thus contribute to a spirit of collaboration, there are specific things you can do to accomplish this goal. First, be punctual to all group meetings. If you can't be trusted to even arrive at the agreed upon time, how can you be trusted with larger responsibilities. To build trust and gratitude, arrive ten minutes early and help set up the meeting room. Your actions will speak louder than your words.

Another way to earn trust is to keep your promises to the group. If you say you'll bring the video camera to a group activity, bring the camera, complete with recharged batteries and an extra memory chip just in case. If you say you'll call the City Council Offices to arrange an appointment with the City Manager, make that phone call and schedule the appointment. And if you say you'll bring the snacks to the next group meeting, bring the snacks and set up the goodies before the meeting begins. And don't forget the napkins.

Either you keep your promises or you don't. No excuses. Just do what you say you'll do. Keep your promises all the time and you'll be a trusted member of the group.

Lastly, be someone who can be trusted with your communication. Don't lie to people. Don't even exaggerate the truth. No one is impressed with embellishment. In fact, a reputation for exaggeration makes you suspect over time. And don't break confidentiality when someone confides a secret to you. Be a man or woman whom others can trust with personal information. In the end, be someone who strives to be honest in all your dealings and is known for keeping promises. That will do more than contribute to a spirit of collaboration with your colleagues; it will bless them as well.

7. Decision by Consensus

The final element of building a spirit of collaboration is the method in which the group reaches its decisions. Although the definition and guidelines for successful consensus making has been describe earlier in this book, I'd like to specifically highlight the way it contributes to the creation of a spirit of collaboration.

If we define collaboration as three or more individuals working together towards a common goal with a collective sense of purpose, sharing, and trust, the process of consensus is the most effective way to include and honor every group member's opinion in shaping a decision or solution to a problem.

Rather than leaving the decision to the group leader or voting by majority rule, the act of consensus guarantees that each and every member contributes to the shaping of the group's decision or solution. Consensus, decided upon only after each group member agrees that he or she "can live with the decision," ensures that the group collectively settles on a decision that meets the satisfaction of all group members. Not the leader's satisfaction. Not the majority's satisfaction. But each and every member's satisfaction. It might not be each member's first and favorite decision or solution, but it's one that he or she can "live with." One that each member can support and stand behind.

In group work, as in life, we don't always get everything we want. And guided by this realization in the process of reaching consensus, each member of the group feels that his or her opinion was considered and ultimately played a determining role in the ultimate decision or solution reached by the group.

Remember, any one member of the group can prevent consensus simply by saying, "No, I can't live with this decision," and the group is forced to further discuss and discover new common ground upon which the group crafts an acceptable decision or solution. Consensus, by design, provides ultimate power to each member of the group, thus guaranteeing that each member listens to, considers, and adjusts to the wisdom of the collective group. This is the heart of collaboration— "to labor together."

Forgiveness

A subject that lies at the foundation of your work with others in small groups, especially in the area of conflict, is forgiveness. Forgiveness is the act of granting free pardon for an offense. In essence, it is the act of letting go of the desire to get even, to make someone pay for the hurt he or she might have caused you during some disagreement or conflict. It is also the act of asking someone to forgive you for an offense you might have caused him or her.

In any group process, people's efforts will often fall short, circumstances will not always accommodate the best-laid plans, and your feelings and those of your group members will eventually be hurt by some incidental or catastrophic event. When we are hurt by someone, be it a critical remark or an act of betrayal, we experience the initial feeling of shock, dismay, or a host of other uncomfortable feelings. But eventually, each of these feelings gives rise to anger—the anger of being injured by another individual. When we are hurt, we ultimately experience anger. One of two things can be done with this anger. We can hold on to the anger or let go of it. We will explore ways to let go.

When we hurt another person, guilt is most often the resulting feeling we must live with—guilt for a remark made in anger, an expectation we cannot live up to, or an act of deception. No matter what we did to bring pain to another person, guilt is our eventual destination if we don't make amends with the one we hurt.

Whether we are prisoners of our anger or prisoners of our guilt, we are held hostage by these powerful feelings until we decide to let go of them. And the only way I know to be free from their suffocating grasp is the act of forgiveness. But to forgive and to ask for forgiveness requires an abandonment of your usual, familiar way of dealing with hurt, anger, and guilt. Here are three principles of forgiveness that will help you when attempting to let go instead of getting even.

> One forgives to the
> extent that one loves.
>
> ✑
>
> FRANCOIS DE LA ROCHEFOUCAULD

Forgiveness is a decision, not a feeling. An erroneous concept regarding forgiveness is that you should feel like forgiving someone before you communicate your forgiveness of the offense. Forgiveness has nothing to do with your feelings. Forgiveness is a decision to consciously let go of your guilt or anger. Initially, forgiveness has more to do with your head than your heart. Don't use the excuse that you don't feel like asking for forgiveness or forgiving someone for an offense. Forgiveness is not a feeling; it is a decision.

Forgiveness requires suspension of the ego. As I stated earlier, your decision to forgive or ask for forgiveness is a difficult task. It requires that you suspend your ego—putting yourself second. This is not an easy process—to occasionally suspend our preoccupation with ourselves. Yet it is essential to the act of forgiveness.

Forgiveness is a never-ending process. Whether we have made the decision to ask for forgiveness or grant forgiveness, the process of forgiving is a never-ending task. Forgiving is not a destination. Rather it is a way of traveling. It is actually something we become over time—a forgiving individual. Forgiving demands of us the greatest of all tasks: the willingness we permit others, and ourselves, to make mistakes.

Asking for Forgiveness

If you have wronged someone in your group and want to ask his or her forgiveness, try the three-step AAA Forgiveness Technique:

1. Admit you were wrong.
2. Apologize for the offense.
3. Ask for forgiveness.

Let's assume you criticized another group member unfairly during a meeting. The next day you feel guilty about your critical remarks. You decide to ask the individual for forgiveness. This is how the AAA Forgiveness Technique works:

YOU: Nathan, do you remember the meeting last Thursday?
NATHAN: I've been trying to forget.
YOU: Well, I was wrong to criticize you in front of the group. (admitting you were wrong)
NATHAN: You bet you were. That was a terrible thing to do. Would I ever do something like that to you?
YOU: No. Probably not. But I apologize for criticizing you. I'm sorry. (apologizing for the offense)
NATHAN: Apology accepted, I guess.
YOU: Would you forgive me for criticizing you? (asking for forgiveness)
NATHAN: Well, yes. Of course I'll forgive you.

Not all attempts at asking someone for forgiveness will go this smoothly. But did you notice how you admitted you were wrong, apologized for the offense, and asked for forgiveness? This AAA Forgiveness Technique can be very useful in dealing with your guilt over something you have done. It can bring you to a place of forgiveness and that's one of the nicest things you can do for yourself. Remember, be gentle on yourself.

Forgiving Others

When someone has hurt or offended you, your initial response can range from mild surprise to rage. Eventually, your hurt can turn to anger. What you do with this anger will determine, to a large extent, the kind of person you will become and the quality of all your relationships. If you choose to hold on to the anger, you can become bitter. If you choose to forgive the person who hurt you, your anger will dissipate. You don't want to be holding on to this anger, for it will only hurt you in the long run. Here are some ways to forgive others.

Forgiving those who are not apologetic. There will be occasions when someone hurts you and is not apologetic, let alone repentant enough to ask you for forgiveness. In this instance, you might forgive the person, anyway.

You might not want to forgive him initially. In fact, you might never feel the desire to forgive him for the wrong he has done you. But forgiveness is not a feeling. It's your decision to be free of the hurt and anger he has brought you. You can use three methods to forgive those who have hurt you and refuse to be apologetic.

The first method I refer to as pretending to forgive. It can be used when the hurt is too recent or too serious for you to even consider a decision to forgive the other person. Here's how the technique works. You place two chairs about three feet apart, facing one another. You sit in one chair and imagine the person who hurt you in the empty chair. Next, you pretend you have decided to forgive this person (even though you have not really made this decision) and you tell the "other person" in the empty chair you have forgiven the offense. Picture the other person's face softening as you say the words. Imagine the other person saying something thoughtful, considerate, or even apologetic. After you have told the person you have forgiven her, just sit in your chair and feel your response to the exercise. Do you feel the same? Do you feel a slight change? Do you still feel the hurt or anger?

The second method in dealing with those who are not apologetic is a technique I call imagining their death. The technique involves you imagining the person has only one day to live. Even though this individual is healthy, happy, and still not apologetic, you are to imagine that person has only twenty-four hours to live. In twenty-four hours the person will be dead. Do you feel the same? Do you feel slightly different? Do you still focus on your hurt? Or are you thinking about the other person? Have your feelings changed about the relative importance of her offense compared with her impending death? You'd be surprised how this will change your feelings toward the person.

The third technique is what I call direct forgiving. After you have decided to forgive the other person for his offense, you share this information with him in person, face-to-face. The primary weakness to this method is that the other person will often respond with denial, justification, rationalization, or blame. He might even deny he did in fact offend you. No matter what response he chooses, you emphasize the fact that you have chosen to forgive him for his offense. You don't have to be the best of friends after the meeting. The single purpose for the meeting is for you to let him know you have forgiven him.

Forgiving those who ask for your forgiveness. If someone who has hurt you comes to you and asks for your forgiveness, you should forgive her, no matter how you feel. Remember forgiveness is not a feeling, but a decision. Forgive her if you wish to be free. If you decide not to forgive, you, not the other person, will carry the weight of anger and resentment.

Forgive those who ask for forgiveness. It's really the only choice you have if you want to be free. Forgiveness may be the most important lesson you'll learn while you participate in and lead small groups.

Conflict is a natural part of all group discussion and of life itself. Rather than avoid or intensify conflict, you can choose to address it directly and constructively, with gentleness and caring. Your willingness and ability to build bridges to those who are disagreeable or hostile, and meet them with openness, fairness, and even forgiveness, can change them. See conflict as an invitation to create common ground, to bring peace, and ultimately, to be more loving. There can be no greater creation in small groups.

∽ Individual and Group Exercises ∽

Boundary Making

EXERCISE 10.1 Communicate a boundary to an individual whose behavior is unacceptable to you. Select someone from your personal life (spouse, parent, child, best friend, or acquaintance) or professional life (coworkers, supervisor, or employee) who did or said something that bothered you. Arrange a two- or three-minute meeting with this individual and share your boundary with her. Complete this pre-meeting form before you meet with this person.

1. Who is this individual? _____
2. What behavior is unacceptable to you? _____
3. Construct your boundary statement. If you _____ , then I'm prepared to
   _____

When you share your boundary with this person, provide some brief introductory remarks about the situation before you communicate your boundary. The purpose of the meeting is not to blame or punish, but rather to inform the individual what you find unacceptable and what you are prepared to do if the behavior is repeated.

How did your meeting go? How did you feel composing your boundary statement? How did you feel asking this person for a meeting? How did you feel communicating your boundary to this individual? How did the person respond? Have you noticed a change in the person's behavior since your meeting? How can you incorporate boundary making into your small group?

Group Conflict Resolution

EXERCISE 10.2 Have your group use some of the procedures outlined in this chapter the next time it experiences either a procedural or substantive conflict. Assign one group member to identify any procedural conflict the group experiences and act as the facilitator to resolve the conflict. Assign another group member to identify any substantive conflict and facilitate the group's interactions during that conflict.

Group Role Playing

EXERCISE
10.3
Have a group member role play one of the five dysfunctional behavior roles in a problem-solving activity. After the role player has played his part in the problem-solving activity, the other group members attempt to modify his behavior using the interventions suggested. Have each group member role play a dysfunctional role. How did your group handle the various roles? Can you see yourself actually using these interventions in a real-life situation? Why or why not?

Afterword

You shape the lives of those around you

—CATHERINE PONDER

THE dinner guests were lined up saying good-bye to Gary and Tricia at the front door, thanking them for the marvelous evening. My wife and I were still in the kitchen, clearing glasses and stacking dishes. It had been a lively gathering of Gary's engineering team from work and their spouses. Vicky and I were invited to the dinner because I had coached his engineers in small group communication skills during the previous quarter.

After walking the last guests to their car, Gary and Tricia returned to the house and plopped down on the sofa, insisting that we sit down and visit.

"That was a fun time," remarked Gary. "And we would never had gotten together had it not been for those workshops of yours, and Lee Nguyen's comment that I needed to be a better listener."

I remembered Lee's comment during one of the group's heated sessions, when he told Gary to "listen to your team without interrupting so much." Gary's face reflected the surprise and the sting of Lee's remark, but the group had developed an atmosphere of unusual openness and trust during its time together, and Gary received the feedback.

He not only heard Lee's words; Gary began to change the way he interacted with his team members by letting them finish their sentences, many times listening for several minutes without interrupting. That's one of the reasons why I liked Gary so much; he genuinely wanted to improve the way he communicated. Gary's dinner party was just one of many ways he tried to understand and enjoy his team members more.

"I remember Lee's comment," I replied.

"Well, that comment changed Gary's relationship with our daughters, too," Tricia said, smiling. "For the past few months Gary hasn't finished one of Shannon or Laurie's sentences or walked away during a disagreement. He's really trying to be a better listener at home."

"I'm not perfect, but I'm getting there," added Gary.

"We're all trying to get there," I whispered to Vicky.

During this lifetime, you will be given countless opportunities to make a positive difference in the groups you participate in and lead. Whether it's working on a problem-solving team at work, organizing a charity fund-raiser, or planning a vacation with your family, you will be involved with helping groups reach a variety of goals.

In your efforts to participate and lead more effectively, remember that every comment and every behavior can influence and shape the group's interaction and productivity. The more openness and trust your group develops, the more successful it will be, not only in terms of achieving the goals of the group, but also in improving the personal lives of each member. You might even inspire a father to be a better listener to those he loves.

You will make a difference in every group in which you are involved. Will your contributions add to the distraction, confusion, and conflict that plagues so many groups? Or will your participation help to encourage, guide, and even inspire your groups to success? You will make a difference. The important question is this: What kind of a difference will you create?

Resources

Chapter 1. Working in a Group

Bales, R. 1976. *Interaction Process Analysis*. Chicago: University of Chicago Press.

Butterworth, Bill. 2006. *Balancing Life and Work*. New York: Currency Books.

Fisher, A. 1970. "Decision Emergence: Phases in Group Decision Making" *Speech Monographs* 37:53–66.

Hirokawa, R. Y., and Poole, M. 1986. *Communication and Group Decision-Making*. Beverly Hills, CA: Sage Publications.

Maxwell, John C. 2004. *The Power of One*. New York: Nelson Reference & Electronics.

Poole, M. S. 1981. "Decision Development in Small Groups I: A Comparison of Two Models." *Communication Monographs* 48:1–17.

Senge, Peter. 1990. *The Fifth Dimension: The Art and Practice of the Learning Organization*. New York, New York: Currency and Doubleday.

Schutz, William. 1969. *Joy: Expanding Human Awareness*. New York: Grove Press.

Chapter 2. Discovering Yourself

Adler, R., and Proctor, R. 2014. *Looking Out, Looking In*. New York: Wadsworth.

Benner, D. 2009. *The Gift of Being Yourself*. Westmont, IL: Intervarsity Press.

Ellis, Albert. 1998. *A Guide to Rational Living*. Englewood, CA: Wilshire Book Co.

Johnson, Spencer. 2003. *The Present*. New York: Doubleday.

Chapter 3. Expressing Yourself Clearly

Fujishin, R. 2011. *Natural Bridges*. New York: Pearson.

Heller, Robert. 1998. *Communicate Clearly*. New York: DK Publishing.

Nielsen, J. 2008. *Effective Communication Skills*. Bloominton, IN: Xlibris Press.

Satir, V. 1988. *New Peoplemaking*. New York: Science and Behavior Press.

Tannen, D. 1991. *You Just Don't Understand*. New York: Ballantine.

Chapter 4. Listening for Understanding

Blanchard, Ken and Johnson, Spencer. 2003. *The One Minute Manager*. New York: William Morrow.

Downs, L. 2008. *Listening Skills Training*. Alexandria, VA: American Society for Training and Development.

Kerman, J. 2011. *Listen*. New York: Bedford, St. Martins.

Chapter 5. Problem Solving in Groups

Craven, Robin E. 2006. *The Complete Idiot's Guide to Managing Meetings and Event Planning*, 2nd Edition. New York: Alpha Publishing.

Crowley, Katherine, and Elster, Kathi. 2006. *Working With You Is Killing Me*. New York: Warner Business Books.

Hirokawa, R. Y. 1985. "Discussion Procedures and Decision-Making Performance: A Test of a Functional Perspective." *Human Communication Research* 12:203–224.

———. 1988. "A Descriptive Investigation into the Possible Communication-Based Reasons for Effective and Ineffective Group Decision-Making." *Communication Monographs* 50:363–379.

Hirokawa, R. Y., and Poole, M. 1986. *Communication and Group Decision-Making*. Beverly Hills, CA: Sage Publications.

Poole, M. S. 1981. "Decision Development in Small Groups I: A Comparison of Two Models." *Communication Monographs* 48:1–17.

von Oech, R. 2008. *A Whack on the Side of the Head*. New York: Warner Books.

Wood, J. T. 1986. *Group Discussion: A Practical Guide to Discussion and Leadership*. New York: Harper & Row.

Chapter 6. Preparing for Discussion

Bing, Stanley. 2004. *Sun Tzu Was a Sissy*. New York: Collins Publishing.

Boulden, George. 2002. *Thinking Creatively*. New York: DK Publishing.

Hartman, K., and Ackermann, E. 2010. *Searching and Researching on the Internet and the World Wide Web*, 5th Ed. New York: Franklin, Beedle, and Associates.

Chapter 7. Guiding Discussion

Benne, K., and Sheats, P. 1948. "Functional Roles of Group Members." *Journal of Social Issues* 4:41–49.

Johnson, D. 1987. *Joining Together: Group Theory and Group Skills*. Englewood Cliffs, NJ: Prentice-Hall.

Pell, Arthur R. 2003. *The Complete Idiot's Guide to Managing People*. New York: Alpha Publishing.

Pollen, Stephen M. 2004. *Fire Your Boss*. New York: HaperCollins.

Chapter 8. Leading a Group

Barker, A. 2007. *How to Manage Meetings.* Philadelphia, PA: Kogan Publishing.
Butterworth, Bill. 2006. *Building Successful Teams.* New York: Currency Books.
DuPree, M. 2004. *Leadership Is An Art.* New York: Crown Publishing.
Greenleaf, R. 2002. *Servant-Leadership.* New York: Berrett-Koeler.

Chapter 9. Building a Cohesive Group

Choninard, Yvon. 2005. *Let My People Go Surfing: The Education of a Reluctant Businessman.* New York: The Penguin Press.
Dyer, W. 2013. *Team Building.* New York: Wiley, John & Sons.
Fisher, B., and Ellis, D. 1990. *Small Group Decision Making: Communication and the Small Group Process.* New York: McGraw-Hill.
Janis, I. 1983. *Groupthink: Psychological Studies of Policy Decisions and Fiascoes.* Boston: Houghton Mifflin.
Maxwell, John C. 2005. *Life at Work.* New York: Nelson Business Publishing.
Shaw, M. 1981. *Group Dynamics: The Psychology of Small Group Behavior.* New York: McGraw-Hill.

Chapter 10. Managing Conflict

Folger, J. 2012. *Working Through Conflict.* New York: Pearson.
Maxwell, John C. 2001. *The 17 Indesputable Laws of Teamwork.* New York: Nelson Books.
Scannell, M. 2010. *Conflict Resolution Games.* New York: McGraw-Hill.
Shaw, M. 1981. *Group Dynamics: The Psychology of Small Group Behavior.* New York: McGraw-Hill.

Index

AAA Forgiveness Technique, 186. *See also* forgiveness

acceptance of others: importance of, 30–31; nonverbal communication of, 61–62; verbal communication of, 63

active listening: advantages of, 68–69; for content, 65–66; for feelings, 66–67; for understanding, 63–68; four steps in, 64–65; guidelines for, 69–70. *See also* listening

ad hominem argument, 113

affection, and group formation, 8

agendas, meeting, 141–42

all-channel network, 157–58

anger, letting go of, 185

anxiety, reducing when speaking, 49–51

arbitration, decision by, 84

asymmetrical realtionship style, 46

autocratic leadership style, 135

behavior norms. *See* norms

Benne, Kenneth, 123

blamer: communication behavior of, 37; how to manage, 178–79; "you-language" of, 178

Blanchard, Kenneth, 136

boundary statement, 176–77

brainstorming process, 89

causal fallacy, 112

channels of communication, defined, 41

check-in period, 88

cohesiveness: competition's threat to, 156; conflict resolution and, 171; defined, 155; by feeling connected, 157–59; by feeling successful, 156–58; by feeling supported, 161–62; by feeling valued, 159–61; group-think phenomenon of, 164–65; trustworthiness, factor of, 162–64

communication: as all-channel network, 157–58; components of, 40–42; dysfunctional patterns of, 37–38; empathic, 63–64; four levels of, 43–45; gender differences in, 45–47; guidelines for listening, 69–70; guidelines for speaking, 47–49; learned behavior, 36; nonverbal, 39–40; transactional process, 40; verbal, 38–39. *See also* active listening; guiding behaviors; nonverbal communication; verbal communication

communicator, critically thinking of yourself, 31–33

compliments, 160–61

compromise, decision by, 84

conflict: advantages of, 170–71; characteristics of, 171–72; defined, 11, 169; forgiveness, 185–88; interpersonal, 175–77; myths concerning, 169–70; procedural, 172; substantive, 172; as unavoidable, 169

conformity to norms, 9–10

consensus: defined, 85; how to achieve, 84–85

control, and group formation, 8

controller: communication behavior of, 177–78; how to manage, 177–78

conversation. *See* verbal communication

creativity techniques, 92–95

cultural awareness, 13–15

decision making: by arbitration, 84; circular nature of, 91–92; by compromise, 84; by consensus, 84–85; groupthink threat to,

164; by leader, 83; by majority rule, 83–84. *See also* problem-solving process

decoding process, 41

defensive climate: certainty, 54; control, 52–53; defined, 51; evaluation, 52; neutrality, 53; strategy, 53; superiority, 54

democratic leadership style, 135

devil's advocate role, 165

Dewey, John, 87

discussion. *See* group discussion

distractor: communication behavior of, 179–80; how to manage, 180

diversity, power of, 13–15

dysfunctional communication patterns: of blamers, 178; of controllers, 177; of distractors, 179–80; of ghosts, 180; of pleasers, 179; intervention strategies for, 177–81

eighty/twenty rule, 159

either-or fallacy, 112

Ellis, Albert, 27

empathic communication, 61

encoding process, 41

equifinality concept, 6

ethical communication: Credo for Ethical Communication, 113–14; environment, 115; group, 115; individual, 114–15

eye contact, 62

false analogy, 112

feelings: of being valued, 159; caused by conflict, 185; of connection, 157–58; listening for, 66–68; social importance of, 157; of success, 155–57; of support, 161–62; of trust, 162–64;

Fisher, Aubrey, 10

followers: attitudes and skills of, 128–30

forgiveness: asking for, 186; defined, 185; granting of, 186–18

gender, and conversational behaviors, 45–47

gestures of acceptance, 61–62

ghost, 38; communication behavior of, 180; how to manage, 180–81

goals: formulation of mini-, 155–56; as group-formation criteria, 8; satisfying personal, 156–57

Greenleaf, Robert, 139

group development models: four-phase linear, 10–12; multiple sequence, 12–13

group discussion: in all-channel network, 157–58; analysis/testing phase, 125–26;

dysfunctional intervention in, 177–81; guiding behaviors for, 124–25; information sharing in, 123–24; negotiating skills in, 126; role of followers in, 128–30; social dimension of, 126; substantive conflict in, 173–75; summarizing of, 124–25

groups: defined, 3; four essential elements of, 3–4; reasons for joining, 7–8; social dimension of, 9; systems theory of, 3–7; task dimension of, 9. *See also* leader of groups; meetings; members of groups

groupthink: how to prevent, 165; how to recognize, 164

A Guide to Rational Living (Ellis), 27

guiding behaviors: for dysfunctional patterns, 177–81; focusing task of, 123; social, 126–28; task, 123–26

guilt, letting go of, 185

Hersey, Paul, 136

inclusion, and group formation, 7

inferences: deductive, 110; defined, 110; inductive, 111; logical fallacies in, 111–13

information sheet, 105

impromptu speaking: one-point impromptu speech, 144–46; standard impromptu speech, 146–48

intercultural awareness: competition versus cooperation dimension, 72–73; individual versus collective dimension, 71–72; low-context versus high-context dimension, 72

Internet research, 100–101

interpersonal conflict; causes of, 175; managing, 176–77

interviews, research, 101–2

I-statements, 42–43; advantages of, 42–43; to communicate appreciation, 160; personal opinions as, 44

Janis, Irving, 164

Jung, Carl, 82

laissez-faire leadership style, 135–36

leader of groups: accepting role of, 140; as decision-maker, 141–44; defined, 134; managing conflict, 172–77; preparing for meeting, 141–42; preventing groupthink, 164–65; productive attitudes of, 148–50; running effective meetings, 142–44; as servant, 138–40

leadership: autocratic, 135; defined, 134; democratic, 135; functional approach to,

137; laissez-faire, 135–36; personality determinants of, 135; situational approach to,
136–37
library research, 100
listening: barriers to, 60–61; communication
acceptance when, 61; importance of, 58;
ineffective styles, 59–60; process of, 58–59.
See also active listening; communication
logical fallacies, 111–13

meetings: acknowledging others in, 143; agendas, 141; how to effectively run, 140–44;
when to end, 144. *See also* problem-solving
process
members of groups: acceptance of, 30–31,
61–63; approval myth of, 81; common
task of, 3; in conflict, 11, 82, 168–77; feeling connected, 157–59; feeling successful,
155–57; feeling supported, 161–62; feeling
valued, 162–64; groupthink attitude of,
164; ideal number of, 3; information sharing by, 123–24; mutuality/interdependence
of, 5; personal goals of, 156–57; socializing
together, 158–59; trusting one another,
162–63
men, 45–47; conversational strategies of, 46;
suggested communication behaviors for,
46–47
messages: active listening to, 64–66; defined,
41; encoding and decoding, 41; nonverbal
communication of, 39–40; verbal communication of, 38–39

negotiating skills, 126
newspaper resources, 100
New York Times Index, 100
noise, 41
Nominal Group Technique (NGT), 89
nonverbal communication: of acceptance, 61–
62; active listening to, 62; encoding/decod-
ing process of, 41; impact of, 39; matched
with verbal, 64; principles/characteristics
of, 39. *See also* communication; verbal
communication
norms: challenges to, 10; conformity to, 9;
from family of origin, 9; implicit and explicit, 9

opinions: communication of, 44; in managing
conflict, 174, 176; testing, 107
orientation phase, 10–11
overgeneralization fallacy, 111

paraphrasing: defined, 64; when listening for
content, 65–66; when listening for feelings,
66–68
parroting, 69
personal goals, 156–57
pleaser, the, 37; communication behavior of,
179; how to manage, 179
Poole, Marshall, 92
primary tension phase, 11
problem-solving process, 79–95; brainstorming solutions, 89; check-in phase, 88; circular nature of, 91–92; creativity techniques
in, 92–95; decision-making techniques,
82–85; implementation phase, 91; myths of,
80–82; problem analysis, 88–89; reaching
consensus in, 90–91; recognizing logical
fallacies, 111–13; research preparation for,
97–106; standard problem-solving agenda,
87–91. *See also* conflict; decision making;
group discussion; research
procedural conflict: defined, 172; managing,
172–73
proposals: defined, 110; logical fallacies of,
111; testing of, 110–11

questions: active listening, 63–66; to guide
discussion, 124–25; to identify problem,
103–4; to request information, 23; to test
evidence, 108–9; to test inductive inferences, 111; to test opinions, 107–8; to test
relevancy, 109

Reader's Guide to Periodical Literature, 100
reinforcement phase, 11
relational track of group development, 12
research, 103–6; computerized presentational
programs, 106; evaluation of, 107–11; five
categories of, 99–103; importance of, 97–99;
information sheet, 105; sharing/clarification
of, 123–24; visual aids, 105–6

Satir, Virginia, 37
Schultz, Beatrice, 137
Schutz, William, 7
secondary tension phase, 12
self-acceptance: aids to, 28–29; importance of,
27–28; obstacles to, 27
self-discovery: aiding group communication,
19–20; in leadership role, 20; through self-
acceptance, 30; through solitude, 21–23
Senge, Peter, 7
servant leadership, 138–40

Sheats, Paul, 123

S.O.A.R. technique, 73–76

social dimension: cohesion goal of, 156; conflict in, 12; defined, 9; guiding behaviors of, 126–28; in leadership style, 135–40; in linear sequence model, 11; in multiple sequence model, 12. *See also* cohesiveness

speaking. *See* verbal communication

speaking kindly to yourself, 27–29

substantive conflict: defined, 172; managing, 173–75

supportive climate, 51–54; defined, 51; description, 52; empathy, 53; equality, 54; problem-orientation, 52–53; provisionalism, 54; spontaneity, 53

surveys, research, 102–3

symmetrical conversational style, 46

synergy, defined, 5

systems theory of groups, 4–7

Tannen, Deborah, 45–46

task dimension: defined, 9; guiding behaviors of, 123–26; and leadership style, 136–37. *See also* problem-solving process

task track of group development, 12

time management: celebrate your completed tasks, 117–18; decide on your incremental goals, 117; establish due dates for your incremental goals, 117; identify your assignment, 116–17; just do it, 117–18; prepare ahead of time, 117; say no to distractions, 118

topic track of group development, 12

trustworthiness: determining, 163–64; importance of, 163

verbal communication, 35–49; acceptance, 63; dysfunctional patterns of, 37–38; encoding/decoding process of, 41; of facts, 43; of feelings, 44–45; guidelines for clarity, 47–49; of opinions, 44; using I-statements, 42–43. *See also* communication; nonverbal communication

women: conversational strategies of, 45–47; suggested communication behaviors for, 47

You Just Don't Understand (Tannen), 45

About the Author

RANDY FUJISHIN is the author of seven books in the fields of communication and relationships. He has taught Communication Studies at the college level for more than thirty years and chairs the Communications Department at West Valley College in Saratoga, California. In addition to teaching, Randy has worked as a family and child therapist and is a featured speaker for the high-tech industry and Christian organizations throughout the western United States. Most important, Randy is a loving husband and father.